CASEBOOKS ON MODERN DRAMATISTS
(VOL. 18)

DAVID HARE

GARLAND REFERENCE LIBRARY
OF THE HUMANITIES
(VOL. 1240)

CASEBOOKS ON MODERN DRAMATISTS

KIMBALL KING
General Editor

DAVID HARE

A Casebook

Edited by
Hersh Zeifman

GARLAND PUBLISHING, Inc.
New York & London / 1994

Library of Congress Cataloging-in-Publication Data

David Hare : a casebook / edited by Hersh Zeifman
p. cm. — (Casebooks on modern dramatists ;
v. 18. Garland reference library of the humanities; v. 1240)
Includes bibliographical references and index.
ISBN 0-8240-2579-2
1. Hare, David, 1947–   . —Criticism and interpretation. I. Zeifman,
Hersh. II. Series: Garland reference library of the humanities. vol. 1240.
III. Series: Garland reference library of the humanities.
Casebooks on modern dramatists ; vol. 18.
PR6058.A678Z64 1994

822'.914—dc20   94-6740

Printed on acid-free, 250-year-life paper
Manufactured in the United States of America

For my mother, Lily Zeifman,
and in memory of my father, David Zeifman

Contents

General Editor's Note

Learning that David Hare has written sixteen stage plays, eight collaborations, and eleven screenplays for film and television, one might be surprised by the fact that this leading English artist is not yet fifty years old. He was only twenty-two when his first play was performed by the Portable Theatre, and he was a major voice on the British stage before he was thirty. Hare's plays are witty, dense, and intellectually challenging. He never provides easy solutions to the complex issues that arise out of conflicts between powerful social institutions and individual needs. While he has categorized himself as a socialist playwright, Hare presents characters and situations so complex that they defy simplistic analysis along political lines. Formed in part by his apprenticeship at the Royal Court Theatre, he follows in the footsteps of Shaw as a writer who can be immensely entertaining while he challenges the most intelligent audiences. The inextricable bond between public and personal worlds does not produce a deterministic worldview. On the contrary, Hare's works convince us that ethical and moral choices are not only possible, but compulsory, in modern life.

The present volume is the first major collection of essays devoted to Hare, and its editor, Hersh Zeifman, who is a professor at York University, Toronto, is well-qualified to assemble and supervise such a significant undertaking. As co-editor of the prestigious journal, *Modern Drama*, he has been exposed to all the major authors and topics of modern theatre and is ideally positioned to discern Hare's pivotal role on the contemporary stage. Zeifman is also on the executive board of *The Pinter Review* and has published widely on contemporary British and American drama. Previously a co-editor of

Contemporary British Drama, 1970–1990, Zeifman has assembled a distinguished gathering of theatre scholars for this volume, and his own fine interview with Hare sets the tone for a challenging assessment of a leading twentieth-century dramatist.

Kimball King

Introduction

At a press conference during the 1993 Montreal Film Festival, director Howard Davies introduced his film of David Hare's *The Secret Rapture* by stating that he persuaded Hare to "play down the politics" when writing the screenplay—"it was dating quickly," Davies explained. The comment seems especially bizarre coming from the director of the play's original stage production: surely Davies above all others should realize that to mute the politics in a Hare drama is in effect to eviscerate it, robbing the text of one of its greatest strengths. In any case, the political implications of *The Secret Rapture*, despite Margaret Thatcher's recent downfall, are by no means "dated"—primarily because those implications extend far beyond the character of Marion, the text's junior Tory minister whom Davies described as a "thinly disguised version of Thatcher" (Conlogue). Marion may embody the most obvious political reference in *Rapture*, but the most obvious aspect of a Hare drama—while invariably amusing—is seldom the most profound: the political resonances in Hare's work are infinitely deeper, infinitely subtler.

Consider, for example, the character of Katherine, Marion's leftist stepmother who claims to hate the spiritually bankrupt Government Marion represents: "Its loathsome materialism. The awful sanctification of greed" (14). And yet, despite her belief that "this Government's appalling," Katherine easily rationalizes her own desire to share in that greed: "let's face it, given what's going on, it's just stupid not to go and grab some dough for yourself. . . . If we don't make the money someone else will. Well, in my book the arseholes have had it their own way long enough." The response of Marion's "saintly" sister Isobel—"But isn't there a chance that taking some will turn *us* into arseholes?" (39)—elicits only laughter and pity: can someone so "naive" truly exist? Alas, not for long: in the world of *The Secret Rapture* Isobel's decency is ultimately perceived as a personal affront, and so must be eliminated. Interestingly, Hare has labelled the play "a classical tragedy," and has argued that Isobel is "doomed because of a particular quality she has. The irony of the quality she has is that it is goodness" (Oliva 169). What, then, are the political implications of a society in which a lack of interest in materialism is equated with an almost criminal stupidity, and in which goodness is regarded as a tragic flaw?

Such questions lie at the heart of all of Hare's drama. "I believe that to be interested in politics," Hare has stated, "is just part of being grown up. . . . I believe history has a great effect on who you are and how you think" (Gaston 217). We are none of us exempt from political systems and the "ethics" that structure them; there is no escape from the world we have shaped and which in turn has shaped us, however apolitical we might claim to be. According to his friend, the American playwright Wallace Shawn: "David feels that the way power is distributed in society affects the private life of every individual in a very, very deep way" (Gussow 47). As another American playwright, Arthur Miller, has observed: "The fish is in the water but the water's in the fish. You can't extricate individuals from society and hope to create a rounded picture of them" (Bigsby 80). For Miller, "there are no public issues; they are all private issues" (Bigsby 139).[1] Hare would agree: the public and the private constantly commingle in his plays, so closely interwoven that the threads finally become inextricable. In his 1978 Cambridge lecture, Hare summed up this "interweaving" succinctly: "A theatre which is exclusively personal, just a place of private psychology, is inclined to self-indulgence; a theatre which is just social is inclined to unreality. . . . Yeats said, out of our quarrel with others, we make rhetoric, while out of our quarrel with ourselves, we make poetry. I value both, and value the theatre as a place where both are given weight" (69).

In David Hare's sixteen stage plays, eight theatrical collaborations, and eleven screenplays for film and television, both the public and the private—the *effect* of the public *on* the private—are given weight. Hare has been quick to point out, however, that "[a] sense of politics has nothing to do with preaching, polemics, or ideology; it is about the effect that dominant beliefs of the day have on us" (Raymond 16). True to his word, Hare strives to avoid preaching in his drama. "In the theatre," he has noted, "I am saying complex and difficult things" ("A Lecture" 57): there is no place in such a theatre for agit-prop, for simplistic notions of "right" and "wrong." As he stated in the interview included in this volume, Hare is deeply conscious of where the balance of his sympathies lies in his plays, but at the same time he is careful not to "rig" the argument: the ideological differences of his characters are dramatized with admirable fairness. In *A Map of the World*, for example, the idealistic socialist Stephen is by no means, as we might expect him to be, the play's unquestioned "hero," nor is the cynical reactionary Mehta its undisputed "villain." Passionately engaged with his characters' polarities, Hare as dramatist nevertheless manages to remain sufficiently dispassionate, sufficiently beyond the fray, to identify with *both* his protagonists; at times, indeed, Mehta sounds suspiciously like an authorial spokesman (a Me[h]ta-Hare?). "In an ideal production of the play," Hare has commented, "you find yourself agreeing with whoever has last spoken" (Introduction, *Asian* xiv).

Hare's deliberate evenhandedness, his refusal to heed "the clamour for a simpler morality" (Introduction, *History* 13), has infuriated ideologues from both the Left and the Right. This strikes me as yet another sign of Hare's excellence as a playwright: he must be doing something right to offend so evenly across the spectrum. From the very beginning of his career, at least as early as *Knuckle* (1974), Hare was aware "that there was to be something about my plays which would attract the most impassioned opposition" (Introduction, *History* 12). And so it has proved: from *Slag* (1970) to *The Absence of War* (1993), his plays have won applause and condemnation in seemingly equal measure. Even his best-known work, *Plenty*, managed to outrage a large portion of its audiences when it was produced at London's National Theatre in 1978; the National's then artistic director, Peter Hall, while calling Hare "a big talent," couldn't help remarking on his "ability to provoke hostility in audiences" (346). Hare has no real problem with that; rather than preach to the converted, he has chosen instead to convert preaching into probing by posing tough questions in his drama. As he once stated: "All I aim to do is to put a bur under people's skin so that they hate it, they scratch at it, it irritates them, but it's there. It's under their skins and it forces them to think . . ." (Lustig 17). "What I'm really trying to do," Hare commented in another interview, "is drive people mad with argument. To prod their brains into life" (Yakir).

   David Hare: A Casebook—the first collection of essays devoted exclusively to an analysis of Hare's work—is animated by a dozen critics and scholars driven "mad with argument": as a result their essays are invariably lively, opinionated, and contentious. The *Casebook* begins, however, on a quieter note, with an interview I conducted with Hare in my rented London flat in November 1991. Hare is remarkably generous in interviews: affable, articulate, refreshingly candid in discussing what he perceives to be shortcomings in his work. Because so many interviews with Hare have traced the chronological sweep of his theatrical career (see, for instance, his 1975 interview with the editors of *Theatre Quarterly*, or the interview with Georg Gaston published in *Theatre Journal* in 1993), I decided to concentrate on his most recent plays (although his earlier work is also discussed). The interview contains, I feel, the most revealing comments Hare has made to date on his theatre trilogy of the 1990s.

   Following the interview is a trio of "overviews": three incisive essays which range widely over Hare's entire dramatic oeuvre. Ruby Cohn, the author of many books and some hundred articles on various aspects of modern drama (her most recent critical study is *Retreats from Realism in Recent English Drama*), starts us off with an examination of the role played by women in Hare's plays. "More than any other living male dramatist," Cohn writes, "Hare has given voice to women. . . ." John Russell Brown—professor of theatre at the University of Michigan, a prolific and celebrated critic and director, and former Associate Director of the National Theatre—assesses the interplay between Hare's films and his work for the theatre in an essay titled "Playing with Place: Some Filmic Techniques in the

Plays of David Hare," focusing on "what his work as a film-maker has contributed to his stage plays and how he has returned to the theatre to enjoy its own distinct opportunities." And Robert L. King, professor of English at Elms College and theatre critic for *The North American Review*, turns a critical eye on the language of Hare's drama. Hare's plays insist, King claims, "that we take a moral point of view in the face of a morally ambiguous world. The instrument for defining and negotiating that position is language. . . ."

This overview is then succeeded by nine essays which zero in on specific Hare plays. The essays are arranged chronologically in terms of Hare's career, beginning with Scott Fraser's critique of Hare's "juvenilia" (*How Brophy Made Good, Slag*, and *The Great Exhibition*) as "satirical anatomies" (Fraser teaches drama at York University in Toronto and is the author of *A Politic Theatre: The Drama of David Hare*, forthcoming from Rodopi). Finlay Donesky, who teaches at the University of Kentucky and who wrote his doctoral dissertation on Hare, examines *Knuckle* and *Teeth 'n' Smiles*, two of Hare's plays from the mid-1970s, discovering in them what he terms "Nostalgia for the Consensus." *Fanshen*, Hare's acclaimed adaptation for Joint Stock Theatre of William Hinton's massive book on the effects of the Revolution on one Chinese village, is the subject of Janelle Reinelt's essay, an analysis of what Hare's play has in common with the work of Bertolt Brecht. Reinelt teaches theatre at California State University in Sacramento and is the author of *After Brecht: British Epic Theatre*, forthcoming from Michigan; her essay, adapted from that book, is informed by a pair of in-depth interviews she conducted with Hare from which she quotes liberally. John Bull, lecturer in English and Drama at the University of Sheffield, expands on his account of Hare's drama in his book *New British Political Dramatists*, one of the key studies of contemporary British theatre, by reconsidering *Plenty* (both play and film) and *Licking Hitler*.

The next two essays in the volume are especially noteworthy for their assessment of works by Hare which have received relatively little critical attention. Toby Silverman Zinman, professor of humanities at Philadelphia's University of the Arts and editor of the casebook on David Rabe in this series, analyses *Saigon: Year of the Cat*, a film Hare wrote for television. Anthony Jenkins—professor of English at the University of Victoria, author of *The Theatre of Tom Stoppard*, and a professional actor and director—critiques Hare's double bill of 1986, *The Bay at Nice* and *Wrecked Eggs*. Then, in an essay titled "Virtuous Women," Anne Nothof (Athabasca University) examines three portraits of female goodness in Hare's recent work. Ann Wilson, who teaches drama at the University of Guelph and who edited the Garland casebook on Howard Brenton, follows with a rigorous analysis of *Racing Demon*. And Lane A. Glenn, a director who is writing his doctoral dissertation on Hare at Michigan State University, concludes the volume with an examination of Hare's latest plays, *Murmuring Judges* and *The Absence of War*, the completion of his theatre trilogy.

It gives me great pleasure to thank all the contributors to this volume, as well as Kimball King, the general editor of this series, for his encouragement and helpful advice. My final thanks go to David Hare, both for the gift of his time in agreeing to be interviewed and for the larger gift of his wonderfully provocative plays and films.

NOTE

1. Hare is on record as deeply admiring Miller's plays. "Like Orwell, even when he writes badly, he writes bang on the nose," Hare has commented of Miller. "The world, to him, seems to be a courthouse, which, of course, makes for great drama. But he's too compassionate to hand down a verdict" (Bigsby 2).

WORKS CITED

Bigsby, Christopher, ed. *Arthur Miller and Company*. London: Methuen, 1990.

Conlogue, Ray. "In a Race Against Time." *Globe and Mail* [Toronto] 4 Sept. 1993: C6.

Gaston, Georg. "Interview: David Hare." *Theatre Journal* 45 (1993): 213–25.

Gussow, Mel. "David Hare: Playwright as Provocateur." *New York Times Magazine* 29 Sept. 1985: 42+.

Hall, Peter. *Peter Hall's Diaries: The Story of a Dramatic Battle*. Ed. John Goodwin. New York: Harper, 1984.

Hare, David. Introduction. *The Asian Plays*. London: Faber, 1986. vii–xiv.

———. Introduction. *The History Plays*. London: Faber, 1984. 9–16.

———. "A Lecture Given at King's College, Cambridge, March 5, 1978." *Licking Hitler*. London: Faber, 1978. 57–71.

———. *The Secret Rapture*. Rev. ed. London: Faber, 1989.

Lustig, Vera. "Soul Searching." *Drama* 170 (1988): 15–18.

Oliva, Judy Lee. *David Hare: Theatricalizing Politics*. Ann Arbor: UMI, 1990.

Raymond, Gerard. "*The Secret Rapture*: David Hare's X-Ray of the Soul." *TheaterWeek* 30 Oct. 1989: 16–21.

Yakir, Dan. "A Hare's-breadth Away from Controversy." *Globe and Mail* [Toronto] 30 Aug. 1985: E5.

Chronology

1947 David Hare is born 5 June in St. Leonards, Sussex, son of Clifford (a ship's purser on the P & O Line) and Agnes Hare.

1952 Moves with his parents and older sister to Bexhill, Sussex.

1960 Attends Lancing, a public school, as a scholarship boarder.

1965 Enters Jesus College, Cambridge, where he reads English and directs a few undergraduate plays.

1968 After graduation, works briefly for A.B. Pathé, screening Pathé Pictorials in search of material for sex education films. Founds Portable Theatre with Tony Bicât, "to take theatre to places where it normally didn't go." Portable's first play, *Inside Out*—a one-act adaptation of Kafka's *Diaries* dramatized by Hare and Bicât—is performed in Sept. at the Arts Lab, Drury Lane.

1969 Appointed Literary Manager at the Royal Court Theatre. His first play, *How Brophy Made Good*, is staged by Portable in Mar. at Brighton Combination, directed by Hare and Tony Bicât. Directs Howard Brenton's *Christie in Love* and David Mowat's *Purity* for Portable.

1970 *Slag*, produced by Michael Codron, opens 6 Apr. at Hampstead Theatre Club, winning Hare the *Evening Standard* Most Promising Playwright Award. In Sept. *What Happened to Blake* is presented by Portable at the Royal Court's Theatre Upstairs on a double bill with Brenton's *Fruit*, the latter directed by Hare. Becomes Resident Dramatist at the Royal Court [1970–71]. Marries

TV and film producer Margaret Matheson (divorced 1980), with whom he has three children: a son Joe (who plays Richard Forbes in Hare's film *Strapless*) and twins Lewis and Darcy.

1971 *Slag* is produced in Feb. by Joe Papp at the New York Shakespeare Festival's Public Theatre, the first Hare play performed in America and the beginning of a long association with Papp. His adaptation of Pirandello's *The Rules of the Game*, written with Robert Rietty, is staged by the National at the New Theatre in June. The collaboration *Lay By*, a Portable/Traverse Theatre co-production, is performed at the Edinburgh Festival in Aug., where Hare also directs Snoo Wilson's *Blowjob* for Portable. His two-minute play, *Deathshead*, is staged at the Traverse in Dec. Resigns as Artistic Director of Portable.

1972 *The Great Exhibition*, starring David Warner and Penelope Wilton and directed by Richard Eyre, is performed at Hampstead on 28 Feb. In Sept. the collaboration *England's Ireland*, directed by Hare, premieres at the Mickery Theatre, Amsterdam.

1973 *Man above Men* is televised 19 Mar. as a BBC "Play for Today." Appointed Resident Dramatist at the Nottingham Playhouse. Hare and Brenton's *Brassneck*, directed by Hare, opens 19 Sept. at Nottingham. Directs Snoo Wilson's *The Pleasure Principle* at Theatre Upstairs and Vanbrugh's *The Provoked Wife* at the Palace Theatre, Watford. Founds Joint Stock Theatre with Max Stafford-Clark and David Aukin.

1974 After previewing at the Oxford Playhouse in Jan., *Knuckle*, with Edward Fox and Kate Nelligan, is presented in the West End by Michael Codron at the Comedy Theatre on 4 Mar.; it wins Hare the John Llewellyn Rhys Award. Directs Trevor Griffiths's *The Party* for a National Theatre tour.

1975 *Fanshen*, a Joint Stock production based on the book by William Hinton, opens 10 Mar. at the Crucible Studio, Sheffield, and then tours throughout Britain. *Brassneck* is televised as a BBC "Play for Today" on 22 May. In June a heavily Americanized production of *Knuckle* is televised on PBS. Directs his *Teeth 'n' Smiles* (with music by Nick Bicât and lyrics by Tony Bicât), starring Helen Mirren, at the Royal Court in Sept. BBC2 televises *Fanshen* 18 Oct.

1976 Directs Howard Brenton's *Weapons of Happiness* at the Lyttelton, the first new play to be staged at the National Theatre's recently opened site on the South Bank.

1977 Awarded US/UK Bicentennial Fellowship; writes and travels in England and the United States. Directs Tony Bicât's *Devil's Island* for Joint Stock.

1978 *Licking Hitler*, directed by Hare, is televised 10 Jan. as a BBC "Play for Today" (wins BAFTA Best Play of the Year Award). The collaboration *Deeds*, directed by Richard Eyre, is staged in Mar. at the Nottingham Playhouse. On 7 Apr. *Plenty*, directed by Hare and starring Kate Nelligan, to whom the play is dedicated, opens in the Lyttelton at the National Theatre.

1980 *Dreams of Leaving*, directed by Hare, is televised 17 Jan. as a BBC "Play for Today."

1981 Directs a revival of Christopher Hampton's *Total Eclipse* at the Lyric Theatre, Hammersmith.

1982 In Mar. the Sydney Theatre Company premieres *A Map of the World*, directed by Hare, at the Opera Theatre, Adelaide, as part of Australia's Adelaide Festival. *Plenty*, directed by Hare, is presented by Joe Papp on 21 Oct. at the Public Theatre in New York—Hare's first directing assignment in America.

1983 Hare's production of *Plenty* transfers to the Plymouth Theatre on 6 Jan., his first Broadway production and winner of the New York Critics' Circle Award. *A Map of the World*, directed by Hare, opens 27 Jan. at the Lyttelton. *Saigon: Year of the Cat* is televised on Thames TV in Nov. Writes the filmscripts of *Wetherby* and *Paris by Night* (then titled "The Butter Mountain").

1984 Appointed Associate Director of the National Theatre. Directs his film *Wetherby*.

1985 *Wetherby* is released in Mar. and wins the Golden Bear Best Film Award at the Berlin Film Festival. Directs *Pravda*, written with Howard Brenton and starring Anthony Hopkins, in the Olivier at the National Theatre; opening 2 May, it wins the *Plays and Players, City Limits,* and *Evening Standard* Best Play Awards. Fred Schepisi's film of *Plenty*, starring Meryl Streep, is released. Made a Fellow of the Royal Society of Literature.

1986 *The Bay at Nice* and *Wrecked Eggs*, two linked one-act plays directed by Hare, open 4 Sept. in the Cottesloe at the National Theatre. Directs Anthony Hopkins in Shakespeare's *King Lear* at the National.

1987 His opera *The Knife* (with music by Nick Bicât and lyrics by Tim Rose Price), directed by Hare and starring Mandy Patinkin, opens 12 Feb. at the Public Theatre in New York.

1988 *The Secret Rapture*, directed by Howard Davies, opens 4 Oct. in the Lyttelton at the National Theatre.

1989 Release of *Paris by Night* (filmed in 1987), directed by Hare and starring Charlotte Rampling. *Knuckle* is televised 7 May by BBC2 on "Theatre Night."

1990 The first play in Hare's trilogy of British institutions, *Racing Demon*, opens 8 Feb. in the National Theatre's Cottesloe under Richard Eyre's direction; it wins four Best Play of the Year Awards, including the Olivier Award. *Strapless* (filmed in 1988), directed by Hare and starring Blair Brown, is released in April. A radio adaptation of *Pravda* is broadcast 28 Sept. on the BBC.

1991 *Heading Home*, directed by Hare, is televised on BBC2 in Jan. The second play of the trilogy, *Murmuring Judges*, opens 10 Oct. in the Olivier at the National Theatre, directed by Richard Eyre.

1992 Release of the film *Damage*, based on the novel by Josephine Hart, directed by Louis Malle and starring Jeremy Irons and Miranda Richardson.

1993 Howard Davies's film of *The Secret Rapture*, starring Juliet Stevenson, premieres at the Edinburgh Film Festival in Aug. On 2 Oct. the trilogy is completed with the opening of *The Absence of War*, directed by Richard Eyre, in the Olivier; the entire trilogy plays in repertory at the National through Nov. Marries fashion designer Nicole Farhi.

David Hare

An Interview with David Hare

Hersh Zeifman: I guess the obvious place to begin is with *Murmuring Judges*, which opened recently [Oct. 1991] at the National Theatre. I was wondering why you chose this particular topic—the criminal justice system—at this particular time.

David Hare: Well, it's my intention to write a trilogy about British institutions. Having done the Church in *Racing Demon*—I suppose that the Church was a sort of metaphor for other British institutions. *Racing Demon* was about how liberals fight, when the essence of Christianity is to turn the other cheek—how Christians organize themselves to fight evil, so to speak. Also, how do liberal institutions function without rules. And then I wanted to take some British institutions where power is the only reality—where the rules are very, very strong—and examine the way they connect or rather fail to connect. You know, the most striking thing about the British judicial system is that the various parts of it—the police, the Bar and the Bench, the prisons—don't relate to each other. And so *Murmuring Judges* is a study of the way Britons are more interested in their own peer groups than they are in the reality of what they're actually doing. At the centre you have somebody who is being *mashed* by this process, and then you have a group of people who are only interested in their own part of the process.

HZ: Why a trilogy? Is it the three estates?

DH: Yes. The main reason for a trilogy is that I felt able now to do an English canvas. I wanted there to be three plays which could be played together, which would present a whole canvas

3

of British life. And which were researched, in that I went to pay my dues to real life by finding out what was actually going on on the ground, but which were not in any way documentary. They are works of fiction—the stories are made up, the characters are made up, they are works of the imagination. But they're works of the imagination which I hope are enriched by trying to find out what people's real lives are like.

The basic idea that it came out of was realizing that we have had, for the last ten years, sort of ideological prima donnas who are dancing on the top of the society, producing an ideology which they say the society is meant to believe in—as it happens, an entrepreneurial ideology. And at the bottom or in the middle of the society, we have all the people who are actually dealing with the tensions that are created by that ideology. It seemed to me that Thatcher's survival and prosperity had actually been guaranteed and ensured by clergymen who were willing, for £8,000 or £9,000 a year, to act as surrogate social workers, dealing with all the problems of society at the grassroots level. And in the same way the police, although they're much better paid (they earn £20,000 a year), are the people at whom all the criticism for what is wrong with the society is being flung. All the grave divisions that have been created by this very self-indulgent philosophy at the top, all those tensions that have been created by that philosophy, the police are having to mop up. So I wanted a trilogy about the people who do the dirty work. You know that line in *Murmuring Judges*, the very emotive line Barry has: "Let's hear it for the guys who keep turning up"—it's a trilogy about the guys who keep turning up.

HZ: And the third one will be on Parliament?

DH: I'm not yet saying what the third one's on. I think everybody just assumed that's what I'd do next. In fact I'm not very keen to do it, simply because if I write about government it will have to be about the ruling class. And I'm not really very interested in the ruling class. I'm interested in the effect of the ruling class on people's lives lower down the system, the lower middle class.

HZ: There was obviously an incredible amount of research that went into the play—the programme cites two research assistants, for example. Did you ever consider that this might be the kind of play to be done with a Joint Stock-type workshop?

DH: Yes—for both plays. *Racing Demon* originally came out of an idea that I would create Synod, which is the Church's parliament, in the Cottesloe Theatre. And I think the original plan was that I was going to work with Max Stafford-Clark, and that we were going to create a Joint Stock kind of show where we researched. Similarly, at the beginning of *Murmuring Judges* I was going to send the actors out into different parts of the legal system. But then I realized I'm no longer, if I ever was, a classic documentary writer. I'm not interested in documentary as a form at all, and I find the vindication of work by the excuse that it actually happened really depressing.

You know, people send me documentary stuff all the time. They think that I'm an expert on the Church. What do I feel about women priests? What do I feel about homosexual clergy? Should gay priests be allowed to marry? I don't have any views on these subjects. I'm not a journalist; I'm not a polemicist. But I *can* try and show you what it's like to be a gay priest who daren't come out of the closet in a South London parish, and I hope I can make you feel for him. But I don't have any sociological brief at all, any polemical or political brief. What inflames my imagination is character, character and narrative. All I'm doing in researching, in fact, is being led to characters and people who interest me, and so I have to have people called research assistants because they're people who lead me to other people.

HZ: The actors presumably could have done that as well.

DH: Yes, but I don't want it complicated by the actors' own thoughts about the subject matter. I'm very, very protective about the subject matter, which I never discuss with anybody. With *Murmuring Judges*, because of the quite extraordinary design of Bob Crowley, the set was integrated into the writing of the play, so that we had some idea of what the play was going to look like before any of it was written. With a designer like Bob who's a great creative theatre mind, your approach can be influenced because you have some idea of what you can achieve. The charge room—which is the basic image of *Murmuring Judges*, *the* key image of the play—I talked through with Bob at some length. But otherwise I'm extremely protective of the material.

HZ: I notice that you haven't directed the premieres of any of your last three plays. In a 1989 interview you stated that theatre directing is no longer as fulfilling as it once was for you. Is that still true?

DH: Yes. I stopped getting any satisfaction from the job. I'm not talking about the work, or what the work was like; it's just that at a purely personal level I stopped enjoying it. I originally took up directing because I felt that the tendency of all directors, however good, was to make your work more like other people's: they tend to feel safe if it resembles something that they know. I found early on that I wasn't sure that directors were getting what I felt to be my voice and nobody else's. But now people are so familiar with my work, in this country at least, that Howard Davies or Richard Eyre not only can make the music of my plays sound exactly how I want the music to sound, but they can enrich the work with their own way of approaching the actors or way of staging it that's better than anything I can do.

HZ: The *literal* music of *Murmuring Judges*—the use of Mozart— is wonderful. Presumably you chose *The Magic Flute* deliberately, in that it too portrays a closed and "secret" society.

DH: And the play has a triangular structure, while of course *The Magic Flute* has the famous three chords. Also—I aim, I don't know if I succeed—the whole structure of the evening is meant to have the grace of a Mozart opera, so that it has choral passages, it has ensemble passages, then it has duets, solos, arias. The prison scene—the love scene (what we call the love scene) between the prisoner and lawyer—is intended to be like a long duet in a Mozart opera, before the play does indeed become a Mozart opera. We worked very hard on satisfactions of form.

HZ: There's that breathtaking moment at the end of both acts when the separate parts of the triangle suddenly come together, accompanied by the music of Mozart—it's a fabulous moment.

DH: Well, those are the things that theatre can do. You know, in the last ten or fifteen years we've all been on the defensive about theatre in this country, and certainly in the United States. We've been going through a period of enfeeblement, and when these periods come then people start asking "What can theatre do at all?" And what theatre can do are those extraordinary collisions of the kind that you get in *Murmuring Judges*, which *only* theatre can deliver. I'm trying in the trilogy to be as flamboyant in the use of form as I possibly can be. *Racing Demon* is quite austere, but it is in a very bold style, namely direct address—people coming out and praying directly to God. I was very struck by a brilliant remark of [William] Empson's, where he says that the English theatre died when the subplot died. What he meant was that with nineteenth-century scenery, with the arrival of rooms with walls, all that stuff, plays just became one story in one room. What I'm trying to do with epic narrative, with subplot, is to create a theatre that goes back to Elizabethan ideas of plot and subplot. I was very, very influenced by going to see three Shakespeare plays at the RSC [*The Plantagenets*—the three parts of *Henry VI* conflated into two, followed by *Richard III*] all in a day. And the aim of this trilogy is that eventually you'll be able to see in one day an entire canvas.

HZ: So you envision it being performed literally as a trilogy?

DH: It will be performed in 1993; you'll be able to turn up at 10:30 in the morning and stay until 10:30 at night.

HZ: Bring your little lunch and a cushion?

DH: It's all I live for. (*Laughs.*)

HZ: You state that *Racing Demon* is quite austere; how much of that has to do with its original playing space? Was the play written specifically for the Cottesloe [by far the smallest of the three National Theatre auditoria]? Are you very aware, when writing, of the theatrical space you're writing for?

DH: Sure. The trilogy has been compromised in that, when I wrote *Racing Demon*, the one thing we all agreed on was that an actor should not have to raise his or her voice to address God. In a historical pageant play, like *Becket* or *Murder in the Cathedral* or something, when a character speaks to God it's rhetoric. But when a character speaks to God in *Racing Demon* we all wanted it not to be rhetorical, for God really to exist so that you could talk to Him without having to "theatricalize." That's why the Cottesloe was so important, and also so that the audience would be among the action. It simply became impractical to sustain a trilogy of this cost in the Cottesloe: you can't economically justify twenty-five actors in a four-hundred-seat theatre.

HZ: Once again in *Murmuring Judges* the "conscience" of the play resides specifically in its female characters, Irina and Sandra. How do you react to feminist criticism of your plays as misogynistic, in that the women are stereotypes—either "negatively" (as in *Slag*), or "positively" with all those icons of goodness?

DH: The thing is that you're damned if you do and damned if you don't. In *Murmuring Judges* it's simply true about the police and the law that they are male professions, and that women tend to be one step back from them. And given that they're one step back they maybe look at them with a slightly more critical eye because they don't belong to the club. That's not a piece of imaginative fiction, that's just a fact about how those male clubs are organized, and any policewoman will tell you that it's not an easy line about whether you fall in with the sexism. You are offered stereotypes as a policewoman: you can either be flirtatious or you can be hatchet-faced. To just be a woman in the police, particularly at the lowest level, is not easy. And so it's not only justifiable that those characters would be the people one step back, it's also realistic.

The general run of feminist criticism seems to me that you're criticized either because the women are too good or because they're villainesses. If they're villainesses you're called misogynistic, and if they're not villainesses—if they're good— you're told you're stereotyping. So frankly I find most academic feminist criticism of my work completely inane; it's never struck me as anywhere near the mark. But the only thing that annoys me is when that criticism becomes censorious, because it implicitly becomes a "you shouldn't." In *Licking Hitler*, for instance, a woman who has originally been raped goes on enjoying sex with the man who has raped her. It is then put to me, "You shouldn't show this." And I say, "Well, do such things actually happen?" And the feminist answer is, "Yes, they do happen, but it's undesirable to show them." Right? I say "Where do you think all the imaginative sympathy of the work is? Do you think it's with the man?" They say, "No, it's quite clearly with the woman. But sexual stereotypes are reinforced on television all night long; therefore *you*, the progressives, should sort of clean up when your hour comes on. You should counterbalance. So although such things do happen, they should not be shown." Now that to me is censorship, and just as insidious as the Lord Chamberlain's blue pencil. Because if we're really saying that you can't show what actually happens, you can only show what you would *like* to happen, then I don't know how a playwright can operate. That's the only feminist criticism that touches me; it annoys me in the way all censorship annoys me.

HZ: Let's return for a moment to the issue of goodness in your plays, however gendered. I find really interesting the Rebecca West quote you use as one of the epigraphs in *The Secret Rapture*: "Only half of us is sane. . . . The other half of us is nearly mad."

DH: That's a wonderful piece of writing.

HZ: What it suggests to me is that the two sisters in the play are symbolically two sides of the same person, which then further suggests that there's a potential for goodness in everyone. In the preface to *Major Barbara*, Shaw writes "It is quite useless to declare that all men are born free if you deny that they are born good"—a sentiment that strikes me as absolutely crucial for socialism. Is that something you more or less believe? Is it *important* for you to believe that there's at least the kernel of potential goodness in people?

DH: Well, you know, when I was writing *Pravda* with Howard Brenton, I realized that the nihilist is free in a way that the progressive is not free—Evelyn Waugh is a wonderful writer because he doesn't believe in human perfectibility. Once you are allowed to say that human beings are trash and that what they feel doesn't matter very much and that there is nothing but cruelty in human life, then you have wonderful comedy and a wonderfully savage way to write, because you're free as a writer to do what you bloody well want with the characters: you have absolutely no responsibility. Look what freedom that gives you as a writer; when we unleashed Lambert Le Roux [the central character in *Pravda*], we unleashed him with total relish.

But while Waugh's work is very funny, ultimately it's quite tiring. I wouldn't like to be left alone with just his work; I need other work as well—

HZ: You wouldn't choose it for *Desert Islands Discs*.

DH: Exactly. That's exactly what I mean. It's a bracing corrective, but I finally don't find his view of the world true. It's a tempting position for a writer, but I still believe that people, however apparently ghastly, do have some capacity for change. Because if they don't, there isn't really much point in works of art, I find. I don't mean that works of art need to be improving, but if we are to be moved by representations of our life, those representations must contain some sense of possibility. It's like the famous Mao remark which I've always loved, in *A Thousand Observations*, that a wise man may make one that is foolish and a foolish man may make one that is wise. And that's true at the end of *Secret Rapture*—maybe Marion will do something good for once in her life.

Not only is it better for people to be allowed to express the—for want of a better word—compassionate side of their nature, but the way that side of their nature has had to be suppressed in recent years has been shaming to the British people. One of the most remarkable things about Thatcher's downfall was a sense of national cleansing: there was an extraordinary sense of "we have been going along with something of which we are basically ashamed." John Major became hugely popular because he was palpably a nice man; there was a tremendous relief in this country that at last we had somebody leading us of whom we weren't ashamed. There was a sort of hilarious attempt by the Right to pretend that her downfall had been a conspiracy, but it is apparent to everybody that her downfall came from a profound change in national mood. And she was a victim of that change in mood, not of a conspiracy or of a tragic downfall: she simply ceased to reflect the mood of the country. So it's not only that people *need* to be able to do good things, which I think they do, but also that it's more rational. Even if people were born in original sin, and even if it were true that greed is the only motivator and that people only live for themselves, you still need checks and balances in a society to make sure that that instinct doesn't get out of hand.

HZ: I'm curious as to how you respond to criticisms of *specific* dramatizations of goodness in your plays. Did you see the profile of Clare Higgins [who played Katherine in the original NT production of *The Secret Rapture*] in the recent *Plays and Players* [Nov. 1991]?

DH: Yes, I did. It was very interesting.

HZ: She mentions that a friend of hers, after seeing the play, commented that the "good" sister Isobel was the most fucked-up and evil woman on the stage, and that that kind of innocence is dangerous.

DH: Well, that's right. I mean, it's right in the sense that I've always thought that, in the first half of the play, Isobel has no theory of evil. She doesn't realize that people are doing her harm, and for that reason she's not able to fight evil. But then in the second half, by the time she comes to fight it, she's trapped: she's in a situation in which whatever route she takes leads to trouble. So yeah, she has an inadequate way of dealing with the world, just as I think Lionel in *Racing Demon* has an inadequate approach to the world. It isn't good enough to wander around pretending that everybody means good; they don't.

HZ: But there's still an important difference here, isn't there? Because finally Isobel is a character one senses you admire—

DH: No, I don't think that's true. No. She's a character I love, and that's different.

HZ: O.K. She's a character you love, whereas a lot of audience members find her irritating.

DH: Absolutely. I'm way out of key with everybody else. (*Laughs.*) But then that's always the case. I mean, it's my experience that people are never going to take from a play what you intend. That's different from "misreading." They don't misread it; what they do is run the play by their own life and experience and then they come to a particular conclusion. There's nothing I can do about that. I know where the balance of *my* sympathies lies in a play, although it changes with the years.

HZ: Can you give me an example?

DH: Well, the most famous—not famous; nothing I've ever done is famous (*laughs*)—but the most sort of conspicuous example was with the two productions of *Plenty*. When we produced the play in London, both Kate [Nelligan] and I were gung ho for Susan. And because we were so gung ho for her, we alienated the audiences and we unbalanced the play. Because when I wrote it, there was meant to be a balance between her and her husband. She chooses one path and pays a price for that: the price is madness and isolation; he chooses the other path, the path of consent with the society, and the price is inertia and repression. And it was meant to be a classical play offering those two balances—those two tendencies. But because we were so pro Susan, we unbalanced the play in London.

HZ: So that the audience doesn't see the choice that Brock has made, and the fact that that destroys him.

DH: That's right. The first thing I did in New York, unconsciously even, was to put both actors on the poster instead of just Kate. So that in London it was the study of a woman, and in New York it was the study of a woman's relationship and what it meant to the man. As soon as those two things were balanced out, the play became a much better play. And Susan was less irritating because I, as the director, wasn't trying to rig the play.

HZ: In the introduction to *The History Plays*, you state that you didn't do much rewriting of *Plenty* for New York, except to change a few lines whose references were too British.

DH: Wasn't it rubbers and condoms, or something like that?

HZ: Well, being an academic—that is to say, a pedant—I naturally checked the two texts pretty closely. And I found some changes that went beyond the merely "local." Was this an attempt to try to "control"—as much as you can—an audience's reaction to Susan? I'll give you an example: at the end of scene six in the original, just before Susan shoots at Mick, Mick says to Alice, "She is actually mad," whereas in the New York text he says, "Why doesn't she listen?"

DH: Because we thought the word "mad" was prejudicial. I take out the directly prejudicial. I mean, once somebody is said to be mad you cease to listen to what they've got to say, you've categorized them. So I always try to take out prejudicial lines. The line that caused the most contention among the actors in *Secret Rapture* was Irwin's line to Isobel about Katherine: "There's such a thing as evil. You're dealing with evil." And the actress who played Katherine in New York said she used to turn off her monitor when the line came up because she disliked it so much; she said it prejudiced the audience against her. I felt that from Irwin's point of view, who in a way is involved in a fight to the death against Katherine, it was justified. But I knew why Mary Beth [Hurt] wasn't very happy with it.

HZ: You're right; that line tells us much more about Irwin than it does about Katherine.

DH: This is very interesting—I mean, I've only just thought of this—but I've lately been working with Louis Malle on a film based on a novel [Josephine Hart's *Damage*]. And I realized that when I'm working on narrative with Louis, who knows more about narrative than I will ever know, at every point he and I are asking the question: "What will the audience be thinking at this point?" In a film, I do think you are always trying to answer in some way that question. When I write a play, I don't think that at all. My experience of a play, of an evening in the theatre, is that it works by silting up—different people get different things at different times—and the effect of it is cumulative, whereas a movie does seem to be linear: you have to guide the audience down a particular path. In a play I'm not conscious of doing that at all. But while I say I'm not conscious of trying to manipulate what the audience think in a play as much as I am in a movie, it is nevertheless a good idea to take out things that will positively mislead.

This issue of removing prejudicial things—for eight weeks Richard [Eyre, the director] asked me to remove a speech in *Murmuring Judges* where the lawyer goes to the prison and says that one young male in three has been convicted of a crime, and then she says that it's not very sensible putting young males in prison: "Being a criminal's an adolescent phase, it's like wearing an ear-ring or listening to pop, it's mildly annoying but it won't last for long." Right? Now Richard begged me to take this speech out, and I didn't, and then sure enough I opened *Time* and the reviewer, while describing the play as the best play of the season, nevertheless said that Hare's ideas are absolute balderdash because he seems to think young criminals shouldn't be punished. Now, I *don't* think young criminals shouldn't be punished; the *speech* doesn't say that; the *character* doesn't say that. But I know why a critic walks away thinking that that's what I think. When I read *Time*, I said to Richard we've got to take that speech out. Right? And he said, "Oh, you mean the only way I can get rewrites out of you is by sixty million midwesterners reading a travesty of what you actually think."

(*Laughs.*) And I said, well, it did concentrate my mind wonderfully to read that.

HZ: Could you talk a little bit about influences on your writing? Do you feel there are any specific ones—I mean, playwrights whose work you admire and who you feel have influenced you in some way?

DH: I've always been very frightened to say this, but I don't feel any. I feel much more that if there are writers I admire, and I admire quite a few, I'm far more likely to *avoid* what they do, on the grounds that their world is not mine. There are certain areas I would never think to stray into, because I would get very nervous if I began to think that this was becoming like something that, say, Athol Fugard would write. Because Fugard so completely controls his own world, and I would not wish to wipe my shoes on the mat on the way in.

HZ: Right—I didn't mean "influence" quite so literally; I was thinking of much subtler echoes or resonances. For instance, when I hear the last line of *A Map of the World*, which is Mehta saying "Madeleine. Michael. To London. Let's go," I can't help hearing an echo of the last line of Beckett's *Waiting for Godot*: "Let's go."

DH: Oh, really? Well, I don't, you see. But I never do.

HZ: The echo makes a kind of ironic sense: *Godot* is a circular play in which the characters never move, while your play is all about movement.

DH: Yes, it is. To me *A Map of the World* is a mess. It may be a rich mess—I mean in that there's all sorts of stuff in it—but the formal problems of it are very profound, I think. And the "Let's go" line is a sort of cheat, in that it's an attempt to pretend that the evening has had a shape which I'm not quite sure it *has* had.

HZ: I found the critical response to *Map* in London simply incredible. Most critics couldn't seem to distinguish between the play proper and the movie embedded within it—which makes total nonsense of the play.

DH: I was just bewildered by this. We had a lot less trouble with it in Australia. You know, Australia has a very peculiar theatre culture—it's jackdawish, with all sorts of influences—but there's a love of formal experiment and freedom from naturalism, which there is much less in England, and the result was no Australian critic had any trouble understanding exactly what was happening when. It mystified me; I think that critics in this country have very little formal understanding of what you're trying to do with style or form at all. They simply think of plays as television plays.

HZ: So it's all content.

DH: The way a play says it is not considered at all.

HZ: You said a few minutes ago that you admired a lot of writers. Does ideology come into this? Is it possible for you to admire a playwright whose ideology you find distasteful?

DH: Of course. In a way, playwriting is a craft. I can weigh a play in my hand like sliced meat: I know how much effort it's cost; I know, within fifteen minutes, how much the playwright's put into it; I know what it means to him or her; I know the density of the effort that they've made. Those people who make that density of effort, and it's very clear who they are—well, it's not true to say that I don't mind what they're saying, but it's true that you can't not respect people who go on struggling with form, struggling with the real problems of the day, who stay writing contemporary material. And this I do feel very, very strongly about—that this whole retreat into historical romanticism which has beset the modern theatre is just a cul-de-sac. To keep writing about the present day is the job. And anyone who goes on being engaged with the present day, and who goes on putting into it that density of effort, as I would call it—density of imagination, even—of course you respect them.

HZ: Are there contemporary playwrights you care to mention whose work you feel reflects that density of effort and imagination?

DH: Well, Fugard obviously. [David] Mamet goes on trying to be involved in the real day. Christopher Hampton, I would feel very strongly; Caryl Churchill, certainly. Now, Christopher's politics are very different from my own. Caryl's politics I'm sure are completely different from my own. But you can't not know that Caryl is serious. She's fantastically talented: everything she writes is very, very interesting. She's just the real thing. You don't go saying, "Ooh, I hope they toe the line. Ooh, I hope they say something I agree with." Caryl's a great mind, so you go to find out what Caryl's thinking now. And it's exciting to find out what Caryl's thinking about. Even if you don't like a particular play, you want to find out where she's going next.

Take her play *Ice Cream*. I mean, plainly *Ice Cream* is not Caryl's greatest work; Caryl would not pretend it was her greatest work. But she's someone who's going on evolving, and will evolve to something that you know will come out of *Ice Cream*. And sometimes, like with my play *The Bay at Nice*, you just have to say, "I'm sorry, I need this play to go on. I just actually need to see this play. I know it's not the greatest play ever written, but we'll look at it and I will learn, and only by writing that will I be able to write the next one."

HZ: Do you mean *Bay* specifically, or are you referring to the double bill with *Wrecked Eggs*?

DH: I don't like the second play at all; I still haven't really cracked it—

HZ: So to speak.

DH: Sorry. (*Laughs.*) But it had to go on. I would have felt very unfulfilled if it hadn't gone on. But it plainly is there to lead to something else.

HZ: Do you feel at all uneasy about having so much of your work done at the National Theatre? I hate to throw 15-year-old interviews back at you, but in the interview you gave *Theatre Quarterly* in 1975 you stated that if playwrights can possibly survive in the commercial theatre, then their work shouldn't be blocking up the subsidized stages.

DH: I've never felt I *could* survive in the commercial theatre. You know, somebody pointed out to me the other day that there wasn't a British film that had taken in as much money in London as *Pravda* did as a play. But *Pravda* was still unmovable to the West End, because the cast was twenty-five; and also Tony [Hopkins] felt, I think rightly, that he couldn't play it eight times a week. That kind of role is like being asked to play Lear eight times a week; it can't be done. So I've never been a commercial writer: I've never had a commercial hit, in a commercial theatre—except on Broadway. The economics of my plays are very difficult.

HZ: Could we talk for a minute about your films? To what extent do you feel that the films nurture the playwriting, and is it that way as opposed to vice versa?

DH: Well, because I'm sort of at the moment committed to five years of work at the National, writing three plays, then obviously I feel the stage plays are the centre of my work. I went off for a romance with the movies, really, and it was great fun while it lasted. The necessary time and energy that you need to be a first-rate film-maker, I don't feel I have.

HZ: Do you feel that the plays you wrote after starting to make films were different because of the films?

DH: No. The claim that was made about my plays from the very beginning was that they were filmic. I was much more nourished by the cinema when I was young than I was by the stage. And when I grew up, the stage was the prisoner of the closed set, the one-room play, the psychological drama, etc.—which has never been my interest. It was from the cinema that I got all the richness, the sense of life's passage, history on the hoof, you know, that you went to Truffaut or Louis [Malle] himself or Godard for.

HZ: So was it European films you were attracted to more than American films?

DH: Yeah. And British. When I was a kid, war movies and *Doctor in the House* and everything—the whole pageant—was at the cinema. So, yes, when I started working in the theatre, yes, I thought, why shouldn't it have the same freedom as the cinema to move where it wants to, to show the passage of time boldly? Why shouldn't it? Why shouldn't you tell stories that are just as melodramatic as the stories the movies tell? Why shouldn't the fun of the cinema be on the stage? Certainly I felt that. But that also coincided with a way of looking at things which was not suited to box sets. You know, I've never wanted to put three characters in one room and let them get at it.

So my plays have always been fluid; they always had that movement. In fact, the reverse is what usually people want or ask for—namely, to make a film of *Pravda*, to make a film of *Secret Rapture*, to make a film of *Racing Demon*, all of which people want to do. And I am lost for any way to—I just don't know how to adapt things for the cinema that so depend on the live audience. In every case I've drawn a blank.

HZ: In the King's College, Cambridge lecture you gave in 1978, you spoke about the pervasive cynicism paralyzing public life and the extraordinary intensity of people's personal despair. Would you give the same lecture today?

DH: No. I think one of the *good* effects of Thatcherism is that it's had the effect in this country of a huge ideological shake-out. It shook things up, in that for a long period, the period that *Pravda* records, people were not ready to fight: they rolled over incredibly easily. When this woman arrived, everybody just curled up and gave in to her. The liberal establishment just didn't know how to fight the forces of change; it didn't know how to organize. Now I think one of the things she did which was good—its *effect* was good, just like you might say that a diarrhetic or a chronic laxative is good for you—was to make those of us who disagree with the Right organize ourselves about what we believe and how we intend to defend what we believe. I think most people are a bit mentally fitter than they were in the late seventies because of that.

HZ: It must have taken guts to give that lecture at that particular time.

DH: Yes. The lecture was very badly received.

HZ: Especially by the Left.

DH: Well, it was a decisive point in the road. I knew I was breaking ranks from certain mealy mouthed pieties of the Left: everybody was going on pretending that the organized Left meant something to the life of the country, and the word "revolution" was still being bandied around. It ceased to be a meaningful word in this country, I think, in the 1930s. There was also the idea that the theatre existed purely to effect political change, which was so popular in the sixties and which indeed I subscribed to in the late sixties. The lecture *was* a breaking of ranks. And at the time it was extremely unpopular and attracted a great deal of abuse. But what I wanted to say was "Now come on, wake up, we have actually got to redraw the lines here." It's not doing the theatre any good to pretend that plays exist just to put over a point of view, because that idea's counterproductive, it doesn't work. Even if it were desirable, plays don't work like this. And it was not a popular thing to say at that moment. Now, if anything, it's become a cliché.

HZ: One last question. I was sad to read about the recent death of Peggy Ramsay; I was wondering if you could comment about the role an agent can play in a playwright's life.

DH: I don't think she was an agent really. I mean, she was officially your agent, but to a number of writers—[Joe] Orton obviously, and David Mercer, and Christopher [Hampton] and me and a number of others—she was somebody who at the absolutely crucial, formative moment when you began to write plays made you feel those plays were plausible. You know, it's very difficult now to remember how contentious a young playwright's work is. Most younger playwrights, if they're any good at all, what they're doing is very, very unusual. And to have as I had this woman, who was the best-recognized judge of a play in the country, come and say that my plays belonged with that body of work that she thought were the leading plays of the day, at a time when I was about to sail into very, very rough critical weather—well, it was irreplaceable.

I don't know whether I would have got through that period without her, without that belief she had. Particularly in *Knuckle* and that whole time when we were fantastically embattled. She simply had the distance and the passion to say that it is the expectation of any serious writer to sail into a lot of trouble. And she always said I was in for trouble all the way. "But," she said to me, "you are on a longer burn than any playwright I know." And she said that from the very beginning. She said that it wasn't worth discussing what they think of *Knuckle*, because *Knuckle* doesn't matter. What matters is what I'll be doing in twenty years' time. And so she always thought that I would have a very long writing span, which has luckily proved to be true. In a profession where people burn out very quickly, or have very fierce, brief periods of writing, I'm sort of on a second, possibly third, wind. I mean, you are very conscious as a playwright that you go through periods in which the urgency of what you want to say coincides with your ability to say it, and that that is cyclical: it does come and go. I know quite clearly that some plays of mine are botched up, and they're botched up in periods where the mix isn't right. You just have to go through those periods, and hope you'll come back into the periods where it all gels again.

Rare Hare, Liking Women

Ruby Cohn

"Raymond loved women. . . . It's very rare," says a wise woman in *Strapless* (70), and one might extend the statement to embrace the author/director of that film, David Hare. More than any other living male dramatist, Hare has given voice to women—on stage, film, and television. With that introduction, I sound as though I am setting Hare up only to knock him down, in a predictable feminist fashion.[1] Hare's treatment of women characters is not, however, invariant, and I hope to unveil its nuances.

A graduate of public school and Cambridge University, Hare has drawn most of his characters—female and male—from his own middle class. More often than not, Hare's men accommodate to their privileged position in an immoral society—usually in England—but his women are less complacent. From the schoolteachers of *Slag* (1970) to the black barrister of *Murmuring Judges* (1991), Hare's women tend to fit badly into a bad society, and a few of his heroines "struggle . . . against a deceitful and emotionally stultified class . . ." (Introduction, *History* 15).

Hare believes "that I didn't write until I wrote *Knuckle* [1974]. . . . Up till then I was writing purely satirical work" (Oliva 165). It is therefore unkind to begin this examination with a "purely satirical work," but *Slag* is too heraldic to ignore. The very title prophesies other witty, enigmatic Hare titles—*The Great Exhibition, Knuckle, Teeth 'n' Smiles, Plenty, The Secret Rapture, Racing Demon, Murmuring Judges*. Never actually

23

mentioned in the play of that name, "slag" is defined in the
Oxford English Dictionary as "a piece of refuse matter separated
from a metal in the process of smelting"; presumably by
extension, slag is British slang for cheap "refuse matter" sex, as
in Hare's "I own up to the slag I want" (*Brophy* 99) or "Couple of
slags here say anyone fancy a blow-job?" (*Teeth 'n' Smiles* 14) or
Pinter's Max to Ruth: "You think you're just going to get that big
slag all the time?" (*The Homecoming* 80–81).

As the title *Slag* reverses the letters of "gals," Hare's play
reverses the sexes of *Love's Labor's Lost* but borrows its basic
situation. Shakespeare's male scholars forswear intercourse with
the opposite sex, and Hare's female teachers forswear intercourse with their opposites, and thus lose all the girls of their
private boarding school. Disingenuously, Hare in 1975 defended
his early play: "[T]he point is that [*Slag* is] really a play about
institutions, not about women at all. . . . It's about every
institution I had known— . . . ever more baroque discussions
about ever dwindling subjects. But it happens to be peopled with
women, partly because it was the sort of play that I thought I
would enjoy going to see—women on the stage, represented as I
thought more roundly and comprehensively than was then
usual" (Itzin and Trussler 110–11). Hare's own uncertainty of
tone—a play "not about women at all," who are nevertheless
well-rounded characters—is reflected in uncertainty of critical
interpretation, even though *Slag* won him an award as the
Evening Standard's Most Promising Playwright. Although we see
only a hint of the institutional school, Hare's preoccupation with
institutions predicts his trilogy of the 1990s.

The "baroque discussions" of *Slag* emanate mainly from
Joanne, the militant feminist and Marxist film critic, but it is also
she who brays obscenities, which were still titillating in 1970—
fuck, bugger, crap, clit, wank, cunt, arse, fartarse, and the
succinct sentence: "[Women] bang like shithouse doors" (24). On
her failed suicide attempts, Joanne ruminates: "You've heard of
haemophiliacs, well I'm a haemophobiac, couldn't keep the
wretched stuff flowing" (70). With her versatile lexicon, Joanne is
at once rebellious and ridiculous. The loner of the pedagogic trio
in the elite boarding school—inept at games, contemptuous of
her colleagues, scornful of titled pupils, sexually inexperienced—

Joanne closes the play in the lack of closure to which Hare became partial.

Ann and Elise are less clearly delineated. Thirty-two years of age—"She's old" (40)—Ann, the school's owner, is at once snobbish, realistic, and communitarian: "But my experience of men is what makes me a woman" (49). As her school disintegrates, Ann keeps a stiff upper lip in her lying letters to her mother: "It is a constant struggle to keep in tune with new ideas. However, a new cricket pavilion will go some way. . . . [Joanne and Elise] are a constant source of help to me" (68). Finally, Ann hopes to resuscitate the school: "Circulate Burke's Peerage for new pupils" (77).

If Joanne is a satirized feminist, and Ann a satirized patrician, Elise lies in some nebulous terrain between the two. She spends much of her stage time knitting for her unborn son, father unknown. Of the three, Elise alone is unrepentantly female, even baring her breasts on stage. She accuses her colleagues: "You've lived so long on other people's behalf you've ceased to recognize yourselves" (76). But Elise is in no position to accuse, since her pregnancy is a graphic lie finally deflated in "a great wet fart" (77).

Although *Slag* reads today like the witty, misogynistic romp of a clever young man, it does announce Hare's serious theme of living with lies, since that is what his English female trio do. Ann's lie is a facade of community, Elise's is her fantasy pregnancy, but the most blatant lie is Joanne's intransigent feminism. Although the trio may undertake to rebuild their all-girls' school, Hare's implied norm is harmonious heterosexuality. Yet Hare gives his Elise a disarming line, which may be turned against him: "This is not the way women speak together, it's not the way they live. It doesn't ring true" (74).

As Hare's dramaturgy grew in assurance, some of his women ring more true and less strident. Hare's wit gains focus in his recurrent critique of middle-class professional women, but he also portrays women who are themselves critical of their—and his—class. Sometimes at the center and sometimes on the sidelines of their respective plays, these women are burdened with a conscience often lacking to men. A conscience who smokes, drinks, and runs a shady night club, Jenny Wilbur is

only a secondary character in Hare's first West End production
and favorite play, *Knuckle*.[2] Hare once described Jenny as "the
most admirable person I've ever drawn" (Itzin and Trussler 114),
but *drama* thrives on less admirable persons. Hare himself
realized: "Jenny sees bad things done and condemns them, but
she herself is not much changed" (Introduction, *History* 13). She
bewilders the gun-running protagonist Curly, who sketches her
in two conflicting verbal portraits: "White-knickered do-good
cock-shrivelling cow" (72) and ". . . the hard, bright, glistening
girl" (85).

Before Curly expresses these polar views of her, Jenny
herself delivers a distinctive monologue:

> Young women in Guildford must expect to be threatened.
> Men here lead ugly lives and girls are the only touchstones
> left. Cars cruise beside you as you walk down the
> pavement. I have twice been attacked at the country club,
> the man in the house opposite has a telephoto lens, my
> breasts are often touched on commuter trains, my body is
> covered with random thumbprints, the doctor says he
> needs to undress me completely to vaccinate my arm, men
> often spill drinks in my lap, or brush cigarettes against my
> bottom, very old men bump into me and clutch at my legs
> as they fall. I have been offered drinks, money, social
> advancement and once an editorial position on the
> *Financial Times*. I expect to be bumped, bruised, followed,
> assaulted, stared at and propositioned for the rest of my
> life, while at the same time offering sanctuary, purity,
> reassurance, prestige—the only point of loveliness in
> men's ever-darkening lives. (66)

Jenny's account of indignities makes up in energy what it lacks
in proportion. Three men are obsessed with Jenny: one threatens
her with a knife, another commits suicide and leaves her a bar,
and a third, Curly, announces: "I'm propositioning you" (52).
She of the "incandescent vagina" (41) taunts Curly to uncover
the truth about his sister's disappearance, and he finds that his
father is the rankest culprit in the moral sewer of Guildford. The
self-styled "point of loveliness" for three men, Jenny Wilbur is a
strong secondary character, but she remains subsidiary to the
investigation of the "business practice" of father and son—that
venerable theme of realistic drama.[3]

Some fifteen years later, Frances Parnell functions comparably in Hare's *Racing Demon* (1990). A sophisticated Londoner from an ecclesiastical family, Frances lacks Jenny's colorful language, but she too is aware of providing "the only point of loveliness in men's ever-darkening lives"—specifically, in the lives of two men, both Anglican clergymen. Frances withdraws her sexual favors from young Tony when she is aware of his ruthless ambition, and she withdraws her comforting presence from middle-aged Lionel when she is aware of "Letting [him] imagine" (61). A minor character, Frances inherits Jenny's moral rectitude in a play about insidious business in the Anglican Church (which scants the controversial Church problem of female clergymen). Like the males in *Racing Demon*, Frances directly addresses God, but she alone is selflessly accusatory, for Hare has endowed her with little self, beyond her appeal to two clergymen in conflict.

Two other subsidiary women are neatly balanced in *Racing Demon*—Heather, the neglected wife of the humanistic clergyman, and Stella, an abused black woman evangelized by the unscrupulous clergyman. Ignorant of the central conflict within the Church, these two auxiliary women are victimized by that conflict, the one losing her sanity and the other her freedom, but Frances retains both qualities as she flies away from an increasingly hypocritical England, to close this first play of Hare's projected trilogy on British institutions.

Between *Knuckle* and *Racing Demon*, Hare conceived other supportive and conscience-carrying women who are on the sidelines of masculine matters in their respective plays.[4] The ambitious male journalist of his television play *Dreams of Leaving* (1980) is teased by an enigmatic beauty who challenges his accommodation with a crooked system. *A Map of the World* (1982) and *Saigon: Year of the Cat* (1983) trace Hare's emergence from English insularity to a broader canvas. The intricate plot of the former winds around a movie based on a novel, based on events into which I will not digress. All three genres—movie, novel, "real event"—pivot on an erotic triangle: an Indian novelist and an English journalist, political opponents, are also rivals for the sexual favors of Peggy, an American actress. A minor character, Peggy has no connection with the world conference on hunger, the reason for the encounters of the other characters. The Indian novelist, whom Peggy marries, summarizes his fiction: "The actress questions her easy promiscuity and is made to realize adulthood will involve choice" (222). In Hare's play, however, we have only his word for it, telling instead of showing Peggy's maturation.[5]

The teleplay *Saigon* offers a less secondary and more moral woman, who nevertheless is sheltered from the world of men. At the end of the Vietnam War English Barbara, a blonde *"almost 50"* bank official (85), engages in a love affair with a CIA agent who is half her age, while panic replaces orderly withdrawal from Saigon. The play provides little confirmation of CIA Bob's confession to Barbara: "Every time I saw you, you made me feel guilty. . . . That's why I stopped coming to see you" (140). Still, that little marks Barbara as another Englishwoman of conscience. Unlike her sporadic lover, she shows concern for her subordinates, including the Vietnamese. Bob forgets to destroy the files of the Vietnamese who have worked for the Americans, and, leaving, he mumbles: "God forgive us" (151). But Barbara utters no such prayer. Like Jenny before her in Hare's work, like Frances after her, Barbara is cleanly on the sidelines of the dirty world of men.

In *Pravda*, Hare's 1985 play co-written with Howard Brenton, Rebecca Foley has a degree in investigative journalism, but she serves mainly to support her crusading journalist husband, and finally to condemn his acquiescence to a powerful publisher. Rebecca's husband is an incidental victim of a megalomaniacal newspaper tycoon, and she is even more incidental—as Hare himself recognized: "The character of the wife is just the worst-written part" (Oliva 173). A year later, in 1986, Hare created a pair of non-English, morally sound women for each of his one-acters about an imperiled marriage—*The Bay at Nice*, set in Soviet Russia, and *Wrecked Eggs*, set in the United States. Written for the actress Blair Brown, in admiration of her "sense of everyday" (Oliva 176), the plays are slight vehicles with decidedly uneveryday situations. In these plays of moral women on the sidelines or in slight plays, one can argue that Hare faithfully depicts the sexism of contemporary society.

When women are leading characters in plays based in that same society—from *Teeth 'n' Smiles* (1975) to *Murmuring Judges* (1991)—Hare's attitude varies. Occasionally, the women are in the *Slag* lineage of living lies, but at least as often they are imbued with the moral fervor of the sideliners. Hare himself has insisted: "Women are characteristically the conscience of my plays" (Nightingale 6). Moreover, conscience is enhanced by consciousness of the cost of morality in a period of greed.

Teeth 'n' Smiles is unique in Hare's oeuvre, uncandidly autobiographical, enfolding rock songs, and almost allegorizing the decline of England after the hopeful revolutions of 1968. Set in 1969 at the Cambridge May Ball, the play was originally "to be all about Maggie, but actually she is only on the stage for about forty-five minutes" (Kerensky 186). During that time, however, Maggie rises from an alcoholic stupor to martyrdom.

Through an energetic exposition we learn that Maggie met Arthur when she was a seventeen-year-old folk singer and he was a Cambridge student—writing songs for her, shaping her persona, and claiming to love her: "[Arthur] invents me" (38). Apparently disillusioned that their popular music inspired no revolution, Maggie rejected happiness along with Arthur, substituting drink, self-pity, easy sexuality, and easier decon-struction. She is scornful of Arthur's (verbal) idealism: "It's all gotta mean something . . . that's childish, Arthur. It don't mean anything" (52). And equally scornful of her manager's cynicism. When one of the band members conceals his drugs in her bag, Maggie accepts arrest: "O.K. Try prison for a while, why not?" (72).

In the original production Helen Mirren's Maggie commanded the theatre with flair. Even before she sets foot on stage, Maggie's drunken condition is on everyone's lips: "She starts drinking at breakfast, she passes out after lunch, then she's up for supper, ready for the show" (12). The first set and the first scene close on Maggie's song "Passing Through," which confirms what we have heard about her: "If you don't scream honey / How do they know you're there" (30). In one way or another, Maggie screams, and we know she is there. She makes mincemeat of her Cambridge student interviewer (a young Antony Sher) as she derides his sexual fumbling. In the second set Maggie insults the Cambridge audience instead of singing, and she is punished beyond measure. In swift succession her manager fires her and announces Arthur's new love. Maggie accepts the band's betrayal and disappears during their third set. But she returns in style, setting fire to the concert tent, excoriating her manager, bestowing Arthur on her rival, and finally turning her back on us: "Remember, I'm nobody's excuse. If you love me, keep on the move" (85). Maggie may not spark a revolution, but "on the move" she threatens Cambridge with conflagration: "Police. Ambulance. Fire brigade. You just got to score the air-sea rescue service and you got a full house" (79). Arthur may have molded her art, but Maggie alone has the will to fail when the world around her is driving toward success. Onstage, Maggie's mobility resonates in a whiskey-voiced nobility that refutes failure.

More subdued and elegant than Mirren's Maggie, Kate Nelligan shoulders the burden of conscience in Hare's works of the late 1970s. A teenage heroine of World War II is common to the teleplay *Licking Hitler* and the stage play *Plenty* (both 1978). The very title *Licking Hitler* puns on the success and subservience of a British Political Warfare Unit, whose mission is to undermine German morale by broadcasting seemingly casual conversations between far-flung Germans during the war. Formed to lick or vanquish fascism, the unit adopts or licks up the tactics of fascism. Archie Maclean from the Red Clyde is "one of our most gifted writers" (123), or inventor of scurrilous lies about citizens of the Third Reich. Anna Seaton, later designated by Hare as "the conscience of the play" (Introduction, *History* 13), translates Archie's defamations into German, a language she learned during summers in a family *Schloss* on the Rhine.

Lonely and young enough to sleep with her teddy bear, upper-class English Anna at first protects herself from working-class Glaswegian Archie by jamming a chair under the door-handle of her bedroom. After she removes it, Archie rapes her. Anna nurses her wounds in silence, and they begin an affair: "I don't know what he thinks about anything. We've never had a conversation. We just have a thing" (120). Humiliating Anna during working hours, Archie finally terminates the "thing" by reporting to his superior that Anna has "tried unsuccessfully to get him to sleep with [her]." In spite of her protests—"But it's not true" (124)—she is forced to resign. In a much criticized conclusion Hare resorts to anonymous voice-over to trace the postwar careers of the unit. Archie filmed documentaries, and then Hollywood potboilers. Anna spent ten years in advertising before rejecting its lies; marriage, adultery, and promiscuity were punctuated by a hysterectomy. Having traced these trajectories, with no communication between them, Anna sees Archie's latest film and writes him "complaining of the falseness of his films, the way they sentimentalized what she knew to be his appalling childhood and lamenting, in sum, the films' lack of political direction" (127). Sentimentalizing herself, Anna closes her letter: "I have remembered the one lie you told to make me go away. And I now at last have come to understand why you told it." She then declares her love for Archie, but: "He never replied" (128).

Hare has conceded that the voice-over is clumsy, but he is silent about its untruth. On the one hand, he acknowledges that "both Anna Seaton and Archie Maclean are trapped in myths about their own past from which they seem unwilling to escape" (Introduction, *History* 13). Anna's myth inflates a "thing" into love, and Archie mythologizes his working-class roots, but we see the play's events through Anna's eyes, and since she and Archie "never have a conversation," how does she recognize "the falseness of his films"? We have only her word that Archie sensed the "corrosive national habit of lying" (128), and although she claims to understand what she calls his "one lie," we are not made privy to that understanding.

Feminists have criticized Hare for Anna's post-rape affair with Archie, and the playwright has pleaded that "such things do regrettably happen" (Introduction, *History* 13), but the play itself does not grapple with *why* they happen. Does Anna submit to Archie through fear? sexual attraction? self-deception? If Anna is, as Hare claims, the conscience of the play, she should not be trapped in a myth about her past, including the myth of a meaningful love affair with Archie.

In *Plenty*, a wittier and less submissive Kate Nelligan enacts Susan Traherne, who spends World War II in France as a subversive agent and peacetime in Britain as an equally subversive agent.[6] Hare has described *Plenty* as "a play about the cost of spending your whole life in dissent" (Introduction, *History* 14). He has also claimed that people can "go clinically mad if what they believe bears no relation to how they live" (Myerson 28). What enthralls in the theatre is the ambiguity of whether Susan Traherne's behavior is dissent or madness. Clear, however, is the mounting desperation of Hare's most resonant heroine.

The play opens on a naked man in a nearly bare house—the obverse of plenty. Susan Traherne is on the point of leaving her husband and giving their Knightsbridge home to a longtime woman friend. The next scene flashes us back twenty years to wartime France where a teenaged Susan greets a British airman who has just parachuted down. Susan soon reveals her fear, and it is the man who saves their supplies from a rival claimant in the French Resistance: "Gestapo nothing, it's the bloody French" (139). After the war Susan is restless and supercilious about "people who stayed behind" (146), so that her future husband Raymond Brock asks: "You don't think you wear your suffering a little heavily? This smart club of people you belong to who had a very bad war . . ." (147).

Hare shades Susan's dialogue, however, not with overt suffering but with cutting deflation of an increasingly prosperous Britain. She abandons her export job and office "mating dance" (152) to seek impregnation by a working-class stranger: "Deep down I'd do the whole damn thing by myself. But there we are. You're second-best" (164). After eighteen sterile months, Susan abandons that project, and when the young man appeals to her emotions, she shoots at him, but guns are not her forte. We next see Susan right after the Suez "blunder or folly or fiasco" (173), married to the diplomat Brock, and scathing about the diplomatic corps. Susan imperils Brock's career by refusing to return to Iran with him, and yet she threatens a senior diplomatic officer with suicide if Brock is not promoted: "I think you have destroyed my husband, you see" (194). But it is Susan who proceeds to destroy Brock, after destroying their common property: "A universe of things. . . . What are these godforsaken bloody awful things?" (199). A few weeks after Susan abandons Brock, she shares a tawdry hotel room with the nameless pilot whom she rescued during the war. When he leaves her, she slips into a drug-induced fantasy of the Resistance, where she responds radiantly to a Frenchman's welcome: "There will be days and days and days like this" (207).[7]

Earlier, a perceptive Brock has charged: "When you talk longingly about the war . . . some deception usually follows" (159). But longing talk about the war is itself deception for Susan, denying its danger and Anglo-French rivalry. Susan Traherne's dissent is oblique: she is contemptuous of the English pride in plenty, of the hypocrisies of the British diplomatic corps, of the resolution with which individuals pursue their selfish goals. She confesses to the erstwhile pilot: "I have a weakness. I like to lose control" (203). Like Anna Seaton in *Licking Hitler*, Susan Traherne is trapped in a myth about her past, a myth she does not wish to control.

Until *Plenty* Hare's protagonists tend to be loners, but Susan is not only married; she also has a woman friend, who lounges in and out of love until she feels old enough "to do good" (197) to unmarried mothers. Although Brock reclaims his Knightsbridge house from that friend, she can presumably continue the good deeds, which never cross Susan's mind. Caustic, violent, and only intermittently scrupulous, Susan Traherne does, as Hare claimed, dissent, but it is a self-indulgent dissent that serves no social purpose. Except for stimulating theatre.

When Hare shifted from the stage to film, he refocused on women without conscience, but they are no longer satirized, as in *Slag*. Visual beauty replaces verbal wit. *Wetherby* (1985) seems to be warmly affectionate to its protagonist because of the luminous presence of Vanessa Redgrave, but also because, fifteen years after *Slag*, Hare was less sanguine about middle-class schoolteachers with repressed sexuality. Deftly interweaving his Jean Travers as mature woman (Redgrave) and as student in love (Joely Richardson, Redgrave's daughter), Hare titles his film for a Yorkshire town where feelings smoulder unexpressed. Hare's Jean Travers *traverses* class boundaries when, as a teenager, she falls in love with a working-class airman. By the end of *Wetherby* a mature Jean Travers, sharing a drink (and perhaps a bed?) with her best friend's husband, has been shaded as an unwitting murderer; suppressing her own emotions, she has effectively killed two passionate men. As a teenager, Jean is unable to articulate her need of the young airman she loves, so he departs for the Orient where he is killed in a gambling den. As a middle-aged teacher, Jean refuses to confess her emotions to a stranger, so he challenges her repression by shooting himself before her very eyes.[8]

Jean's responsibility for these two deaths is never flatly stated in the film, but it is implied when three repetitions of the young airman's violent death are enclosed within clips of the suicide of the young stranger. And yet responsibility does not mean blame—"Was it your fault?" (118). The double violence teaches the teacher Jean to free her own feelings. Not only do she and the investigating policeman make love, *"all the tension going out of them"* (130), but Jean and her best friend's husband approve of her student who leaves Wetherby to live in London with her boyfriend: "Good luck to her. . . . To all our escapes" (132). Neither an escapee nor a rebel against repression, Jean Travers has nevertheless learned the power of passion.

We see a harder woman in *Paris by Night*, the movie Hare scripted soon after *Wetherby*. This time the repressed and professional woman (Charlotte Rampling) is an efficient political Conservative. The overriding ambition of Clara Paige has driven her husband to drink, and their child to loneliness. Before entering politics, husband and wife shared a business with Michael Swanton, who went to prison for crooked dealings in which the three were accomplices. Free but disgraced, Swanton begs Clara for money but is refused.

Paris by night resembles Wetherby as a site of unmoored passion for a usually inhibited Englishwoman. Startled by a mysterious telephone caller—"I know who you are" (5)—Clara Paige abruptly leaves London for her Paris mission, but on impulse she abandons her post to enjoy the French capital with a handsome young stranger, Wallace Sharp. Another impulse dictates a tender parting so that she can walk alone, but she is suddenly confronted with Michael Swanton on the Pont des Arts. Believing herself followed by him, she gives vent to still another—but far more violent—impulse: she pushes Swanton off the bridge into the Seine below. By morning, Clara is back at work—a lone but admired female figure in a world of men. In London Clara's son has undergone an emergency appendectomy. Promising to leave Paris at once, she suddenly recognizes Swanton's distraught daughter, and the once cool English Tory turns again to Wallace, to spend a passionate night: "*Small howls of pain from CLARA, as if WALLACE were trying to get the truth out of her*" (61). But Clara's life congeals in lies.

Back in England Clara resumes political business as usual, while her husband and her lover in their separate cities read of the discovery of Swanton's body. The lover seeks her out in England, and she confesses the murder, but promises him a divorce and a new life: "If we're honest, we can make a fresh start" (78). It is an insuperable "if." In London Clara's husband, gun in hand, accuses her of killing Swanton, and of having a lover. Clara counteraccuses her husband of incriminating them to Swanton, whereupon he lifts the gun and fires five shots: "CLARA *slumps to the ground, dead*" (83).

"You're my first naked Tory" (59), Clara's lover informs her during their Paris night, and that is true of Hare as well. Bright, ruthless, and seductive, Clara Paige preaches morality while practicing hypocrisy, but the film gradually undresses her. Hare himself has claimed that "Clara Paige is not such a terrible person," and that, in filming, "We simply did not know what our response to Clara was" (Introduction, *Paris* vii, ix). Some of us, however, do know our response to murder, however inadvertent, a response guided in the film by the hard light on and hard lines of Charlotte Rampling's resolution.

Clara's lover assures her that she has a softer side, and Hare's *The Secret Rapture* (1988) dramatizes a (metaphorically) naked Tory as Marion, and her soft-sided sister as Isobel.[9] The critic Philip French has summarized the resemblances between the play and the film: ". . . a female Thatcherite politician with a weak husband, financial chicanery visited upon the innocent by unscrupulous entrepreneurs, a woman shot . . . at point-blank range by a desperate man. . . ." However, Clara is shot by her wronged husband, and her last words are a spiteful accusation. Isobel is shot by the lover who wronged her, and her last words are humorously self-effacing: "I haven't got shoes [on]. Still you can't have everything" (78).

In *The Secret Rapture* Hare seems fascinated by both sisters—the energetic evil of Tory Marion, who is first seen removing a valuable ring from her dead father; and the subdued tolerance of Isobel, who is last seen as a radiant ghost (in the original production, although not in either version of the published text). Drawing its title from Catholic theology—the moment when the nun becomes the bride of Christ, or death—*The Secret Rapture* is Manichean, with its satanic and angelic sisters, whose dialogue is at times so arch that the play has to be enlivened by their father's alcoholic widow Katherine. In performance reprehensible Marion was a satirized Conservative, but Hare groomed virtuous Isobel for tragedy. Although it was lavishly praised, the play seems to me to confirm the improbability of binary divisions.

Hare's film *Strapless* (1990) avoids that dramatic error. As in the play *The Secret Rapture*, we view two contrasting sisters, but in the film they are Americans living in England. Dr. Lillian Hempel (Blair Brown), in her mid-thirties, is a physician at a National Health Service London hospital, and her feckless younger sister (Bridget Fonda) has vague aspirations toward becoming a designer. Wooed and wedded in a whirlwind romance, Lillian assumes political responsibility only when she is abandoned by her seductive but shifty husband. Lillian's sister Amy, having indulged freely in sex and drugs, finds herself pregnant but refuses an abortion. In the film's final sequences both sisters coo over newborn Mary, and both sisters wear black strapless evening gowns for a hospital fund-raising ball: "They shouldn't stand up. But they do" (85). As do the two sisters, in their respective careers, while the evanescent lover smiles enigmatically, perhaps in memory of his brief marriage, perhaps in desire for another woman.

In *Strapless* a man—Raymond Forbes—is dedicated to plenty. An entrepreneur who buys and sells, he showers Lillian with expensive gifts before he runs afoul of the law and disappears from her life. Cool and suave, he is not a naked Tory, but an international speculator, for whom the fun is in the chase, as he acknowledges in a sexual pun: "I love that feeling of soon she will come" (36). But in spite of two close-up kisses, we witness no passion between Lillian and Raymond; rather, she is almost hypnotized by his pursuit.[10]

The most passionate scene in the film is one of reciprocal fury between the two sisters. Doctor Lillian turns on Amy: "Have a child? Are you nuts? . . . What will you do? Go to college? They don't give diplomas for dreaming. Let alone diplomas for fucking!" Amy countercharges: "Oh, you're always so kind. So patient. So tolerant. And in that kindness, doctor, there's such condescension" (43–44). By the end of the film, all condescension spent, Lillian acknowledges her arrogance: "You have certain feelings. And then you must pick up the bill. . . . You've always known that. But it's taken me time" (79). "Pick up the bill" seems a curiously monetary image for a National Health doctor with a social conscience.

Hare's irresponsible sister of the 1960s behavior and his professional sister of the selfish 1980s learn to blend private tenderness and public responsibility. A scene of birth—Amy's baby—is followed by a scene of death—Lillian's cancer patient. Lillian has lost a husband, and yet he sends her a gift—a tiny silver horse in the script, a toy jockey on a horse in the film. In *Strapless* no one is killed, no blow is struck, and women finally emerge independent of men. The film devotes more footage to women's professional skills than Hare's other two films. After Dr. Lillian Hempel agrees to chair the hospital protest committee, *Strapless* concludes upon a fashion show in a worthy cause; we watch from behind as each strapless, seductive woman's back parts the curtain to face an audience.

For all his good intentions, however, and divergent sisters, Hare's metaphor rings false. The naked breasts of *Slag* are absent, but Amy exults about her strapless designs—"Let them stand up on their own" (80). Hare may intend to embrace all independent women, but the metaphor is inaccurate, for strapless gowns preserve the proprieties not by means of women's breasts—"on their own"—but because of strategically placed supports. And the strategically placed supports in most Hare plays are men.

On the sidelines, or front and center, Hare's women of principle tend to depend upon men. In *Knuckle, Wetherby, Licking*

Hitler, and *The Secret Rapture*, women are assaulted by men, and in the three films women *need* particular men, however unable to articulate that need. As early as *Knuckle* Jenny rejects liaisons, but she thrives as a talismanic symbol in a bar frequented by men. Maggie's art is as sexual as Madonna's, and Anna Seaton sentimentalizes her erotic "thing." Susan sheds a husband for a nameless lover. Only in *Strapless* do both sisters weather affairs with men; Amy dismisses the faraway Argentinean father of her baby, whereas the protagonist Lillian is nostalgic about the man who bigamously married her, only to vanish. Yet the film itself recalls him to our view. Still, *Strapless* is the first Hare drama to close on independent professional women "on their own," however inapt the metaphor.

Murmuring Judges (1991) pursues professional women—on the stage. Having relegated women to the periphery of *Racing Demon*, the first play of his projected trilogy about British institutions, Hare in his second play sets *two* women front and center—Police Constable Sandra Bingham and junior barrister Irina Platt. Deftly shifting between their respective worlds in contemporary London—the police station and the law court—and the prison that shades both worlds, Hare dramatizes British justice as an oxymoron: the overworked police cannot begin to contain crime, the prison is governed by its own brutal laws, and the legal eagles fly by their own rarefied codes.

Although Sandra has had an affair with a seasoned detective, and Irina has known love in her native Antigua, Hare focuses on the professional lives of the two women—in a patriarchal context. Sandra, who has been brought up as a boy by her policeman father, is ambitious to rise in the force; Irina, who serves as the black female token of a prominent jurist, is ambitious to defend the innocent. Separately, both women are advised that they are members of "a team," but conscience as well as sex distinguishes them from their colleagues.

Reviewers faulted Hare for the intricacy and/or improbability of his plot, in which the two professional women separately pierce to the lies that victimize an Irish laborer. Reviewers also complained of Hare's lectures in the mouths of Sandra and Irina—in Irving Wardle's phrase, "a pair of young puritans" (1282). And indeed both smart young women wear their conscience a little heavily, particularly black Irina haranguing her silver-haired benefactor on English prison and English privilege: "It seems so obvious to an outsider. Do you really not know? All this behaviour, the honours, the huge sums of money, the buildings, the absurd dressing-up. They do have a purpose. It's anaesthetic. It's to render you incapable of imagining life the other way round" (91).

To his credit, Hare expands his own ability to imagine life the other way round. *Murmuring Judges* is not a Manichean reduction: the victimized prisoner is guilty, and the police show humor and humanity. The higher echelons of the judiciary are men of culture who admit a black woman—provided she abides by their rules. Despite reviewers' contradictory complaints—on the one hand, that Hare was parading his research; on the other, that he was saying nothing new about judicial corruption—the playwright is theatrically informed and informative about the judiciary.

Hare's dramatic problem is his conscience-carrying women protagonists. Although one is black and the other white, they are both colorless on stage. In the theatre the villain steals the show, so that a playwright presents a virtuous protagonist at his or her own peril. Dipsomaniacal Maggie of *Teeth 'n' Smiles* and hysterical Susan of *Plenty* may accomplish nothing constructive in the world, but they seethe with theatrical life. In *Murmuring Judges* Sandra appreciates the rough masculine humor of the force, whereas Irina is impassive before the sophisticated wit of the leading members of the judiciary, but both are pale figures in their respective worlds; small wonder that they are puzzled about "when it's time to say no" (98).

Boldly, Hare gives the two women a scene together, in which a casually dressed Irina appeals to Sandra, out of uniform, to help her imprisoned client by incriminating the police: "You've chosen a woman. . . . You thought I'd be easier. I sort of resent that." But since "*both smile*" (95), the resentment dissolves into mutual sympathy—a sympathy that is so wholly dependent on their sex that Hare bolsters it with scenic directions: "IRINA *picks up on* [SANDRA's] *tone.* . . . IRINA [*is*] *confident she has* SANDRA's *interest.* . . . IRINA *waits, knowing* [SANDRA] *is hooked.* . . . IRINA *makes a slight movement towards* [SANDRA] *with a card.* . . . *[There is] a real warmth suddenly between the two women.* . . . *They both smile together, joined by the thought"* (96–98). The thought is Sandra's remark that Irina's alternative bar has no counterpart in the constabulary: *". . . there's nothing called the alternative police"* (98). Nevertheless, *Murmuring Judges* closes on Sandra's decision to act as though there were, or eventually might be. Sandra does not telephone Irina with the crucial evidence; she keeps it within the constabulary. In Hare's last scene a panoramic sweep against the prison background finally narrows on Sandra, who steps downstage center: "I want the Chief Superintendent. *(She waits.)* I wonder. Could I have a word?" (109).

During the course of *Murmuring Judges* Sandra has too many words, and Irina even more. Yet it is not so much the quantity as the quality of his heroines' words that is sometimes so dispiriting—unfailingly earnest, without the silky wit of the judges or the rough humor of the policemen (and women). It would, however, be well worth the wait if Hare could, in the third play of his "institutional" trilogy, create a female protagonist who can dispense with dotting her *i*'s and crossing her ethical *t*'s.[11]

NOTES

1. See, for example, Michelene Wandor, *Look Back in Gender: Sexuality and the Family in Post-war British Drama* (London: Methuen, 1987), or June Schlueter, ed., *Feminist Rereadings of Modern American Drama* (Rutherford: Fairleigh Dickinson University Press, 1989). Contrary to (my) expectation, there is no mention of Hare in Susan Carlson, *Women and Comedy: Rewriting the British Theatrical Tradition* (Ann Arbor: University of Michigan Press, 1991).

2. *Knuckle*'s inclusion in *The History Plays* is puzzling, since *Teeth 'n' Smiles* would seem more suitable. Jenny's position is so secondary that Bull barely mentions her in his astute analysis of *Knuckle* (70–73).

3. Nightingale comments on Hare's surprise at receiving letters of thanks for the father-son subject "he thought not central to it at all" (1).

4. Chronologically, the women of *Fanshen* (1975) belong in this group, but since the play is an adaptation of an account I have not read, and, more importantly, since the play is so atypical of Hare, I do not discuss it. However, see Cave for a view of the importance of *Fanshen* for Hare's later work, since it "charged overt theatricality . . . with a powerful sense of purpose" (203).

5. The bare-bones situation resembles Stoppard's *Night and Day*, where a woman in Africa (rather than Asia) is erotically involved with two journalists. See Cave for a much more sympathetic view of Peggy (208–9).

6. The film of *Plenty* displaced Kate Nelligan with the (film) star Meryl Streep, and the flashback with conventional chronology. In short, a conventional film.

7. Hare's direction preserved the ambiguity between Susan's memory and drug-induced fantasy. See, for example, Gussow's review (20).

8. The disturbed young man is named Morgan, like the madman in the Karel Reisz movie of that name written by David Mercer. Morgan's suicide resembles the opening scene of Christopher Hampton's *The Philanthropist*.

9. The London production of *The Secret Rapture* titillated by its Edwina Currie details, whereas the New York production leaned on Margaret Thatcher. The latter version was the occasion of Hare's heated diatribe against the *New York Times* reviewer, Frank Rich.

10. I ignore Hare's several statements about the powerful love story in the film, preferring to focus on what the film actually contains. Like most playwrights, Hare is not his own most acute critic, but then playwrights have more important things to do.

11. The harshest judgment of Hare's women charges: "Essentially Hare does not write about women at all but rather as blanks on which he can imprint an external, male pressure; and to such pressure they respond only with pain or madness or, if they are secondary characters, with baffled dismay" (Chambers and Prior 186). It is true that Hare's women all suffer male pressure, but that pressure elicits scorn for the established verities. It is also true that secondary women characters are often dismayed, but they are rarely baffled. I have tried to trace Hare's gradually growing respect for professional women—Maggie Frisby, Susan Traherne, Jean Travers, and Dr. Lillian Hempel; three endearing scenes reveal Jean Travers's rapport with her pupils; nurses, doctors, and patients reveal high regard for Dr. Lillian Hempel's medical skills.

Perhaps Hare's next heroine will have no need at all of masculine succor.

WORKS CITED

Brenton, Howard and David Hare. *Pravda: A Fleet Street Comedy.* Rev. ed. London: Methuen, 1986.

Bull, John. *New British Political Dramatists: Howard Brenton, David Hare, Trevor Griffiths and David Edgar.* London: Macmillan, 1984.

Cave, Richard Allen. *New British Drama in Performance on the London Stage: 1970 to 1985.* Gerrards Cross: Smythe, 1987.

Chambers, Colin and Mike Prior. *Playwrights' Progress: Patterns of Postwar British Drama.* Oxford: Amber Lane, 1987.

French, Philip. "Hare and the Tortoise." *The Observer* 4 June 1989. Excerpted in *File on Hare.* Comp. Malcolm Page. London: Methuen, 1990. 78.

Gussow, Mel. "Two Sparkling Performances Light Up the West End." *New York Times* 30 July 1978, sec. 2: 4+.

Hare, David. *The Bay at Nice* and *Wrecked Eggs.* London: Faber, 1986.

———. *Dreams of Leaving. Heading Home, Wetherby* and *Dreams of Leaving.* London: Faber, 1991.

———. *How Brophy Made Good. Gambit* 5.17 (1971): 83–125.

———. Introduction. *The History Plays.* London: Faber, 1984. 9–16.

———. Introduction. *Paris by Night.* London: Faber, 1988. v–x.

———. *Knuckle. The History Plays.* London: Faber, 1984.

———. *Licking Hitler. The History Plays.* London: Faber, 1984.

———. *A Map of the World. The Asian Plays.* London: Faber, 1986.

———. *Murmuring Judges.* Rev. ed. London: Faber, 1993.

———. *Paris by Night.* London: Faber, 1988.

———. *Plenty. The History Plays.* London: Faber, 1984.

———. *Racing Demon.* Rev. ed. London: Faber, 1991.

———. *Saigon: Year of the Cat. The Asian Plays.* London: Faber, 1986.

———. *The Secret Rapture.* Rev. ed. London: Faber, 1989.

————. *Slag*. London: Faber, 1971.

————. *Strapless*. London: Faber, 1989.

————. *Teeth 'n' Smiles*. London: Faber, 1976.

————. *Wetherby*. *Heading Home, Wetherby* and *Dreams of Leaving*. London: Faber, 1991.

Itzin, Catherine and Simon Trussler. "From Portable Theatre to Joint Stock . . . via Shaftesbury Avenue." Interview with Hare. *Theatre Quarterly* 5.20 (1975–76): 108–15.

Kerensky, Oleg. *The New British Drama: Fourteen Playwrights since Osborne and Pinter*. New York: Taplinger, 1977.

Myerson, Jonathan. "David Hare: Fringe Graduate." *Drama* 149 (1983): 26–28.

Nightingale, Benedict. "An Angry Young Man of the Eighties Brings His Play to New York." *New York Times* 17 Oct. 1982, sec. 2: 1+.

Oliva, Judy Lee. *David Hare: Theatricalizing Politics*. Ann Arbor: UMI, 1990.

Pinter, Harold. *The Homecoming*. London: Methuen, 1965.

Wardle, Irving. Review of *Murmuring Judges*. *Independent on Sunday* 13 Oct. 1991. Rpt. in *Theatre Record* 11 (1991): 1282–83.

Playing with Place: Some Filmic Techniques in the Plays of David Hare

John Russell Brown

Only a very few dramatists have made films. Many have written filmscripts and been involved with the cinema's revisionary processes; but they have not been in charge of that complex collaboration which leads to the finished film: from idea and story to development, casting, setting, shooting, editing—the manifold processes which collect and then order a film's fixed images of reality. David Hare is one dramatist who *has* done all this: only the camera itself has escaped his direct control.

Many English-speaking dramatists have written plays about theatre—*The Entertainer*, *Noises Off*, *A Chorus of Disapproval*, *A Life in the Theatre*—and still more have created plays in which the leading characters are performers before live audiences—*Burn This*, *The Real Thing*, *Amadeus*, *The Tooth of Crime*, *The Birthday Party*, and (to widen the idea of performance) *Waiting for Godot*. But David Hare, the dramatist, writes as a film-maker about film-making. His play, *A Map of the World* (1983), begins with an international conference on poverty set in a luxury hotel in Bombay, but then everything that has been seen so far is revealed as having been a representation of reality, not reality itself. The whole opening scene had been created carefully by its characters, so that it could be recorded by camera, and subsequently edited, for the making of a movie. The dramatist is at home with all this business and has used his inside knowledge to awaken questions about the truth of what art can present about life, and about the efficacy of humanitarian goodwill. This

45

is not unlike the way in which Shakespeare used his familiarity with theatre to juxtapose theatrical performance and the lunacies of authority, love, and sexual strife in *A Midsummer Night's Dream*.

This dramatist also understands those enthusiasts who feed greedily upon a film's plausible and engrossing illusion of reality. Whereas Hamlet had believed that a play was the thing to "catch the conscience of the king," Hare's characters turn to the cinema as a rather desperate escape from the intolerable crises of conscience in their own actual lives. At the end of the first scene of Act II of *The Secret Rapture* (1988), Irwin and Rhonda are discovered in an intimate moment by Isobel, Irwin's lover. He is almost speechless, *"looking at* ISOBEL," while Isobel is *"standing thinking, taking no notice of* RHONDA"; so the initiative has to be Rhonda's:

> RHONDA: Well, anyway, I'm going to the flicks. Excuse me.
> ISOBEL: We'll come with you.
> RHONDA: I'm sorry?
> ISOBEL: I'd like to come.
> (IRWIN *looks across amazed,* RHONDA *puzzled.*)
> RHONDA: It's very violent. I saw the trailer. It's one of those Los Angeles crime things. Rooms full of blood. Then the cop says, "Right, I want everyone here to help look for his ear . . ."
> ISOBEL: Sounds fine. I'd like that. No really.
> (*She turns and looks at* IRWIN.)
> That would be good. I mean it. Let's all go to the cinema. . . . Then we can have a good time. (58)

The dramatist himself has not been carried away by the power of cinema; Hare remains critical of these characters. Besides, he has turned back from film-making, which at one time used all his creative energies, and is writing again for the theatre. With *Racing Demon* (1990), he brought a theatre-person into his play. This is Ewan Gilmour, an out-of-work stage actor, who is the lover of clergyman Harry Henderson. But Ewan is not glamorized in conventionally theatrical ways: he wears simple, unremarkable clothes, and speaks in a Glaswegian accent; he is terse, not voluble, when he is angry, and seems to be without very much guile; he is first seen reading a comic, with a pile more at his side. Ewan is given a chance of earning easy money by selling his story to a cheque-book journalist, but he does not incriminate Harry: this actor is loyal to his friend. In a play about weakening faith and duplicity, in which the other characters seek solutions to nothing more than their own difficulties, Hare has introduced someone from the "unreal" world of theatre who stands true to the intimate and scarcely-spoken feelings which bind two people together. The contrast with the successful and self-concerned film actors of *A Map* could hardly be greater. So, in assessing Hare's work as a dramatist, it may be profitable to notice both what his work as a film-maker has contributed to his stage plays and how he has returned to the theatre to enjoy its own distinct opportunities.

I

The most fundamental difference between the film and the other arts is that, in its world-picture, the boundaries of space and time are fluid. . . . In the plastic arts, as also on the stage, space remains static, motionless, unchanging, without a goal and without a direction. . . .

Hauser 227

David Hare has, from his earliest plays, tried to buck this "static" limitation which others have seen as natural to the stage: he has constantly played with space. In *Knuckle* (1974), he took Curly successively from one location to another, in a quest for information about his sister who had disappeared; each new setting showed this central character in a new light. In *Teeth 'n' Smiles* (1975), he brought a loud and trendy pop group to a gig within the precincts of a Cambridge college, banishing time-honored proprieties and leaving the place itself barely recognizable. In *Pravda* (1985), written with Howard Brenton, the newspaper proprietors are not kept on their own turf; they are also shown in a garden, an Exhibition Hall, a London Club, a bungalow in Weybridge, a Greyhound Stadium, the Yorkshire moors, a TV studio.

In the shorter of two one-act plays of 1986, *Wrecked Eggs*, Hare brought two of its three characters from New York City to a cottage in Rhinebeck in upstate New York, displacing them from the habitat of their professional lives. This drama turns on a further change of context, for during its action the set is filled with preparations for a large party to celebrate the couple's divorce. Only one guest will come, however, and she and the hostess are left alone on the brink of this event; this very theatrical moment of quiet recognition is the heart of the play. A violent outburst then follows which alters what is about to happen, and revalues the entire action. It may seem that only the change which has been effected in the potential of the single set could have caused this detonation: the characters are confronted with a crisis by a visual transformation of the setting.

In many ways these manipulations of stage place operate very simply. Computerized switchboards have now brought a more filmic fluidity of scene to the theatre and endowed a dramatist with a much stricter control over an audience's attention. No longer are *dramatis personae* confined within the three walls of a constructed stage set, a limited and defined environment which has to be changed behind a curtain or during a meaningless darkness. Nor does the play have to be enacted before some permanent background which serves for every scene by making minor changes—opening this door rather than that, thrusting out a bed or a table, carrying on flags or flowers, or changing the way the stage and its structure are lit. A more filmic illusion is now possible because stage lighting has become infinitely and finely variable, so susceptible to electronic control that onstage action has almost unlimited mobility from place to place. Hare uses these devices boldly and they become increasingly important in his plays, as if he were eager to bring theatre much closer to the "fluidity" of film.

Hare knows as much as almost anyone about the power of electronic switchboards; he has directed numerous plays at the National Theatre in London and at the Public Theatre in New York, where he has worked with the foremost lighting designers and the most sophisticated equipment. Already in *Plenty* of 1978, he called for an arbitrary change of place by using light and color; the scenery must change silently in full view of the

audience, without apparent human aid. So Susan Traherne
moves from England to France, and back in time, in a seamless
continuation of performance. The penultimate scene is in a seedy
hotel in Blackpool in 1962:

> (LAZAR *turns the nightlight off. Darkness.*)
> SUSAN: Tell me your name.
> (*Pause.*)
> LAZAR: Code name.
> (*Pause.*)
> Code name.
> (*Pause.*)
> Code name Lazar.
> (LAZAR *opens the door of the room. At once music plays.*
> *Where you would expect a corridor you see the fields of France*
> *shining brilliantly in a fierce green square. The room scatters.*)

> SCENE TWELVE

> *St. Benoît, August 1944.*
> *The darkened areas of the room disappear and we see a French*
> *hillside in high summer. The stage picture forms piece by piece.*
> *Green, yellow, brown. Trees. The fields stretch away. A high*
> *sun. A brilliant August day. Another* FRENCHMAN *stands*
> *looking down into the valley. He carries a spade, is in*
> *wellingtons and corduroys. He is about 40, fattish with an*
> *unnaturally gloomy air.*
> *Then* SUSAN *appears climbing the hill. She is 19. She is*
> *dressed like a young French girl, her pullover over her shoulder.*
> *She looks radiantly well.*
> FRENCHMAN: Bonjour, ma'moiselle.
> SUSAN: Bonjour. (205–6)

This closing scene is rather like a walk into the sunset at the end
of an old film: Susan smiles at the stranger, and they look at each
other, about to go. But then Hare directs a pause, in which he
pulls the focus back to Susan by giving her words to speak:
"There will be days and days and days like this" (207). The effect
is complicated because the audience knows what Susan at this
moment does not: her prognostication is quite obviously untrue,
having been denied by what has already been shown on this
stage. In a film, the characters would now start walking into a
real sunset, getting smaller and smaller in the distance; the

camera might show them moving closer together or beginning to dance. But on stage, Susan is life-sized and close to the audience to the very end. Even though her whole self may shine with confidence and well-being on this brilliant summer's day, the darkness and waste of the days to come are summoned up in the audience's mind. Hare has used modern technology to control attention, plucking what he chooses from Susan's individual history and from the real history of a world at war and peace, as if he were a film-maker; but finally each spectator must make what he or she can of the contradiction between stage-present and stage-past. In its playing with place and time, *Plenty* was the most filmic of Hare's plays to date, but nevertheless it was still conceived for theatrical immediacy in performance.

In later plays, Hare refined this filmic device of a slow fade-out of one scene and fade-in to the next. For example, before Isobel, Irwin and Rhonda can leave to go to the flicks and have that "good time,"

> (*. . . we hear the sound of* MARION's *voice as she approaches from the back. The scenery changes as the others leave, and we are in Tom's office—an anonymously decorated room of glass and wood panel, dominated by a big, bare leather-topped desk. The glass runs unnaturally high, giving a feeling of airy emptiness.* TOM *is already at his desk to greet his wife, who approaches, putting down her coat as she comes.*)

SCENE SIX

Tom's office.
MARION: I can't see the problem. There really is no problem. People so love to talk problems up. Family things actually belong at the weekend. A drink on Sunday is lovely. Or lunch. Or walking after lunch. That's the right time for the family. It's crazy when it starts infecting your week. (58–59)

So dramatic images are juxtaposed, the new ones echoing those from the previous scene while marking contrasts with them. As one person moves on, three move off. The glass running *"unnaturally high"* establishes a new *"feeling"*—anonymous, airy and empty—like a cinema screen waiting to show some action drawn from the problems which "People so love to talk . . . up." The effect is fluent, imagistic, expressive, and unconfined by any

one location. It is also contrived, and the play-maker is very
much in charge, insisting that the drama is viewed in his way, as
if he were showing only what the camera records. On one level
of appreciation, the switch of setting, effected without any
apparent difficulty, dominates attention; on another, the
contrasting and yet echoing words offer stabs of superior insight.

Such transitions have become a hallmark of Hare's writing
for the stage and he continually refines and extends their use. At
the beginning of *The Secret Rapture*, a few almost silent figures
and a setting which is only partially revealed engage attention
together, in the manner of a film thriller:

ACT ONE

Scene One

*Robert's bedroom. The curtain goes up on almost complete
darkness. Then a door opens at the back and a dim and indirect
light is thrown from the corridor.* MARION, *in her late thirties,
brisk, dark-haired, wearing a business suit, stands a moment,
nervous, awed, in the doorway. She moves into the room which
you can just detect is dominated by a large double bed, in which
a man is lying, covered with a sheet reaching up over his face.*
MARION *stops a moment by the bed, looking down. She then
turns to go back towards the door.*
ISOBEL: Marion?
(MARION *lets out a scream, not having realized that* ISOBEL
was sitting in a chair at the end of the bed.)
MARION: My God!
ISOBEL: I'm sorry.
MARION: You startled me.
ISOBEL: Don't turn the main light on. (1)

A door opens. A figure is seen in silhouette, and then a bed and a
man in it. The standing and nameless person moves in one
direction and then another; in the darkness, a voice calls out a
name; then there is a scream. A second figure is now seen,
seated; and the man is recognized clearly as a corpse. So the
theatre audience is introduced to the situation and alerted to
danger just as if the dramatist were in charge of a camera by
which he can insist on his point of view and his choice and
manipulation of successive images. But then, characteristically,
having brought Marion and Isobel face to face, as in a film, Hare

uses only words to impel the drama forward, and also to extend the audience's sense of where the action is:

> ISOBEL: I needed some peace. . . . I decided this would be the only place. For some quiet. There's so much screaming downstairs. (1)

The filmic sequence of images had not supplied all the dramatist's needs: once the elaborate opening has provided the exposition, it has no further role to perform, and what follows is conventional onstage drama.

In *The Secret Rapture* and *Racing Demon* scenes flow together, changing place smoothly as in a film, and words illuminate the contrasts and similarities between the images. But in the later play the actual "built" stage set is kept to a strict minimum. The scenic contrasts are between two sets of human figures in disparate situations, rather than between their surroundings. The effect is to enhance the verbal connections between scenes and the effect of "montage"; here the device has something of the eloquence of strict and refined film editing. For example, at the end of the penultimate scene of Act I of *Racing Demon*:

> (*The doors throughout the hall are thrown open. Clergy and laity flock in to take their places. Men in legal wigs and gowns assemble at the central table, as the hall fills.*)
> KINGSTON: Well, here they come. A vigorous morning's debating. Rapier and bludgeon. Absolutely no holds barred. All opinions respected. And at the end, a view acceptable to everyone. Lord, guide our thoughts.
> (*A MALAYSIAN WOMAN rings a small handbell.*)
> WOMAN: The Synod is in session. Let us pray.
> (*At once there is silence. As the prayer in the hall continues, the lights go down until there is darkness.*)
> ALL: Our Father,
> Which art in heaven,
> Hallowed be thy name.
> Thy kingdom come,
> Thy will be done,
> On Earth as it is in Heaven.
> Give us this day our daily bread,
> And forgive us our trespasses,
> As we forgive them that trespass against us,

And lead us not into temptation,
But deliver us from evil,
For thine is the kingdom, the power and the glory,
For ever and ever.
Amen.

SCENE TWELVE

*The church. The lights have gone down through the prayers. At
the end there is total darkness but for two candles in front of
TONY's kneeling figure. Behind him, LIONEL stands,
unnoticed. On TONY's face, a look of intense concentration.
The organ plays, subliminally.* (44)

The whole theatre can be brought into the light to represent the
assembling Synod and to encourage the audience to feel
included in its business. Then as the voice of prayer makes its
requests for "daily bread," forgiveness, and delivery from evil,
and ultimately acknowledges an everlasting "power" and
"glory," the focus in the gathering darkness must be increasingly
on words alone, until two candles and then two contrasting
figures are discovered, the dim light and new silence
concentrating the audience's attention. When these figures
speak, the words they use echo the earlier prayer and contrast
with it: Lionel calls Tony's *name* and at first it is not heard; and
he offers the suppliant a meal—a form of *daily bread*. The
audience may sense that both the *power* and the *glory* are now
almost totally absent, and that *temptation* is close at hand. *For ever
and ever* is replaced by "some other time," words which seem set
for endless repetition:

LIONEL: Tony.
(TONY *doesn't hear.*)
Tony.
(*He hears but, transfixed, doesn't turn.*)
TONY: It's you, Lionel.
LIONEL: You look like a ghost.
(TONY *turns and stares at him.*)
I came in. I wanted . . . to ask you to dinner.
TONY: Dinner? That's very kind. But I can't. I've got . . .
another invitation.
LIONEL: Really?
TONY: In town.

LIONEL: Oh yes?
TONY: I'm going to see . . .
(*He stops. There is a very long pause.* LIONEL *is quite still.*
Then)
. . . someone else.
(LIONEL *smiles.*)
LIONEL: Well, then, some other time.
TONY: Some other time, yes. (*Stares at him a moment.*)
Well, I must be going, or else I'll be late. Good to see you,
Lionel. (*Gets up from his knees.*) I'll see you soon.
(*He begins to walk from the church. Then, towards the door, he*
accelerates and runs out. . . .) (45)

Silences and wordless confrontations are emphasized, so that the
audience sees and hears as the dramatist has willed them to do:
these Christians can scarcely summon each other's attention by
calling their names; trespass and forgiveness are not talked about
easily; neither character can be led out of temptation, or
delivered from what has made him almost ghostly to the other.

For all the filmic devices in Hare's late plays, which free
his characters from conventional stage settings, it is the living
presence of actors on stage which continues to provide the
essential dramatic experience. Here film can provide no
alternative. In *The Bay at Nice*, the other one-act play of 1986,
theatrical and filmic devices work together to draw attention to a
scarcely bearable tension held silently within the mind and body
of Valentina, the central character; and then, in the last moments,
her experience is related to an imagined world established in
wider dimensions and a stronger light than it could ever possess
within a conventionally static stage set. Valentina had known
Matisse in her youth and has been summoned to a Leningrad
museum to authenticate an unsigned picture. By the end of the
play the picture has been on stage since early in its action, with
its back facing the audience; now, after Valentina's daughter has
left,

(*. . . There's a moment's silence. Then* VALENTINA *walks*
across to the chair and picks up the canvas. . . . She holds it out
at arms' length for five seconds. Then, without any visible
reaction, she puts it down. Then she walks across the room and
stands alone. Then her eyes begin to fill with tears. Silently the

ASSISTANT CURATOR *returns, standing respectfully at the*
door.)
VALENTINA: You've come back.
ASSISTANT: Yes.
VALENTINA: I didn't hear you.
ASSISTANT: Have you had time to look at it?
VALENTINA: I've examined it.
(*There's a pause.*)
Yes. It's Matisse. (46)

Slowly the audience learns that Valentina has recognized the
painting by the way in which light is represented as it shines
through the shutters of a window. "The way the sun is diffused,"
she explains. "He controlled the sun in his painting. He said,
with shutters he could summon the sun as surely as Joshua with
his trumpet" (47).

It is for loss of that "power" and "glory" that Valentina has
wept, and the truth of these feelings has been emphasized by the
five-second examination, her silent crossing of the stage, and her
tears. These are theatrical devices, but used with the confidence
of someone used to film, where the camera can hold and fix
attention on motion and silent performance. Valentina has little
more to say, but the dramatist insists on a further vindication of
what she has recognized by a filmic change of setting:

VALENTINA: . . . he said the result was truer and more
beautiful than anything that came as an effort of will.
(*She stands a moment, then turns to go.*)
ASSISTANT: I'll get you a car.
VALENTINA: No. The tram is outside. It goes right by my
door.
(*She goes. He stands a moment, looking at the painting. The*
background fades and the stage is filled with the image of the bay
at Nice: a pair of open French windows, a balcony, the sea and
the sky.
The ASSISTANT *turns and looks to the open door.*) (48)

Neither of the persons on stage sees the brilliant image of
Matisse's painting; that is the film director's and dramatist's
message to the audience.

The close scrutiny brought to bear upon Valentina or
Susan Traherne by the dramatist's control of focus is like that
provided by a close-up on the face of a film actor, when the

drama is sustained by the very being of the performer, with all its secret and manifest individuality. But here the actress is present on stage; the audience sees her completely and responds to her actual presence. Each performer will reveal something a little different from another and, for all the dramatist's cunning, the performer is finally in charge. Not surprisingly, Hare, as theatre director, has entrusted these stage roles to actresses— Irene Worth and Kate Nelligan—whom he can trust to hold attention in silence and to endow the roles with quiet, unforced, and unmistakable life.

In later plays such burdens are shared more widely among their casts, and their silences are sometimes superseded by the highly theatrical device of soliloquy—speeches on their own behalf, in the manner of plays from earlier theatres where asides and direct address to the audience were common. *Racing Demon* is a play about four parish priests, two bishops, and some churchgoers, so that here old-fashioned soliloquies blend easily with prayers addressed to the Almighty, as if to another person above the stage or present in the mind of the speaker. Thus, after encountering Tony in church following the Synod, Lionel is left alone to pray:

> (LIONEL . . . *[s]teps forward and looks up to heaven.*)
> What can you do, Lord? You tell me. You show me the way. Go on. You explain why all this hurt has to come. Tell me. You understand everything. (*Steps back.*) Why do the good always fight among themselves? (45)

Lionel's backward movement introduces a theatrical device which cuts off prayer for his last sentence: this makes a strong impact, one which closes the scene and the first act of the play. If the Synod has been an occasion for lighting the audience as well as the stage, thus involving its members more directly in the situation and dialogue, then, after the backwards step, the concluding sentence can be addressed to those listeners. Perhaps the auditorium lights have begun to come up for the intermission. Lionel has been speaking to the "Lord," almost as if to a distant, overhead camera, but now dramatic illusion shifts again. He steps out of character and out of his own place, to offer a question to any and every one who is attending the perform-ance. Filmic mobility and passive attention yield to an essentially theatrical device as the author breaks the bounds of the stage world; the character steps out of a dramatic illusion and into a place from which he can communicate directly with an audience. This is not representation or filmic illusion; it is encounter.[1]

II

David Hare does not play according to a single set of rules, but mixes techniques from cinema and stage in order to focus attention where he decides it should be, and on occasion to break illusionistic reality and so challenge an audience's understanding. This can be seen again in his theatrical use of a device found variously at the end of his television and cinema filmscripts where he builds up a final statement by a series of cuts from one place, or one focus, to another. In the concluding minutes of *Licking Hitler* (1978), a blank screen is followed by five separate still shots, each accompanied with voice-over, and each set in a different place; then there are two more shots, the first moving inside a house and the second viewing its exterior, while the voice continues (126–28). At the end of *Wetherby* (1985), the audience is shown a school, the inside and outside of a house, and then a pub, each shot dominated by one or more of the film's leading characters; and then, in the last shot, the camera pulls away, so that Stanley and Jean are seen as *"two among many"* (130–32)—as customers in the pub who are looking around in silence. A similar multi-focused conclusion can be seen, to some extent, in the last moments of the stage play, *The Bay at Nice*: the viewing of the painting; the tears; the Assistant's entry; the vast projection of the subject of the painting; the open door.

The wide variety of viewpoints in the last moments of this short stage play may have suggested, in turn, the restless movement of the camera at the end of the filmscript *Paris by Night* (shot in 1987), which also focuses, at one point, on a representation of reality, not reality itself. After a fatal pistol shot, the audience is forced to look from place to place: first the view of a child asleep, then of a man in a car, then of a woman dead; then back to the car to show the woman's handbag and two drawings, which had been sketched on a napkin much

earlier in the film; then, once more, back to the child who is now
waking up (82–83). Using the precise focus of a camera shot,
Hare has no need here for words in order to establish a wide
context and differing modes of perception.[2]

Only a few years after these experiments, *Racing Demon*
was given a multiple ending, but modified yet again. Its last
scene begins with Lionel alone in his living room, *"speak[ing] into
the empty air"* a soliloquy of loss and helplessness. Then "TONY
... *appear[s] in the church, in another area of the stage,"* and he too
soliloquizes. At this point, "FRANCES *appears at the other end of
the area. All three are oblivious of each other."* She speaks as if
addressing the "Lord," in familiar talk rather than in prayer, as a
means of settling her own mind:

> A last look round, Lord. To close the subject. Like pulling
> down a blind. I am going, Lord. . . .

All three change their modes of address before the play is
done—Tony to self-doubt, Lionel to urgent prayer, and Frances
to contented daydream (like Valentina remembering the
sunlight): "And then you turn and head towards the sun."
Frances's words give the cue for *"(The stage darkens),"* and for the
play to finish with each of the three characters in focus,
simultaneously (87–88). In this experiment, which may have
been suggested by the multiple focuses at the close of his films,
the dramatist depends on the actors' performances and not on
scenic images. In doing so Hare has drawn on theatrical devices
which in recent years have been more common in opera or
musicals than in spoken drama. The persons of the drama are the
living images which conclude the play, separate and yet viewed
simultaneously. The three stand together but they do not speak
to each other; each is alone in a darkening world.

III

Hare's mingling of theatrical and filmic experiment
distinguishes him from other dramatists who use their
knowledge of film-making in writing stage plays. Trevor
Griffiths's *Piano* (1990) is a play obviously indebted to Chekhov,

whose characters, situations, action, and style it imitates and modifies assertively. But in the concluding scene a lighting change effects a shift of focus, as if the playwright had ordered a panning shot from one group of characters to another. The household is assembled:

> (YASHA *fusses up and down, with coats and capes and wraps. Greetings, hugs, kisses: another crisis over.*)
> ANNA: Nothing will change, my friends.
> (*The sun suddenly strengthens. They turn, like spectres, to watch it lift over the hill across the lake.*)

The light change seems to unsettle nothing: they continue to talk idly, remembering Chekhov's death, and they drink champagne. Anna repeats her comforting conclusion: "Nothing changes. Everything will be as it was." But the play is not over yet, for the focus changes. Out of darkness at first, but then in transforming light, the servant Radish makes a different comment (possibly it is a soliloquy; the text is ambiguous in this respect):

> RADISH: (*From above; unseen*) Grass dies. Iron rusts. Lies eat the soul. . . .
> (*The radiance spreads upwards; reveals* RADISH *and* ZAKHAR, PETYA [*a child*] *between them, holding their hands, on the plank bridge.*)
> (*Looking down on the spectres below*) . . .
> Everything's possible.
> (*Fade to black.*) (55)

And so, at the author's direction, the play ends with a firm counterstatement which is given force by technical means, as if the author were manipulating attention in a film.

Instead of playing one focus against another, Stephen Poliakoff, in *Coming in to Land* (1986), introduced filmic techniques by calling for television screens in banked array and, later, in large size, so that his characters see images of themselves, and the audience sees them too. He calls for these television images to be stopped in mid-action, so that they are held still for inspection and re-interpretation. More inventively, Poliakoff sought to increase the field of vision for his stage drama to filmic dimensions. He called for a vast mural to stretch across the back wall of the stage:

> *The mural shows people arriving on a shore with blue and white*
> *water behind them, shadowy travellers facing an idealized*
> *glowing city on a hill, across an expanse of green.*
> *Somebody has drawn one major piece of graffiti on the mural,*
> *a monster emerging out of the blue water with its teeth bared.*
> (54)

As Halina, the heroine, is interrogated about seeking entry to
Britain from Poland, the mural, already double in its message
because of the monster, is further modified by the presence of
nameless supernumeraries in front of it, all clamoring for
attention. In the following scene, as if altering the focal width of
the camera, the official's office gets larger and more menacing.
There is also an inset picture to be shown:

> PIERCE's *office now fills the stage. The door is oddly large for*
> *the scale of the walls. Around and above the door is misted glass*
> *looking out on the passages beyond; we can glimpse the mural*
> *on the back wall, now looking smudged and diffused through the*
> *glass.*
> *There is a small picture on the wall of people on a golden*
> *beach mirroring the mural outside; it is the only ornament on*
> *the wall.* (60)

The dramatist has asked the scene designer to give multiple and
changing form to the "world" in which he wishes his characters
to be viewed, and in stage directions he has explained what he
wants the audience to see. But there is little in the action or
dialogue to impress these effects on the viewer's attention; he
has played a filmic trick without integrating it with the
presentation of his characters in speech and action.

Hare's way of switching from place to place between short
scenes, while fading in and out with sound and image, is also
found in the plays of other writers. Experience of working on
filmscripts and a daily exposure to television seem to have
encouraged many dramatists to think in terms of short episodes
with changing locations, rather than of long scenes with a single
setting which are sustained by talk, a series of cleverly motivated
entries and exits, and a developing story or action. Short
episodes are used to provide a sudden change of viewpoint, a
quick turn of events, a new reaction, or an escalation in the
passage of time. Harold Pinter's later plays, *Betrayal, Victoria*

Station, and *Mountain Language*, offer many examples. In much earlier plays, such as *The Caretaker* (1960), episodes had stopped and others started with no change of location, and with only a change of lighting to indicate a change of time. So, for example:

> DAVIES: You see, the name I go under now ain't my real one. It's assumed.
> *Silence.*
> THE LIGHTS FADE TO BLACKOUT.
> THEN UP TO DIM LIGHT THROUGH THE WINDOW.
> *A door bangs.*
> *Sound of a key in the door of the room.*
> DAVIES *enters. . . .* (44)

Little is changed by the device of a cut from episode to episode, beyond a new disposition of the characters. But in *Betrayal* (1978), time changes forwards or backwards; and the setting changes too, drawing attention to the change of fortune for the characters. In *Mountain Language* (1988), lights snap off and on again between episodes to effect a change of scene; and in the course of a single episode, lights go "*to half*" and the "*figures are still,*" while voices continue "*over,*" and then the reverse sequence follows (33–35). Here a change of light is part of the play's action and the means whereby the dramatist, like a film-maker, can indicate a new pressure on the institution's inmates. The different "takes" in Pinter's plays operate to forward the action and reveal the varying potential of the *dramatis personae*, but filmic device does not alter radically the audience's mode of perception.

In contrast, Hare uses filmic devices in many and challenging ways, tightening and refining his hold over an audience's attention. In *Plenty*, *The Secret Rapture*, and *Racing Demon*, a sequence of episodes fade into each other and give an effect like that of montage in film: continuity as well as contrast is marked. An audience is given a sense of context beyond that expressed by a single stage set or by a single response of the *dramatis personae*. Hare's filmic effects can open up a view of the larger world in which the characters operate. Often the consequences of the characters' actions are thus expressed in a way which goes beyond their own understandings.

IV

By using a film-maker's techniques in the theatre and so controlling what an audience sees and senses, Hare might be accused of taking responsibility away from his actors and manipulating an audience's reaction to his drama. As viewers in a cinema have little chance of escape from what the camera has captured for them to see, in the form in which the editor has chosen to present it, so for these stage plays the audience's response is very carefully controlled from offstage, or out front, by manipulation of light, sound, and focus. How the action is perceived has been decided by the omniscient dramatist and has been specified in stage directions before the actors have started rehearsals.

But this is only half the truth. The audience's attention is being directed so that it will view the actors' performance with close attention and unusual subtlety, but the actors are not "fixed" by this process. In *Plenty*, how does Susan say "There will be days and days and days like this"? How does she vary those three "days," and by what sensations is "this" given definition? In *Racing Demon*, how do the various clerics and Frances hold the stage in close-up for soliloquy or prayer? The actors have to supply the necessary substance to these moments of special scrutiny which the dramatist has provided and forced the audience to observe. Speech and performance remain the mysterious heart of these plays, even when presented with artful and inescapable technique; and this centre is ultimately the responsibility of the actors.

The end of *The Secret Rapture* shows how Hare draws back from taking responsibility away from his actors. In the very last moments, after Isobel has been killed by Irwin and preparations are being made for her funeral, Marion and her husband come together in a house which she has just restored to its condition at the beginning of the play:

> TOM: Oh God, you feel wonderful.
> MARION: Yes, so do you.

There is scarcely any verbal or visual preparation for this, and nothing, at this moment, to lend credibility to these words. And for the actress, another and larger challenge is yet to come; the text continues:

> MARION: Yes, so do you.
> (*They kiss again. Then he takes a couple of steps back, smiling, slightly adjusting his tie.*)
> Tom. I love you.
> TOM: I'll be back soon.
> (*He pauses, and laughs a small laugh. Then turns and goes out. MARION is left alone. She sits on the sofa at the centre.*)
> MARION: Isobel. We're just beginning. Isobel, where are you? (*She waits a moment.*) Isobel, why don't you come home? (81–82)

In these very last moments, Marion has to address her dead sister as if she were still alive and present before her. Then she senses that Isobel is not actually there, and so puts the possibility of her return into words, in the form of a question that she expects to be heard. Conviction, simplicity, lucidity, and a changing awareness of a non-physical presence: all these are required, and now the author does nothing more to help the actress, or to intervene. (Perhaps Tom's "*small laugh*" is intended, by its awkwardness, to help Marion's clear words to register more assuredly in contrast.) The printed text asks for neither fade-out, nor blackout, nor final curtain; decisions about all that will depend on what the actress has provided in her performance.[3]

In an introduction to the published filmscript of *Paris by Night*, Hare describes vividly what he looks for in performance. Having told how the film came to be made, he explains that the main difficulty had been in casting Clara, its central role, because she had to be "a notably strong woman, and what's more one who was, in the cant phrase of the trade, 'unsympathetic'" (vi). But all along he had maintained that Clara was "not that different from you or me" (vii). When Charlotte Rampling accepted the part, these difficulties vanished: "It was no longer

important [that the film] should be made. It was absolutely vital"
(viii). For Hare her performance clinched everything:

> In the fourth week, in the Halcyon Hotel in Notting Hill
> Gate, we found ourselves shooting the scene in which
> Clara lays out her philosophy of life to Wallace after they
> have made love. Clara is talking from her own experience,
> jumbled up with a certain amount of confused political
> prejudice, yet a mixture of things—the context in which
> she speaks, the tenderness with her lover, the play of the
> light, Charlotte's exquisite conviction in the role—
> combined to produce in those of us watching a feeling of
> total disorientation. We simply did not know what our
> response to Clara was. We were watching a woman whose
> head was apparently full of careless and half-thought
> scraps, yet in the image of her and her own self-awareness
> was something so moving that you could not tell if beauty
> was confounding truth, or if the two, as I suspect they are
> in life, were so mixed up that nothing could unlock them.
> We were all robbed of our usual reactions. This is
> something I have so long wanted to do as a writer that a
> profound and lasting contentment came upon me in that
> room, and it persisted through the remaining weeks of
> shooting. For as long as we worked, the process of art did
> what it has always promised: it comforted, it clarified, and
> set everything in order. (viii–ix)

Of course, the film was something else: images of that revelatory
moment. The spell had lasted only for "as long as we worked."

Ironically, it is films and not stage plays that are said to
have "the *appeal* of a presence and of a proximity that strikes the
masses and fills the movie theaters. . . . The feeling of credibility,
which is so direct, operates on us in films of the unusual and of
the marvelous, as well as in those that are 'realistic'" (Metz 5).
But such attraction is the contrivance of the film-maker: the
chosen sequence of images, the sense of the inevitable which
comes from the movement portrayed in those images. So the
running of a film assures its audience that "there it *is*; it is
happening." But *what* is there? Only very rarely and fleetingly is
it an impression of truth from within the very being of hero or
heroine:

> For a film heroine to exhibit, for even a fraction of a
> second, a gesture or an intonation that is true implies the
> success of a most difficult enterprise on the part of the
> film-maker; it is something that occurs once in a year,
> producing a shock in the viewer, and each time it occurs it
> renders forty films, retroactively devoted to the pure
> Plausible, obsolete in a single stroke. (Metz 246)

Hare's experience while working on *Paris by Night* was an
experience of a different order; it depended on the entire
presence of the actress and her closeness to the watchers, and
their mutual suspension of disbelief.

When Hare returned from film-making to write for the
theatre he knew how to manipulate the audience's viewpoint
and focus. He is now able to encourage a perception of contrasts,
connections and convergencies, and a sense of critical risk. But in
the theatre he does not have to select a single and irrevocable
image of any moment; nor does he have to edit, frame or
manipulate that image. His task is limited to bringing the heart
of the drama forward for attention and offering an unrestricted
view of its performance, in all its subtle "confusion," "beauty,"
and "truth." For some of the audience and, perhaps, for himself,
there may be a moment of disorientation and "a profound and
lasting contentment," because the actor is there on stage, totally
present, with an "exquisite conviction" which clarifies and places
the whole play in some "order" which is beyond the contrivance
of the dramatist.

Perhaps Hare returned to write for the theatre to escape
from the omniscient role of film-maker and to discover a new
sense of the world in which he lives. Each time the actors
perform in his plays, they enjoy the freedom to create their roles
afresh as they bring the action to a full conclusion; and so they
may provide the author with a vindication which goes beyond
what he had imagined. The end of *The Secret Rapture* depends on
what the actress brings to her role; that of *Racing Demon* on the
performances of two actors and an actress. The filmic elements in
the plays of David Hare are at the service of his romantic quest
for a halcyon truth which is essentially, and very simply,
theatrical.

NOTES

1. The distinction between prayer and soliloquy in this passage was even stronger in the first published version of *Racing Demon* (London: Faber, 1990), where Hare provided a *double* "shift." In that edition, Lionel begins by speaking to himself *before* launching into prayer: "I tried. Lord knows I tried. He [Tony] wouldn't listen. I did all I could. He just ran out the door like a madman. It was out of my hands. (*Steps forward and looks up to heaven.*) Where are you, Lord? You tell me . . ." (49). Lionel's movement forward and turning his eyes upwards helped to differentiate prayer from soliloquy, and thus helped to prepare us for his shift *away* from prayer in his concluding sentence.

2. A further circumstance may provide another clue that this filmscript and this play are connected in their author's mind. As Clara and Wallace sketch each other's faces on the napkin, so, in the last moments of *The Bay at Nice*, Valentina tells a story about Matisse sketching his mother's head on a spare telegram form: "His hand did the work, not the brain. And he said the result was truer and more beautiful than anything that came as an effort of will" (48).

3. One difference between two productions of this play provides further demonstration of its author's reliance on his actors' performances. In London at the National Theatre, for its first production, the director, Howard Davies, added a new entry for Isobel at the end of the play; the scenery opened up (in the manner of the last scene in *Plenty*) to show the garden of the house bathed in sunshine where Isobel was entering slowly and calmly, to be present in sight of her sister for a final tableau, a tangible representation and reinforcement of Marion's state of mind. In the second production in New York, directed by Hare, the text was adhered to faithfully: the scenery did not open and the dead woman did not re-enter. Here the actress playing Marion carried the conclusion: the context in which she speaks, her new tenderness and, perhaps, the play of light, all prepared for the last moment. But then, finally, everything depended on an "exquisite conviction" in performance. In the event, the New York performances did not please the principal critics of the city. The production was withdrawn and the author became involved in a public dispute with Frank Rich of the *New York Times*. This outcome, very different from the play's reception in London, could be the result of an inadequate performance or an inadequate response. Perhaps the latter is the more likely, since the dramatist was making unusual demands on his audience's attention.

WORKS CITED

Griffiths, Trevor. *Piano*. London: Faber, 1990.

Hare, David. *The Bay at Nice* and *Wrecked Eggs*. London: Faber, 1986.

———. Introduction. *Paris by Night*. London: Faber, 1988. v–ix.

———. *Licking Hitler*. *The History Plays*. London: Faber, 1984.

———. *Paris by Night*. London: Faber, 1988.

———. *Plenty*. *The History Plays*. London: Faber, 1984.

———. *Racing Demon*. Rev. ed. London: Faber, 1991.

———. *The Secret Rapture*. Rev. ed. London: Faber, 1989.

———. *Wetherby*. *Heading Home, Wetherby* and *Dreams of Leaving*. London: Faber, 1991.

Hauser, Arnold. *The Social History of Art*. Trans. Stanley Godman and Arnold Hauser. Vol. 4. London: Routledge, 1962. 4 vols.

Metz, Christian. *Film Language: A Semiotics of the Cinema*. Trans. Michael Taylor. New York: Oxford University Press, 1974.

Pinter, Harold. *The Caretaker*. Rev. ed. London: Methuen, 1962.

———. *Mountain Language*. London: Faber, 1988.

Poliakoff, Stephen. *Coming in to Land*. London: Methuen, 1986.

Language and Values in Hare's Plays

Robert L. King

> As soon as a word is spoken on stage it is tested.
>
> Hare, "A Lecture" 59

> We have no sooner uttered words than we have given impulse to other people to look at the world, or some small part of it, in our way.
>
> Weaver 285

David Hare's works do not participate formally in the debate over meaning that began with the language reformers of the seventeenth century, but they often use the very terms that have framed that debate and, as a result, they challenge audiences to examine their own values. For many of Hare's characters, the issues are momentous: whether words are signs of things; whether abstract terms carry values or whether the audience supplies them; whether meaning is so indeterminate that political or social discourse is futile. Assertions about meaning range from the absolute, out-of-fashion conviction of Irwin in *The Secret Rapture* ("There's such a thing as evil. You're dealing with evil" [57]) to contemporary reader-response theory as voiced by the novelist Mehta in *A Map of the World*:

> The reader brings to the book his own preconceptions, prejudices perhaps. He misreads sentences. A tiny incident in the narrative is for one person the key to the book's interpretation; to another it is where he accidentally turns two pages and misses it altogether. (222)

To be sure, Hare does not speak in his own voice in his plays and films, but it is still clear that he concedes no moral ground to advocates of indeterminacy. While a sense of loss pervades his various treatments of meaning, Hare does not despair of language's efficacy. Indeed, he insists that we take a moral point of view in the face of a morally ambiguous world. The instrument for defining and negotiating that position is language, and Hare's most complex attitudes toward its usefulness are manifested through dramatic speech, delivery, and lighting.

In his essay "Four Actors," Hare endorses Vanessa Redgrave's commitment to values and equates her inner state with something "real":

> [Redgrave's] values are curiously nineteenth century. More than anyone I have met she believes in the great abstract nouns, with capital letters, like Youth and Enthusiasm and Wickedness and Art. These nouns are real to her, and inform all her acting. (168)

In contrast, the Thatcherite Marion in *The Secret Rapture* makes a more modern, pragmatic observation:

> I don't believe this. This is most peculiar. What is this? A *vow*? It's outrageous. People making *vows*. What are *vows*? Nobody's made vows since the nineteenth century. (63)

As a speech act, a vow represents the highest kind of responsible usage because it makes a spiritual pledge against the vagaries of time to come: the values of the self will remain constant regardless of circumstances. As Hare sees it, Redgrave's belief works in a similar way. This creative, meaningful connection between the inner self and speech ("acting" in Redgrave's case) can be the source of values in a world, like Marion's, that has lost touch with them.

The pun on "characters" in the following exchange from *Knuckle* stresses this inevitable human participation in creating meaning; the reminder of a literary *character* indicates the opportunities and limitations facing the playwright who often speaks through unreliable speakers like these:

> MRS DUNNING: I wonder why all the words my gener-
> ation believed in—words like honour and loyalty—are
> now just a joke.
> CURLY: I guess it's because of some of the characters
> they've knocked around with. (36)

In Hare's film *Wetherby*, Morgan contrasts meaningful
abstractions and those terms applied by our century to the inner
self:

> Well, I don't know. I only know goodness and anger and
> revenge and evil and desire . . . these seem to me far better
> words than neurosis and psychology and paranoia. These
> old words . . . these good old words have a sort of
> conviction which all this modern apparatus of language
> now lacks. (123)

Morgan, we know in this flashback, is already a suicide; the
"good old words" were evidently churning within him in
irreconcilable conflict. If the "modern apparatus of language"
lacks an objective framework, and hence "conviction," personal
passion is no more sure a guide:

> ROGER: Define your terms.
> (MORGAN *looks at him.*)
> MORGAN: They don't need defining. If you can't feel
> them you might as well be dead. (123)

In *Wetherby* and elsewhere, Hare fudges the terms of any formula that would equate feeling with morality, yet he constantly
challenges us to examine how feeling prompts us to act on our
values. Morgan is at best an ambiguous spokesman, and his list
of abstractions is morally indiscriminate. The words carry
"conviction" because of their moral weight independent of a
political or social context.

When Hare gives a character such absolute moral diction,
the lines are delivered with force or fervor, but the speaker,
ironically, does not always have the moral dedication necessary
to justify the tone. In *Pravda* (co-written with Howard Brenton),
Lambert Le Roux's first-act curtain speech uses biblical diction
("cast out") and articulates a traditional religious belief about life
as a struggle. However, Le Roux himself has just sacked many
employees arbitrarily; his amorality gives a frightening under-

current to the surface meaning of his words: "We have cast out the bad. There was bad on this paper. Life is a fight between the good and the bad" (58–59). Clergyman Tony Ferris's delivery is likewise insistent in *Racing Demon* but, unlike his more experienced fellow priests, he would impose his convictions on others: "People must be converted. There is only one religion. . . . And the only way to God is through Jesus Christ" (49–50). In *Wrecked Eggs*, when Grace becomes *"suddenly vehement"* over the morality of gentrification in New York, she states the issue in an unexceptionable way, but she herself writes copy to defend the practice she condemns. So the audience should not necessarily trust Grace's delivery as an index of her values or of the play's:

> The question is never "Is this right or wrong?" (*She shakes her head, suddenly vehement.*) It's not "Shall we do this?" "Should this be done?" No, it's "Do we like the guy who's doing this? Is he a nice guy?" (77)

Even when a speaker seems truly committed to a moral course, delivery can still betray him—as Judd tells Chesnau, the advocate of a humane evacuation from Vietnam in Hare's television film *Saigon*: "Lately you've become very loud. Whether you're right or wrong, it's not very effective. You're not going to make anyone change their mind." Forceful, apparently sincere delivery is divorced from the speaker's ethos; indeed, Chesnau's passion effectively diverts attention from the moral question: "[R]aising your voice . . . [is] self-indulgent," Judd continues. "And it doesn't have the effect you require" (124).

In the above passages, Hare confronts us with deliberately obscured uses of right and wrong as topics of argument; his common thread is the character of the speaker, but that source of rhetorical ethos can be as empty as the language people use. Peggy makes this point succinctly in *A Map of the World*: "Principle, indeed! People do what they want to, then afterwards, if it suits them, they call it principle." Stephen objects in language that flatly identifies morality and reality: "Certain things are important. Certain things are good." Peggy's response stresses the personal pronoun, emphatically returning values to their source in the individual: ". . . when he [M'Bengue] says 'principle,' we listen. It's at some cost. It's at some personal expense. But your principles come from a store on the corner and

cost you nothing" (190–91). Peggy's diction, however, undermines her apparent moral superiority, for she defines principle
in monetary terms ("cost," "expense") that apply to M'Bengue as
well as to Stephen. Few would dispute Peggy's claim that the
character of the speaker leads us to "listen"; we have the
authority of Aristotle that "character may . . . be called the most
effective means of persuasion [the speaker] possesses" (25; bk. 1,
ch. 2). Dramatic fictions necessarily present us with appearances,
but Hare's characters—like the politicians produced by modern
image-makers—also use diction that appears ethical, and their
onstage critics, like Peggy, often speak in the same terms.
Through this challenging presentation, Hare apparently wants
his audience to approach speech as he expects it to judge the
twelve scenes of *Plenty*:

> Each of these actions is intended to be ambiguous. . . . This
> ambiguity is central to the idea of the play. The audience is
> asked to make its own mind up about each of the actions.
> In the act of judging the audience learns something about
> its own values. ("A Note" 87)

We are to decide whether words like the "good old" ones carry
values; whether their use by various speakers is responsible—
that is, whether the speakers mean what they say and accept the
consequences of their words; and, frequently in a Hare play,
whether speech can effect any true social or political change.

Hare sets forth the premises for our judging without
connecting them to any clear conclusion. When, for example,
Robbie questions Grace's speech in *Wrecked Eggs* (cited earlier) as
"kind of pointless," Loelia invokes the standard that Hare seems
to endorse: "She feels it, Robbie." She adds that, as a result of
that personal feeling, Grace's belief deserves "respect." Robbie's
"I do respect it" moves the exchange toward resolution until he
adds, "However, I also happen to think she's wrong" (77).
Robbie doesn't tell us if Grace is wrong in her feelings, her
beliefs, or in her ambivalent yoking of the two. The audience
hears an unambiguous, absolute moral term ("wrong") in a
dramatic context that prohibits sure interpretation.

In *The Bay at Nice*, Valentina's delivery and style are
convincingly forceful; in the following exchange, her sudden

reaction indicates genuine emotion, and her short sentences and simple diction suggest conviction:

> SOPHIA: . . . I still have the right.
> (VALENTINA *suddenly gets angry*.)
> VALENTINA: Don't use that word. You have the *right*?
> What does it mean? It doesn't mean anything. Be a person.
> Do what you have to. Don't prattle about rights. (24)

Again, we are left in a muddle. After all, Valentina is an ultimate judge of meaning for the play's central dramatic metaphor, the onstage painting of uncertain provenance, and she posits the same belief that Hare subscribes to elsewhere: "Be a person." Yet, she is no advocate for personal freedom in her domineering tone ("Don't use that word") and her quasi-satiric juxtaposing of "prattle" and "rights."

A more obviously reductive treatment of the bond between values and the self appears in *Pravda*:

> LE ROUX: . . . Moral feelings? They pass. A second. What
> are they? Little chemical drops in the brain. A vague
> feeling of unease, like indigestion. A physical mood. Too
> much dinner. "Oh, I have a feeling," then in the morning
> it's gone. You're there. You're the owner. You're a fact.
> (42)

"Owner" is reminiscent of Peggy's "cost" and "expense"; it is on the same level of measurement as "fact," relatively low in relation to worth. Hare laments the passing of the great abstractions, but he will not substitute a positivist view in their place. His practice rejects that position, for literal, material, and factual meanings are favored not only by Le Roux, where we might expect them, but also by Tony Ferris in *Racing Demon*, whose absolutist point of view allows no shades of meaning when he judges others. He can call a questionable connection— that Lionel Espy's manner of spiritual counselling caused a man to abuse his wife—a "fact" (48), and he compares his spiritual power to a machine: "I can throw on three extra generators" (66). Concerned about "statistics" and "numbers" (16) of churchgoers, he is rhetorically inept, antagonizing the people he would change. He is even capable of turning a prayer into a self-assertive lecture to God: "Christ didn't come to sit on a committee. He didn't come to do social work. He came to preach repentance. . . . God, please help Lionel to see this" (20). Hare's concerns with the ways in which language means are all projected through the style of Tony Ferris: the worth of moral absolutes, meaning and reality; the self as source of meaning; the limitations of literal diction; the efficacy of speech.

Early in *Racing Demon*, Tony and his lover, Frances Parnell, break off their relationship in natural dialogue that subtly insists on the superiority of language of moral worth. Tony, the clergyman, may not realize that he hides behind empty fashionable terms; Frances, the non-believer, surely knows that ethical linguistic categories ("sinning" and "lying") can accurately label personal behavior. Tony draws unreflective ease from the broad, shallow pool of contemporary usage: he speaks of "a caring and loving relationship" and of "a long-term commitment," he would "share what I think" and "communicate my thoughts" (7–8), but his verbs are cant terms that promise open disclosure as they withhold it. "Share" in current usage often qualifies as a euphemism for "tell" in the patronizing sense of the word; it suits Tony well. Against these gutted terms, Hare ironically plays off the sad filler "I mean." Four times in one speech Tony falls back on that expression; it introduces either incomplete thoughts or qualifications that prevent clear meaning ("sort of" and "you understand"):

> I mean, I know this sounds terrible, but the fact is, our relationship . . . well, *we* understand. It's a caring and loving relationship, with some eventual purpose. It's in the context of . . . well, of our future. Of one day marrying. I mean we've sort of joked about it. But I think that's what we've both thought. Haven't we? (*He pauses. She doesn't answer.*) I mean, you know I would *never* . . . the physical experience, I mean you understand it's always in the context of a long-term commitment. (7)

Tony's most revealing verbal strategy may be his mystifying use of "context." Traditionally, locating words in context led to greater precision by setting limits on their application; lately, appealing to "context" has become a way of dodging responsibility by politicians and other people on the defensive. Tony's abuse of the term in the modern manner comes through sharply, for he appeals to a context that doesn't even exist: "It's in the context of . . . well, of our future." As he falters on, Hare artfully displays his confusion through multiple verbal clues: (1) the juxtaposition of his filler "I mean" to "you know" and "you understand"—an unconscious admission that the burden of meaning is transferred to Frances; (2) his failure to articulate a complete thought despite the absolute and emphatic *"never"*; (3) the contrast of *"never"* with "always," which in turn contrasts with "long-term" and the relative connotations of "context"; and (4) Tony's qualifying "context," his signal of clarity, with "if you like" and with fragments of sentences and thought.

In this same scene, *Racing Demon* finally rejects Tony's expression and subscribes to the standards that Frances's style evokes; her moral diction provides the boundaries for the most serious dialogue, and she reduces Tony to silence at the scene's end. After his rationalizing speeches, she—who has had far less to say—renders Tony wordless by raising the linguistic subtext to the play's surface:

> FRANCES: Why is there one word you're frightened to use?
> TONY: Which one? (*Frowns.*) What word?
> FRANCES: I'm not a Christian, so it doesn't frighten me.
> TONY: I have no idea what you mean.
> FRANCES: (*Smiles*) The word is sin. Why don't you use it? You've been sinning.
> (*He looks at her, silenced.*)
> Well, isn't that what you think? (9)

As a Christian, Tony should know that "sin" has an objective meaning outside all his self-serving talk. Others, like Frances, need not accept such moral categories, but one who does can no longer center meaning in the self.

The correspondence between self-centered meaning and general values is mocked by Valentina in *The Bay at Nice*. To her daughter's axiom, "In their private life, a person must be free to live as they choose," she reacts first with an incredulous raising of her eyebrows and then with a belligerent question: "My goodness me, your principles are convenient. You call that an ideal?" (20). Her casual "goodness" anticipates similar Hare examples in social discourse of words drained of their spiritual values; Streaky in *Racing Demon*, for one, reacts to talk of damnation with a "gracious" (51). Valentina will not accept the hypocrisy that drapes fine-sounding names over selfish behavior:

> How convenient. Goodness. An ideal. Which also coincides with what you want. How perfect. . . . For me, it had a different name. I never called it principle. I called it selfishness. (20)

Again, absolute diction ("ideal," "principle") establishes the gulf between naming and reality when the speaker alone is free to determine meaning. Frances Parnell is more honest than Sophia when she tells Tony: "I didn't make love in any 'context.' Whatever that may mean. I made love because I wanted you" (8). By way of contrast, Stephen in *A Map of the World* turns heavy irony on Peggy for rationalizing her desires under the name of "freedom": "Gosh, well, thank goodness" (191).

Unlike Frances and contrary to Samuel Johnson's maxim, Peggy may be a hypocrite in her pleasures. Her offer to be the prize in the debate between Mehta and Stephen debases both personal desire and the ideal behind the form of open verbal exchange. Peggy would attach the high-sounding terms "freedom" and "principle" to her offer, but Stephen insists that it be given a more proper name: "That's not freedom. My God, that's bartering" (193). This negative judgment, expressed in a metaphor of trade, constitutes one of the poles in Hare's scheme of linguistic things. The simply measurable or transactional lacks the inherent worth of the good old abstractions, no matter how strongly they resist defining. Hence, Tony's unwitting pun damns him to us and to Frances when he concludes an appeal based on his emotional confusion with "I'm not sure I can *afford* that any more" (9; emphasis added). Hare is too thoughtful an artist to suggest that we operate from either one extreme, the tangible, or the other, the abstract; instead, they are mixed together dramatically, as at the very end of *A Map of the World*. The Stephen actor[1] defines his car technically ("It's a steel-grey, 2.4 litre 1954 Alvis") as prelude to "It's my whole life." The figure who has spoken for higher values earlier in the play becomes, as actor acting, the enthusiast for a thing that he identifies with his whole being. Mehta's response, "Yes. I am sure," ironically confirms the confusion of object and worth (228–29).

As the winner's trophy, Peggy is a stage presence during the men's debate, a constant reminder that her body as a sexual commodity occasioned the speeches over principle. The debate deals directly with the political efficacy of language. To address that topic, one in which Hare has a deep professional concern, the adversaries raise the collateral, preliminary ones about meaning. On that level, the clear winner is Stephen. At the outset, Mehta tries to *"bait"* Stephen with a condescending tone, but Hare calls attention to Mehta's limited vision by having Peggy interrupt him just as he uses a term of calculation:

MEHTA: . . . But I had not reckoned—
PEGGY: Victor! (212)

This implicit comment on Mehta's values is then amplified by Stephen's charge that Mehta poses as "a finished human being" who is "objective" and without "emotions." In a characteristic Hare development, Mehta's own words then expose him, for he calls his emotive label of Graham Greene ("charlatan") "an objective fact" (212), a willful wrenching of *fact's* meaning to defend a personal position. Mehta takes the strategic ground of many contemporary politicians with the appeal to objectivity; like them, he goes on to base his ethos on a personal narrative of doubtful relevance: "My mother died when I was born" (213). Having misnamed linguistic value as objective fact, Mehta should not be persuasive when his endorsement of "the value of [the West's] material prosperity" (214) makes the same basic error again.

Mehta, then, confuses matters on the most fundamental level where any distinctions between referential and moral meanings are made. Nonetheless, he delivers the most impassioned attack on bureaucratic abuse of language, and he speaks unequivocally in support of an author's "individual integrity" (215):

MEHTA: . . . this now-futile United Nations.
STEPHEN: Futile? Why futile?
MEHTA: Futile because it no longer does any good.
(*He gets up again, shouting.*)

> Words! Meaningless words! Documents! ... A
> bureaucracy drowning in its own words and suffocating
> in its own documents. . . . [I]n this universe of idiocy, the
> only thing we may rely on is the lone voice—the lone
> voice of the writer—who speaks only when he has
> something to say. (214–15)

Lest we hear the unfiltered voice of David Hare sounding
through Mehta, we should recall that a stage direction like
"shouting" often signals something akin to bluster, loud delivery
overriding objections. Stephen returns us to the beginning level
of solid evaluation when he censures Mehta for delighting in the
"dismal statistic" and for opposing "information" to "hope"
(216–17). Aside from other points that Stephen scores against
Mehta, the most telling one stands unrefuted—that despite "the
points of order" and "verbiage," political discourse achieves
worthwhile goals: "Crises are averted, aid is directed." The
factual ring to Stephen's claims is strengthened by his calm
delivery, contrasting sharply with Mehta's shouting; he remains
seated, only *"leaning forward"* for emphasis (218), while Mehta
stands in an attempt to dominate physically where he cannot
argue winningly.

In the play's final scene, the "real" Mehta further qualifies
the appearance of power that the Mehta actor conveys in the
debate; he is far more sensitive to the inability of an artist to
convey subtleties of meaning. *That* Mehta—as an outgrowth of
the earlier one—seems more like a spokesman for the dramatist
himself; he remains, though, only one of many voices competing
for the trust of the audience. In *A Map of the World*, as in *Pravda*,
Hare sets differing styles against each other as part of his
challenge to us to work through meaning for ourselves. In Act I,
M'Bengue glosses "boring" almost as a rhetoric instructor would
(185). In Act II, the search for a crossword puzzle answer
satirizes tendencies to surrender control of meaning to the
speaker's intention; "Zionism" can be "the plague of the earth" if
"it's got seven letters" and if that's "what the compiler thinks"
(196–97). Narrowing the word to its letters reduces the literal-
minded approach to its absurd, amoral conclusion. By the time
we reach the penultimate scene, we should be like M'Bengue in

seeing through the socially sanitized words and phrases that Martinson applies to the UNESCO conference he has supervised:

> MARTINSON: The occasion was perfectly handled. And in a way, although tragic—the tragedy eats into my soul— but also, we must say, the way things fell out has also been elegant.
> M'BENGUE: Elegant?
> MARTINSON: Convenient. (226–27)

Throughout his works, Hare invites us to be critics of language as social action. The rewrite of fairly accurate news copy in *Pravda* (60–62) could be lifted from the play and used as a teaching technique in a study of slanting. Scene seven of *Plenty* illustrates with devastating cultural force how ready-to-hand negative political terms are (Susan's catalogue includes "Suez Canal," "Nasser" and "fiasco") (172–73). Patrick in *Knuckle* translates a once current phrase, "peace with honour," into its true meaning of "surrender": "Peace with honour—peace with shame" (78). In general, Hare is content to illustrate such negative examples briefly, but his television film *Licking Hitler* locates black rhetoric near its dramatic core. *Pravda* shows us misuse of language on the grand scale of media influence; its more fundamental theme is the loss of ideals that make responsible discourse possible. During the interval of *Fanshen* (as a Chinese term, the very title calls attention to meaning) two characters rehearse the speeches that they will deliver in Act II; political rhetoric in that play has the power to redirect society. The resolution of *Wrecked Eggs* turns on Loelia's opening herself to new meanings and to a self-informed awareness of her inner qualities:

> GRACE: I'm just saying you have certain qualities I envy. Qualities which aren't just . . . momentary.
> LOELIA: Like what?
> GRACE: Loyalty. Courage. Perseverance.
> (*There is a pause.*)
> If you don't use them, you're going to feel lousy. (93)

These are the very qualities that would lead a person to stay on, as Loelia finally does. *The Secret Rapture*, from its title through to its romance-like ending, celebrates Isobel's self-possessed virtue.

And the question of meaning also supplies a continuing dramatic image in *The Bay at Nice*; the authenticity of the canvas we see from behind parallels verbal authenticity. The inner self creates a validity that cannot be literally expressed:

> VALENTINA: . . . I didn't know Matisse well. But I understood him. I understood what's called his hand-writing. I love this phrase. Do you know what it is?
> PETER: No.
> VALENTINA: It's a painting term. Which is indefinable. It's not quite even signature. It's more than that. It's spirit.
> (33)

The spirit of the word in the Christian tradition is the Logos, Christ as the word of God; in *Racing Demon*, Hare draws on survivals of that rich tradition to create a beautifully complex treatment of the meaning of spirit and the spirit within meaning. In its original production at the Cottesloe, the smallest of the three auditoria that comprise London's National Theatre, seating was arranged so as to make a cross, with the audience defining its outer edges and allowing for playing space within. When the space becomes a church, it is a natural setting for prayer, a form of speech in *Racing Demon* that leads to entirely credible soliloquies in modern idiom. The theatre audience supplies its own idea of the God addressed by believer and non-believer alike as they search for words to express their inner states. A prayer from the Reverend Lionel Espy opens the play and introduces the question of meaning in the absolute sense that eternity sanctions:

> God. Where are you? I wish you would talk to me. God. . . . You never say anything. All right, people expect that, it's understood. But people also think, I didn't realize when he said *nothing*, he really did mean absolutely nothing at all. (1)

Lionel's somewhat disjointed style and perplexed tone before what he calls the "perpetual absence" (1) of his God project an essential deficiency in his private prayer, the formal means given to him for solace and strength. Uncertain of the unseen God, Lionel ironically has put faith in the custodian of God's Word, the Bishop of Kingston, who assured him that if he gave up his freehold, or life tenure, in his parish (to ease the transition to team ministry), his position would still be guaranteed. As a result, some important events of the play revolve around the moral and legal meanings of the Bishop's word. Lionel's confidence is so supreme that he can mimic the inbreathing of the Holy Spirit when he dismisses the suggestion that he could be removed from his post: "Gilbert gave me his word. (*Blows on his hand, as if to signal the problem being blown away)*" (32). He also characterizes the promise as "freely given" and "in good faith" (33). The first of these phrases traditionally attaches to divine benefits, a proper allusion for a promise given by a bishop, but the theological connotations of "in good faith" have been coated over by years of social and legal usage. Like "goodness" and "gracious" in other passages, Lionel's normal diction carries both the ancient spiritual suggestions and the current secular ones. One set of connotations does not cancel the other out; rather, their unquestioned, slightly uneasy co-existence gives speaker and audience alike a power of selection over meaning.

At the moment of crisis, the Bishop of Southwark over-rules Kingston's promise as he vests himself in the episcopal robes symbolic of power, and Lionel responds, ". . . a friend of mine has been to see a lawyer. . . . I'm afraid you have no argument in court" (78). The conflict between the two men, as Hare dramatizes it through the ways in which meaning works, can never be resolved, for it resides in the refusal of moral language to yield a single meaning in self-centered contexts. When Southwark comments, "No two people will ever agree on theology. . . . But you can insist that, whatever our beliefs, we assemble together and perform the same rituals," Lionel expresses the problem honestly: "I agree. As long as those rituals aren't an organized hypocrisy." The Bishop replies like a literalist who resists the inevitable shifts in meaning that time imposes:

> . . . But what else can we do? Truly? . . . [W]e must rely on
> formulae which have served men well for two thousand
> years. No, more than rely on them. I have begun lately to
> realize we must fight for them as well . . . Oh yes, the
> church's reformers are always great advocates of passion

and—what do you call it?—"commitment." But always in
their own cause. (76)

Admittedly, individual commitment does not determine
meaning by itself; still, Southwark's accusation of "egotism" (74)
against Lionel is unfair because it oversimplifies the process of
meaningful struggle. Earlier, the conflict was set forth in abstract
terms that *Racing Demon* immerses in dramatic contexts of
human exchange; Kingston, the bishop who gave his word,
confronts Harry, a member of Lionel's ministerial team:

> KINGSTON: Is [Lionel] a man of faith?
> (HARRY *looks down.*)
> HARRY: He's a man of conscience. (43)

In the play's brief final scene, "faith" is as absent for Lionel
as God is. Tony, Lionel, and Frances share the stage, but *"All
three are oblivious of each other"*—together, yet distinct and apart.
In alternating speeches, each speaks twice; Tony alone does not
mention God, although he instructs the Almighty from his literal
perspective. He talks down to the Above: "It's numbers, you see.
That's what it is, finally. You have to get them in" (87). In Tony's
last words, "faith" has been replaced by "confidence," a word
with an inherent tension lost on him; its root meaning recalls the
virtue of true belief, but advertisers—like Tony himself, huckster
for a full church—have appropriated it for their own: "It's a
question of confidence. If you don't allow doubt, the wonderful
thing is, you spread confidence around you" (88). As he did in
scene one, Lionel asks for more than "silence"; he concludes with
questions. Frances has the final words; she begins with a pun
("bit") more from show business than legitimate theatre, and
concludes the play with an image of technical transcendence:

> I love that bit when the plane begins to climb, the ground
> smooths away behind you, the buildings, the hills. Then
> the white patches. The vision gets bleary. The cloud
> becomes a hard shelf. The land is still there. But all you see
> is white and the horizon.
>   And then you turn and head towards the sun.
> (*The stage darkens.*) (88)

In production, before the stage went dark, there was near-
blinding light from a multitude of bulbs on the back wall. As at

the end of *Plenty*, stage lighting serves as metaphor for ambiguity of meaning: what allows for clarity of physical vision cannot be applied reliably even to the specific scene it literally illuminates. We know that when Susan opens her arms to a brilliantly lit new world at *Plenty's* close, her optimism is painfully wrong: "There will be days and days and days like this" (207). As an abstraction, *plenty* has been infused with meanings at odds with its positive ones; more specifically, Susan herself has spoken of her "glittering lies" in France (166). In *Licking Hitler*, the verbal metaphor of bright light also falls short of a positive ideal:

> ANNA: . . . In retrospect what you sensed then has become *blindingly* clear to the rest of us: that whereas we knew exactly what we were fighting against, none of us had the whisper of an idea as to what we were fighting for. (128; emphasis added)

In *Knuckle*, Curly argues that harsh light exposes the evil of our time because people no longer can rationalize that "they were ignorant or simple or believed in God": "[A]t last greed and selfishness and cruelty stand exposed in white neon: men are bad because they want to be" (71). The theatre audience, often literally in the dark, also gets a false promise from strong light in *A Map of the World*: "*brilliant light*" announces the "real" Mehta in scene nine (220). Although it "is in the matter of meaning" (221) that Mehta appears, his theorizing over reader response (cited previously) and his comments on the values of his fictional characters complicate interpretation rather than ease it. In *Strapless*, the medium of film allowed Hare to give something of a double perspective on blinding light: as Lillian Hempel faces the walkway in the fund-raising fashion show at the film's end, we see the back of her head against the field of brightness she is about to enter. Hare freezes this final shot, a moment of personal commitment and inner feeling held against the swings of meaning that acting inevitably brings about.

The pun on "acting" as doing and performing returns us to Hare's praise of Vanessa Redgrave for her lived belief in abstract terms. Theatre is the place and production the means for Hare to test meaning for himself and for his audience. As a politically sensitive author, he will not surrender meaning to that audience, nor does he abdicate personal control to a deconstructionist theory. Since his work is best realized in performance, two modern theorists are especially pertinent in summarizing how words work in Hare's drama. Both Michael Polanyi and Kenneth Burke are concerned with how language achieves meanings through its audience. Polanyi argues that, although "all our knowledge is inescapably indeterminate," "personal participation and imagination" examine "subsidiaries" (e.g., words) as "bearing upon . . . their focal meaning" (61–70). That is, experiencing language in usage and within contexts leads us to see multiple meanings in metaphor, symbol and universal terms. Burke could be thinking of Hare's "great abstract nouns" when he insists that "things *do* have intrinsic natures, whatever may be the quandaries that crowd upon us as soon as we attempt to decide definitively what these intrinsic natures are" (56–57). Polanyi similarly assumes that we will fall short of certitude in trying to reconcile "incompatibles" in our lives. He could be analyzing Lionel Espy, Isobel Glass, the young Susan Traherne and, maybe, David Hare:

> . . . [I]ncompatibilities . . . make up the whole stance of our lives: the hope that we may be able to do or achieve what we know we must do but which we also know we have not the power to do.

As a result, Polanyi argues, we live—again the applicability to Hare's dramatic worlds is striking—"in a sort of permanent tension" (156). One source of respite from the tension can be found, extending another Burke insight, in language:

> All thought tends to name things not because they are precisely as named, but because they are not quite as named, and the name is designated as a somewhat *hortatory* device, to take up the slack. (54; emphasis added)

Hare would exhort us without giving us a program or sentimental hope. In the "seeing place," theatre, the audience is challenged to see moral language at work in an incompatible world and to think about taking up the slack.

NOTE

1. In *A Map*, characters appear *both* as media figures or participants in a world conference on poverty *and* as actors who play those characters in a film purporting to depict what happened at the conference.

WORKS CITED

Aristotle. *Rhetoric*. Trans. W. Rhys Roberts. *Rhetoric and Poetics*. Intro. Friedrich Solmsen. New York: Random House, 1954.

Brenton, Howard and David Hare. *Pravda: A Fleet Street Comedy*. Rev. ed. London: Methuen, 1986.

Burke, Kenneth. *A Grammar of Motives*. *A Grammar of Motives* and *A Rhetoric of Motives*. Cleveland: Meridian, 1962.

Hare, David. *The Bay at Nice* and *Wrecked Eggs*. London: Faber, 1986.

———. "Four Actors." *Writing Left-Handed*. London: Faber, 1991. 160–83.

———. *Knuckle*. *The History Plays*. London: Faber, 1984.

———. "A Lecture Given at King's College, Cambridge, March 5 1978." *Licking Hitler*. London: Faber, 1978. 57–71.

———. *Licking Hitler*. *The History Plays*. London: Faber, 1984.

———. *A Map of the World*. *The Asian Plays*. London: Faber, 1986.

———. "A Note on Performance." *Plenty*. Rev. ed. London: Faber, 1984. 87–88.

———. *Plenty*. *The History Plays*. London: Faber, 1984.

———. *Racing Demon*. Rev. ed. London: Faber, 1991.

———. *Saigon: Year of the Cat*. *The Asian Plays*. London: Faber, 1986.

———. *The Secret Rapture*. Rev. ed. London: Faber, 1989.

———. *Wetherby*. *Heading Home, Wetherby* and *Dreams of Leaving*. London: Faber, 1991.

Polanyi, Michael and Harry Prosch. *Meaning*. Chicago: University of Chicago Press, 1975.

Weaver, Richard. "Language is Sermonic." *Language is Sermonic: Richard M. Weaver on the Nature of Rhetoric*. Ed. Richard L. Johannesen et al. Baton Rouge: Louisiana State University Press, 1970. Rpt. in *The Rhetoric of Western Thought*. Ed. James L. Golden et al. Dubuque: Kendall/Hunt, 1983. 275–85.

(Re:)Defining the Assault: Hare's Juvenilia

Scott Fraser

The ideological commonality of David Hare's first three published plays—*How Brophy Made Good* (1969), *Slag* (1970), and *The Great Exhibition* (1972)—is their emphasis on the dialectical relationship between public (institutional) and private (individual) moral decay. Yet stylistically, with the exception of the final group scene in *How Brophy Made Good*, the audience is never directly accused of involvement with the amoral onstage world; nor is there an onstage spokesperson who articulates or demonstrates a political alternative to the status quo. Rather, the dialectic is implicitly presented in a group of inherently subversive texts which are in themselves gestures of revolt, and which can be termed "satirical anatomies."[1]

Central to an understanding of how this genre of political drama works is an explanation of its manipulation of audience expectation in terms of ideological content and dramatic structure, as opposed to direct accusation. A point of recognition must first be established with the audience in terms of individual characterization, narrative structure, or dramatic genre so that it can then be parodied and subverted. As David Edgar has pointed out, playwrights like Hare "are employing given forms and structures, but they are not using them as a bridge into people's familiar dramatic experience; they are deliberately disturbing and disorienting the audience by destroying the form and denying expectations." The intention, according to Edgar, is similar to Brecht's *Verfremdungseffekt*, but with a significant difference:

> As in Brecht, the aim is to force the audience to respond analytically; but instead of distancing the audience from the occurrences, these writers involve the audience, provoking them into thought by the very surprise and shock of the images. . . . (31–32)

This shock is what Edward Bond has termed "aggro-effects"—a strategy designed "to disturb an audience . . . , to involve them emotionally . . ." (Innes 113). The result of combining recognizable dramatic structures with such aggro-effects is the creation of a form of heightened realism that implicitly questions the stage action, as opposed to stage naturalism which serves to reinforce the socio-political status quo. By questioning the audience's aesthetic expectation, the dramatic enactment of the text questions the political assumptions upon which it is predicated.

The intended shock effect of such sudden subversions is illustrated by the structural divisions between realism and self-referentiality which characterize *How Brophy Made Good*. The "Author's Note" to *Brophy* states that "[t]he play alternates between 'character' scenes where an actor plays one person and group scenes where character is only occasionally suggested" (84). In agit-prop fashion, the actors are required to step out of character and directly address the audience. Not only does this shift from realism to self-referentiality prevent any emotional identification on the part of the audience by providing the prescribed shock effect, it also emphasizes the text's dialectic between the private individual and his public persona. Indeed, it is this dialectic which generates the text, in that all of the characters are in some way involved with and corrupted by institutionalized modes of communication. Further, the dialectic between public and private life (specifically the corruption of the emblematic individual involved in institutions which act as metaphors for contemporary England) means that the moral decay of the individual becomes a metaphorical reflection of the decay of society.

All of the characters narrate reconstructions of their private past, with media satirist Brophy (whose life is the supposed subject of the text) providing a touchstone for each of their discourses. It is this emphasis on autobiography which helps to create a stylistic and structural unity in the "character" scenes; but as the first group scene states, the audience must beware of sentimentality:

> BROPHY: There was once a time, and such a time.
> SMILES: Distrust him. Distrust all these things. (88)

Brophy's line echoes the opening of Charles Dickens's *A Tale of Two Cities* (1859): "It was the best of times, it was the worst of times . . ." (1), a form of sentimental narrative reconstruction of the past implicitly attacked throughout the text by characters' direct references to Dickens. And the truth of autobiographical narrative is negated not only by Smiles's line, but by Leonard's ensuing "This man is fiction" (88), a point which the text reinforces through its metadramatic artificiality, and which can be made about all of the characters. For example, Smiles, who is both the host of the *Time For Concern* television series and Brophy's lover, believes that "Media matters" (96). But this optimism is directly countered by Brophy, who claims that Smiles's liberal programs "of elaborate social concern" (97) are actually tools of the establishment which reinforce the status quo. Any gesture toward liberalism is thus implicitly subverted by involvement with the media, and this is illustrated in the text by the self-congratulatory nature of the private individual; as Brophy accuses: "The whole point of your awful shows is to prove how bloody liberal you all are" (108). The shift from public forum to private, from the facade of public concern to sentimental reconstruction of the speaker's past, is affirmed by Smiles's ensuing autobiographical soliloquy, in which she describes her mentor, a pacifist liberal philosopher (108–9). The final negation of Smiles's ineffectual liberalism comes from associating her with established liberal culture: Brophy claims that she could never love anyone who did not have "a working knowledge of the novels of Charles Dickens" (109).

If this is the fate of the text's liberal emblem, an equivalent private nostalgia overcomes the public protests of the play's socialist (Peter) and revolutionary (Leonard). Their ineffectuality is suggested by the gap between their rhetoric (oral signification) and actions (visual signification broadened to create satire grounded in irony). For example, Peter's overtly socialist speeches are comedically underscored in Chekhovian fashion by the contextual frames in which they are uttered. Obsessively jealous of the affair between Brophy and Smiles, Peter defends such jealousy with empty rhetoric from the political Left, absurdly attempting to delay Brophy and Smiles's sexual intercourse with long-winded speeches on the sociological impact of a death in one's family and man's place in society. Brophy's response to Peter, "A stitch in time saves nine," exposes the trite nature of Peter's rhetoric, and comically he and Smiles resort to picking Peter up and carrying him off stage (102). Further, Peter's private sexual corruption and his artificial socialism are associated with Smiles's liberalism when Smiles relates how Peter entered her bedroom as she and Brophy were sleeping and talked about "how Dickens understood the need to liberate the working classes," and while he was talking "he put his hand under the covers and started fondling my breast which was naked at the time" (113).

The closest Peter has ever come to actual revolution is through the death of his brother, Gavin; notably, there is no place in the landscape of *How Brophy Made Good* for an actual revolutionary. For while another character such as Leonard may have an exaggeratedly revolutionary profile, he remains equally impotent to produce change. In the second scene, Leonard poses in front of the white light of a slide projector, comically mimicking the personal history related by the other characters: "Slide One will show you the ideological family tree of the left wing. Marx begat Lenin, Lenin begat Trotsky, Trotsky begat Stalin and Stalin begat Leonard Cook, a direct descendent" (92). Leonard's personal history becomes the public history of the political Left in England, his public popularity being revived in the 1970s by a series of media articles on Brophy. Like Peter, however, he deliberately denies his love for Smiles and explains his private frustrations in terms of empty political rhetoric.

Leonard is further equated with Peter when it is implied that they are lovers, and identified as "the ruling class of English socialism" (123). The paralleling of Smiles, Peter, and Leonard in terms of sex and the media serves to illustrate the collective subversion of the English political Left through its incorporation in established British institutions. For example, as Leonard recites in "Poetry of Revolution," control of communications is central to the revolution's aims: "Communications are vital. / Media are the first target of the socialist revolution" (104). Yet the revolution ceases to exist because of its involvement with the media: officially, the failure of the revolution is explained as "a failure of communications" (117).

Thus, while the text is entitled *How Brophy Made Good*, it concerns the corruption of each character who represents a specific political ideology (liberal, socialist, revolutionary), with Brophy providing the narrative (conservative) link between them. If Brophy has "sold out" and been "subsidised by the Arts Council" (94), then those characters who live off him (e.g., Smiles in her broadcast, Leonard in his articles) are more parasitical than he. Yet his sexual obsessions also reflect a personal moral decay resulting from media involvement as well as an increasingly reactionary political stance—his line, "When I hear the word culture I reach for my sex" (95), echoes Nazi politician Hermann Göring's famous phrase, "When I hear the word culture I reach for my gun." Not only is Brophy harassing in his random, obscene telephone calls, but it is revealed that he may have been Gavin's murderer: this, the text ambiguously implies, is how he actually made good. However, as Brophy neither admits to the crime nor is charged, the focus of Gavin's murder becomes the liberal, non-reaction of the other characters: society is implicitly condemned as indifferent to the fate of the actual revolutionary.

Yet there is a sense of integrity based on self-awareness in Brophy's refusing to continue his involvement as a media satirist. In what first appears to be the final group scene, the actors directly implicate the audience in the onstage corruption by stating "*YOU* are how Brophy made good. . . . *YOU* are his prosperity. . . . He is the hero you deserve" (122). The theatrical simplicity of this gesture is followed by a textually unspecified shift into the final "character" scene, both parts being included under the heading "SCENE NINE." Here, the characters of the Left implicate themselves through patently sentimental reconstructions of a past the audience has already witnessed.

Whereas Brophy "rides his horse into the sunset" (124), Peter and Leonard end up being interviewed years later on Smiles's new program, *Where Are They Now?* Ironically, both have joined the institutionalized media establishment: Leonard is now a professor of communications, and Peter works for the Ministry of Communications. The political Right has disassociated itself from public criticism and the Left remains impotent to instigate change.

The juxtaposition of these final "character" and group scenes points to a structural weakness in the text as a whole. While the purpose of the group scenes in *Brophy* is to subvert any realism in the "character" scenes by shocking the audience into an evaluation of its relationship to the events on stage, there is a sense in which their insertion as a separate and competing form of discourse creates an imbalance in the structure of what is primarily a realistic play. This is not to state that realism should be given primacy, but the "character" scenes have a degree of subtlety that makes the text something of a hybrid: an uneasy counterpointing of realism and didacticism.

Hare's text for *Slag* is clearly illustrative of a more implicit manipulation of accepted dramatic and literary tradition as a form of political commentary, evidenced by the opening scene in which three female teachers at a public girls' school pledge to "abstain from all forms and varieties of sexual intercourse" (11). While this provides obvious echoes of Aristophanes' *Lysistrata*, it is most often critically referred to as a parody of the opening scene of Shakespeare's *Love's Labour's Lost*, wherein Ferdinand, King of Navarre, leads Berowne, Longaville, and Dumain in a pledge of celibacy and abstemiousness.[2] While vows in *Lysistrata* may have been recited to inspire an end to war, and in *Love's Labour's Lost* to foster academe, the recitation in *Slag* has a much more contemporary political relevance, that of gender equality and "the establishment of a truly socialist society" (11). But as in *Brophy*, the humour in *Slag* comes from the gap between the articulated theory and its practice, or oral and visual signification.

Within the hermetic community of the girls' school, the three women provide something of a parody of the nuclear family, each having a particular filial, sexual, and political function.[3] Like Smiles, Peter, and Leonard in *How Brophy Made Good*, Joanne is the character in *Slag* who actively subverts her own articulation of rhetoric from the political Left. For while Joanne views sexual activity as political, her belief in the efficacy of self-denial is immediately undercut by the revelation that there are no male employees at the school. Although rhetorically her speeches articulate a then contemporary form of feminism grounded in science, her position is subverted with the revelation that she is a virgin whose only sexual understanding comes from "descriptions and drawings." As Elise states, "Then you don't know what you're talking about" (44). Indeed, as a spokesperson for any form of radicalism, Joanne is particularly inadequate: her frame of intellectual reference is the fantasy world of the cinema; and she erroneously claims to be working-class and an artist, when in fact she is neither.

Diametrically opposed to Joanne, the rebellious child figure and pseudo-socialist, is Ann, the father figure. An upper-middle-class headmistress, Ann, like Brophy, initially voices a "late 1960s libertarianism" (Wandor 109), claiming that the three women "will build a new sort of school where what people feel for people will be the basis of their relationships. No politics" (12). But as *Slag* progresses, she becomes increasingly conservative, and articulates the moral bias of an earlier generation: "If you people wash away the old-fashioned values, what happens to the old-fashioned people who happen to believe in them" (20). Any appeal to the moral validity of her conservative past is negated when Ann's reactionary, anti-feminist stance becomes both masculine (in the lesbian scene between Ann and Elise, it is Ann who takes the masculine role) and violent.[4] Ann and Elise repeatedly submerge Joanne's head in a bath as a form of conditioning, during which it is Ann who articulates the doctrine: "Inferiority is a privilege I wish to preserve. I don't want to be equal. And I don't want my girls equal. And I don't want a socialist community" (50). Finally, Ann admits to attempting to poison Joanne, a response to a political opponent which further links her to Brophy.

Between the ideological opposites of Ann and Joanne is Elise, the mother figure and liberal in the text. In the conflict between Ann and Joanne she does not completely side with one or the other. While on the one hand she is influenced by Ann (the lesbian love affair, the violent practical jokes they play on Joanne), on the other hand she conspires with Joanne (informing her that Ann may be betraying the cause by having an affair with the butcher). She even placates Joanne by claiming to be working-class, a status she later betrays by admitting to having shares in Shell Oil, ICI, and Marks and Spencer, and still later contradicts by claiming to be the daughter of a wealthy communist. But if Elise is meant somehow to provide an image of a middle-class liberal who sees herself as "normal" and her role as one of rearing children, then her act of knitting booties throughout the play for a child that does not (and, given the absence of males, cannot) exist effectively subverts her position.

Taken as a debate on feminism, *Slag* has been described as "anti-feminist . . . , a vicious slur on women" (Hammond 352); and there is validity to the position of critics such as Wandor that, in this text,

> . . . Feminism is represented as non-sexual and indeed in many respects as anti-sexual, as something undesirable and repulsive, to be done violence to. Women are represented, through Joanne and in the world of this disintegrating public school, as incapable of choosing art or the creations of the mind, and horrific and frustrated when they try to choose the pleasures of the body. (111)

But even Wandor admits that the "framework of the play suggests a satire on the public school system" (111). And Hare himself has stated that *"Slag* was about all educational establishments which I've known, including Cambridge" (Ansorge, "Underground" 18). The metaphorical nature of the location is emphasized by the self-referentiality of the action and the school's apparent placelessness: there are few props or stage directions; there are no references to events in the outside world; no character is permitted to leave the grounds; and none of the pupils is ever seen by the audience. Given the slang definition of the word "slag" as a derogatory word for women or for sexual intercourse,[5] Hare's use of it as the title would seem to imply the ideological barrenness of the school.

Throughout the text, the middle-class public school Brackenhurst is constantly being defined by Joanne, and her vision of the future of this community is particularly utopian:

> ... There'll be no moral judgments, or processes of consultation, or export drives, or balance of payments. There is independence of mind and body. The alternative cannot be defined. ... By escaping definition it escapes parody and defeat. (24)

But because of the gap between such theory and its facile application at the school, the alternative society is indeed parodied to the point of Brackenhurst's becoming a dystopia. The sexual role-playing and argumentation can be interpreted as metaphors for control of the ideological future of Brackenhurst. The debates over such varied subjects as sex, leaky roofs, dog feces, and attempted murder are Pinteresque in their use of rhetoric as a weapon in a territorial imperative with subtextual political applications. Significantly, no character is finally seen as a clear victor, and the constant redefining of the alternative society provides repeated opportunity for parody and finally defeat. By the end of *Slag*, the institution is empty but the teachers remain the same: they wait in hope for the children of those in Burke's Peerage to come and begin the same process all over again. In effect, their revolution has been subsumed by the institution in which it was begun. Put in the terms of Joanne's reference to the film version of *Robinson Crusoe*, they attempted "to create a perfect embryo of the society [they] had escaped from" (12).

This applies not only to revolutionary gestures at Brackenhurst but to revolutionary gestures in middle-class England as a whole: "[t]he distinctive English sight of nothing happening and nothing going to happen" (29). John Bull thus interprets Brackenhurst as a metaphor for the state of England and draws a comparison with the metaphorical locale in Shaw's *Heartbreak House*: "The faded gentility of an exclusive school ruled over by would-be progressives—the paradox is impossible and deliberate; in Brackenhurst and in England nothing ever changes" (64). As a metaphor for the inertia of political change in England, *Slag* is certainly effective. Just as *Heartbreak House* focused on "cultured, leisured Europe before the war" (7), Hare's

Slag focuses on cultured, leisured England in the late 1960s. There is a great deal of talk about revolution, but the middle-class characters who articulate the aims of such revolution operate in an entrenched social institution that morally corrupts individuals (in sexual terms) from across the political spectrum, and leaves the revolutionary movement impotent (as Ann comments: "I don't have simple sexual needs. No one who teaches at Brackenhurst does. We're all in the Freud and under-pant class" [49]).

Further, there is a sense in which the women's liberation movement is a character device in *Slag*: these are individuals who self-fashion themselves as mouthpieces of different ideological approaches to feminism and politics. But while there is certainly dramatic legitimacy in creating emblematic characters, so filled with fantasy do Joanne, Ann, and Elise become that they can too easily be interpreted as simply self-indulgent. As Richard Cave has stated:

> Hare's technique is to resort to increasingly bizarre situations to portray how zany his characters are in believing that their solipsism is a fulfilling engagement with reality and this risks diffusing the satirical passion. . . . It becomes too easy as [the text retreats] into fantasy for an audience to dismiss the whole experience as elegant whimsy. The comic method (admittedly very funny) stifles the poignant urgency of the writer's vision. (185)

Feminism and corrupt sexuality at a girls' public school may be employed as a complex metaphor for politics in England, yet so extremely is the metaphor presented that it overshadows the political commentary. But while *Slag* is not completely successful as political drama, as a parody of accepted dramatic styles the text provides an illustration of Hare's willingness to manipulate dramatic tradition: "I regarded *Slag* as an exercise for the proscenium arch. . . . I wanted to assault . . . the conventional theatre" (Ansorge, "Underground" 18). And although parody is essentially a subversive form of literary discourse, it implicitly recognizes the perceived importance of that which it is subverting. Arguably, it is Hare's willingness to deal with accepted dramatic styles that enables *Slag* to move beyond the structural weakness of *How Brophy Made Good*: instead of the structural division between realism and didacticism, there is an incorporation of implicit commentary into the established form, a point reinforced through the artificiality of the heightened realism of the text.

A more complex employment of such implicit commentary in a satirical anatomy of British society is *The Great Exhibition*. As in *Slag*, this text focuses on the middle class, itself a hermetic society—a thematic concern which Hare has described in terms redolent of his description of *Slag*, and as directly related to the amount of parody and implicit political commentary in the text:

> The "seriousness" of many plays is just another word for self-pity. To me a cultivated seriousness is only so much phoney suffering. *The Great Exhibition* is about people who suffer with a capital S—that area of self-ignorance. I'm fascinated by self-enclosed societies—a very middle-class obsession. There has to be a degree of parody about plays with that theme. My plays are intended as puzzles—the solution of which is up to the audience. (Ansorge, "Underground" 18)

And *The Great Exhibition* is essentially parodic, both visually and ideologically subverting audience expectations engendered by the conventions of the well-made play. The opening stage description calls for *"a study/sitting-room"* that *"should preferably be boxed in"* (11), yet any audience expectation established by this visual signification of the fourth-wall convention is denied when the set is physically altered during the action:

> (*The back wall of the set recedes and the two side pieces slide into the wings. . . . The top of the set is hoisted into the flies and the furniture in the middle is either pulled back or lowered through traps. It's essential that this should be a quite magical effect of the whole room receding and flying apart as* HAMMETT *looks at it, darkening. As the stuff flies away, he walks upstage into the newly created bare stage. . . .*) (43–44)

The conventions of the well-made play are called into question not only on a visual level, as these stage directions would imply, but on an oral level as well. Metatheatrical references are made to acting both in public and private life, the implication being that the private relations and public careers of the onstage characters fail because they are based on performance. And the political commentary is neatly incorporated by having the characters involved in the public institution of the ruling Labour Party.

It is illuminating to note that the text's epigraph contains a single-page juxtaposition of a quotation from Shakespeare's *King Lear*, specifically Lear's "unaccommodated man" speech (3.4.103–11), and statistics concerning "The Distribution of Private Property: Percentage of total net private capital in relation to percentage of total population" (8). This intertextual juxtaposition of a middle-class Member of Parliament's private search for self and current political reality is central to the text. The Labour MP, Charlie Hammett, has created his own self-enclosed society by refusing to visit his constituency. As in *Slag*, the isolation appears as an outgrowth of the middle-class environment of *The Great Exhibition*: Hammett states that his constituents "resent me because I'm not working class" (28). Charlie's conservative wife, Maud, is a casting director for a production of *King Lear*, and her references to acting and its relation to reality are political in their implication:

> MAUD: I've always said there are two kinds of people. Human beings and actors. . . . [Actors are] not quite—people. . . . It was nice to know someone outside the theatre.
> HAMMETT: No longer nice.
> MAUD: No longer so far outside the theatre. (19–20)

Extending the premise that actors are "not quite—people," precisely because they are actors, to include all those who "act" is a direct criticism of Charlie's private life and an implicit textual indictment of all politicians, including middle-class socialists. As Maud puts it in terms of the acting metaphor, "Socialism's a talent, like acting" (42).

While the text divides into two acts entitled *"Public Life"* and *"Private Life "* respectively, the similarity of the acts implies that for these characters there is no difference between their public and private personas. As Hare has acknowledged, ". . . Hammett feels himself to be an exhibitionist both in his public life and in his private life. He feels conscious that he's performing in parliament, and conscious that he's performing in front of his wife" (Itzin and Trussler 112). Further, any distinction between public and private worlds is blurred when Charlie describes his courtship of Maud in terms of performance and political rhetoric:

> HAMMETT: . . . And in the following weeks I talked to her about socialism, and as I talked I became so convinced, it became so clear, that I decided to be a politician. My own eloquence, you see. The platform, the business of speaking it all delighted me. I courted Maud with public speeches. My actual proposal drew heavily on *Das Kapital*. (33)

Hammett's linguistic associations concerning the artificial nature of private experience (courtship) and public text (*Das Kapital*) are meant to signify that his private life is a metaphor for contemporary politics.

The closest to revolution that Charlie has come is in joining the Labour party, and the closest Maud comes is in her affair with Jerry. As in *Brophy* and *Slag*, this spokesperson for the alternative culture has his position subverted by the onstage action: not only does he resort to continual substance abuse and obvious paranoia, but he collapses into unconsciousness and must be carried from the room by Maud and Charlie (an act reminiscent of Smiles's and Brophy's removal of the vociferous Peter). And again, sexual activity in the text has obvious political implications: that Maud's affair with Jerry is simply a repetition of the gesture toward socialism that was her marriage to Charlie is suggested from the very entrance of the lover. Not only are both men equated in their sexual relations with Maud, but in the manner in which the relations occur: on a public as opposed to private level. It is the detective, Abel, who overhears the disintegration of Maud's marriage and photographs her infidelity, which "[p]uts the whole thing on a public footing. More or less a performance" (40).

The public nature of even the most private moments of Maud's affair with Jerry is paralleled in Charlie's affair with Catriona, whom he meets when literally exposing himself in public. His exhibitionism is at once an obvious parody of the heath scene in *King Lear* (both men have abdicated their political responsibilities, and both strip in order to determine the nature of "unaccommodated man"), and an attempt by Charlie to escape the claustrophobic environment of his home (a point made with the physical disappearance of the set). Just as Maud is reported to have performed badly in the part of Cordelia, Charlie now fails in his role as Lear. For his gesture of rebellion, his great exhibition, is impotent: the last woman he flashes, Catriona, fails to respond. Charlie's attempt to "render himself naked before his public" is "echoed in the Polaroid shots of Maud and Jerry taken for him by the private detective . . ." (Bull 68). And just as Maud found a marginally more liberal version of her husband in Jerry, so too does Charlie find a marginally more conservative version of his wife in Catriona. Her lack of response to Charlie's flash also serves to emphasize that the failure of his revolt stems from the artificiality of his performance: "You were acting the part, I'm afraid" (51).

Yet, while filled with self-indulgence, Charlie's ensuing analysis of his past is not simply a subversion of his position as speaker but an elucidation of the ineffective tenure of his party (a point which links him with Leonard in *Brophy*):

> I've been four years in Parliament, swept in, as they say, on the Labour landslide of '66. A lot of creepy-crawlies swept in on the froth of that wave. It's like a debating society, some ghastly boys' school, with the whole grotesque inhuman game of charades magnified and ritualized to the highest possible point of futility, the most elaborate conceivable way of not actually talking to each other, of not actually saying anything. . . . (48)

The institution of the Labour Party, like that of the world of the public school in *Slag*, is seen as inherently flawed through its emphasis on ritual (performance) over action (political change). Of this speech, Peter Ansorge has accurately noted that the images employed of the boys' school, the game of charades, and the ritualized futility, are typical Hare preoccupations with the inner workings of the English political system (*Disrupting* 13). Also typical of Hare's technique is the speaker's own subversion of a political statement by ensuing self-indulgence: the speech is followed by lengthy digressions on his baldness and on the "cosmic insolence" of the world spinning before he was born (49).

When Hammett does return to a discussion of his role in politics, it is with trepidation over the implications of the precedent created by his gesture of revolt, his public exhibition: "I fear tonight's the real beginning of my parliamentary career, not the end. . . . I can't even mouth the word 'revolution' any longer" (52). Faced with the notion of actual revolution to facilitate political change, Charlie is as ineffective as he is at exhibitionism, a point reinforced though the structure of the text. Just as Hammett fails to progress toward some form of self-awareness (arguably a trope of the well-made play) and political resolve, so the narrative structure denies closure. The title of the second act, *"Private Life,"* is ironic in the sense that the location is once again Charlie's flat; and while the narrative may be complicated, and revelations may be made, the action is essentially of the same nature as that of the first act. When it is revealed that Catriona has had Abel spy on Maud and Hammett for their entire marriage, Hammett comments on the nature of *The Great Exhibition*, stating that "Maud used to appear in plays by Ibsen in which the characters would come on stage and tell each other what they perfectly well knew already. . . . That's how I feel with you, Catriona. It was called exposition. But it turned out you already knew" (75). Accordingly, the text can be read as an exercise in exposition. With the subversion of the entirety of that exposition, the type of drama which relies on it—the well-made play—is called into question.

Indeed, the conventions of the well-made play are implicitly criticized throughout the second act: Charlie appears rejuvenated from his exhibition and introspection, but he never actually returns to Parliament as he initially plans. Any audience expectation that the characters will somehow gain from their experiences on the Common and reach some sort of self-knowledge expressed through political resolve is subverted along with the textual denial of closure. When Maud enters at the end of the play claiming that she wants to take over Hammett's constituency, only to discover that the secretary of a local union is to be elected, her reaction is an echo of his: Hammett's response is "Class warfare"; Maud's is "Bloody workers always let you down" (81). Such lines recall Hammett's complaint at the beginning of Act I that his constituents resent him because he is not working-class, and thus reinforce on a lexical level the text's narrative circularity. The textual implication is that the characters are unable to become involved in socialism because of their self-ignorance, an ignorance which appears to stem from the very fact that they are middle-class. As with the characters in *Brophy* and *Slag*, the middle-class progressives in *The Great Exhibition* subvert any articulation of political ideology by their self-indulgence and are left politically impotent. Having failed in their public lives, Hammett and Maud are left in private trying to "[l]ose our personalities," their final lines being a simple repetition of each other's name (83).

As a subversion of the expectations imposed by the format of the well-made play, *The Great Exhibition* is remarkably successful, particularly since that subversion occurs in both content and structure. However, while this is a significant complication in form over the earlier texts, the same criticism can be made of *The Great Exhibition* as can be made of *How Brophy Made Good* and *Slag*: that the artificiality of emblematic characters and situations leads to the dismissal of the piece as fantasy. While the equation of public and private life illustrates the hollowness of the characters, and subsequently the class and political party which they represent, it also reduces the political analysis to the simplistic, creating a thesis which superficially posits that all middle-class members of the Labour Party are fools. This is the essential problem of creating a political satire based on caricature, and is the same criticism that can be levelled at agit-prop theatre. As Hare has admitted, part of the difficulty arises both from the restrictions created by the form chosen to be parodied, and the attempt to subvert the private disillusionment which is the basis for a critique of institutional corruption:

> . . . I think people have expectations of plays with one set and a limited number of characters, and I think those expectations are impossible to resist. And although *The Great Exhibition* starts in a room, and then deliberately explodes and opens out to try and confound the audience, I don't think it really succeeded in that. There is something about the ritual of a play in which there is this guy at the centre of the stage with all the best lines, who's being witty at everybody's expense, and whose uniquely subtle psychology we're going to explore during the course of

> the evening, which is limiting, which is dead. Because it
> stops the audience thinking—or rather, they imagine
> they're there to find out what this man on the stage thinks.
> They're not: they're there to find out what *they* think. (Itzin
> and Trussler 112)

While audience expectations are subverted by the dissolving of
the set near the end of the first Act, and the return to Charlie's
flat at the beginning of Act II reinforces the equation between
public and private life, the return also means that *The Great
Exhibition* does not completely escape the conventions of the
well-made play.

While this is a criticism of the genre, and thus of these
three juvenilia, the texts are an effective illustration of the
redefining of the ideological and structural tenets of Hare's
oeuvre. Characters from both the Left and Right remain political
emblems in opposition to or in complicity with public institutions which metaphorically represent the contemporary English
status quo: the media in *How Brophy Made Good* become the
propaganda unit in *Licking Hitler*, and later the press in *Dreams of
Leaving* and *Pravda*; the private school in *Slag* is Cambridge in
Teeth 'n' Smiles; the Labour Party in *The Great Exhibition* is
resurrected in *Brassneck* and *Deeds*, and is comparable to
branches of the civil service in *Plenty* and *Saigon*, the Communist
Party in *The Bay at Nice*, the Conservative Party in *Paris by Night*
and *The Secret Rapture*, the Church of England in *Racing Demon*,
and the judiciary and police force in *Murmuring Judges*.
Throughout these works the audience is seldom directly
confronted, but rather has its aesthetic expectations manipulated,
expectations engendered primarily by conventions of realism
which reflect the political status quo, but which are implicitly
questioned through the heightened realism that is Hare's drama.

NOTES

1.   According to Rabey, "... rather than elect to use a dramatically powerful spokesperson, a dramatist may choose to provide a satirical anatomy of society. ... Satirical anatomies work by referring to a latent sense of morality, all the more striking by its absence from a play's heightened image of our society engaged in its characteristic processes" (4).

2.   See, for example, Bull (63), Grant (122), and Wandor (109).

3.   Curiously, Wandor sees Ann as "the mother figure, Joanne the bullying and brutal father and Elise the vulnerable and submissive child" (110). Yet Ann, the oldest character, claims in the lesbian scene to be the man; Elise appears to become pregnant; and the youngest character, Joanne, is disciplined by both of them for her rebelliousness. It would seem, then, that Ann is the father figure, Elise the mother, and Joanne the obdurate child of the new generation.

4.   Grant has described the sexual game-playing in the text as "Genet-style" (122), and Ansorge has noted that "the lesbian encounter between Elise and Ann [is] included for pure literary parody (a boarding school version of Genet's all women *The Maids*)" (*Disrupting* 12). Parallels might also be drawn to Genet's *The Balcony* (1956) and the sexual role-playing which occurs in Madame Irma's brothel. However, in *Slag* the rebellion is impotently occurring in the hermetic society of the school, whereas in *The Balcony* the rebellion of the outside world has a direct effect on the lives of the characters in the brothel.

5.   Cf. Brophy's use of the word in *How Brophy Made Good*: "I don't nurse my desires. I own up to the slag I want" (99).

WORKS CITED

Ansorge, Peter. *Disrupting the Spectacle: Five Years of Experimental and Fringe Theatre in Britain*. London: Pitman, 1975.

———. "Underground Explorations No. 1: Portable Playwrights. David Hare." *Plays and Players* Feb. 1972: 18–20.

Bull, John. *New British Political Dramatists: Howard Brenton, David Hare, Trevor Griffiths and David Edgar.* London: Macmillan, 1984.

Cave, Richard Allen. *New British Drama in Performance on the London Stage: 1970–1985.* Gerrards Cross: Smythe, 1987.

Dickens, Charles. *A Tale of Two Cities.* 1859. Ed. Andrew Sanders. Oxford: Oxford University Press, 1988.

Edgar, David. "Ten Years of Political Theatre, 1968–78." *Theatre Quarterly* 8.32 (1979): 25–33.

Grant, Steve. "Voicing the Protest: The New Writers." *Dreams and Deconstructions: Alternative Theatre in Britain.* Ed. Sandy Craig. Ambergate: Amber Lane, 1980. 116–44.

Hammond, Jonathan. "David Hare." *Contemporary Dramatists.* Ed. James Vinson. London: St. James, 1973. 351–53.

Hare, David. *The Great Exhibition.* London: Faber, 1972.

———. *How Brophy Made Good.* Gambit 5.17 (1971): 83–125.

———. *Slag.* London: Faber, 1971.

Innes, Christopher. "From Rationalism to Rhapsody." Interview with Edward Bond. *Canadian Theatre Review* 23 (1979): 108–13.

Itzin, Catherine and Simon Trussler. "From Portable Theatre to Joint Stock . . . via Shaftesbury Avenue." Interview with Hare. *Theatre Quarterly* 5.20 (1975–76): 108–15.

Rabey, David Ian. *British and Irish Political Drama in the Twentieth Century: Implicating the Audience.* London: Macmillan, 1986.

Shakespeare, William. *The Tragedy of King Lear.* Ed. Russell Fraser. New York: Signet, 1963.

Shaw, George Bernard. "Heartbreak House and Horseback Hall." *Heartbreak House: A Fantasia in the Russian Manner on English Themes.* 1919. Harmondsworth: Penguin, 1970. 7–48.

Wandor, Michelene. *Look Back in Gender: Sexuality and the Family in Postwar British Drama.* London: Methuen, 1987.

Nostalgia for the Consensus
in *Knuckle* and *Teeth 'n' Smiles*

Finlay Donesky

> [Britain's early-nineteenth-century political dissenters] had feeling and imagination on their side; but they lacked a convincing theory to give the promptings of the heart an intellectual cutting edge. They could mourn the passing of the old world, and dream of a new one; but they could not make sense of the world which was actually taking shape around them. . . .
>
> Marquand 222

> SLOMAN: It's a sort of . . . presumption you have that you're different, Joe. That's all. Nothing else. And you're not. There is nothing . . . objectively. . . to distinguish you from all the rest.
>
> Griffiths 66

The moral and political authority of the postwar consensus in Britain (variously known as welfare capitalism, or Keynesian social democracy) was just about exhausted in reality by the mid-1970s, although it lived on as a compelling myth for an ever-dwindling number of people until dealt a death blow by the election of Margaret Thatcher in 1979. According to leftist intellectuals and academics such as Raymond Williams, Stuart Hall, David Marquand, Robert Hewison, Tom Nairn, and Alan Sinfield, the consensus failed largely because the socialist principles it rested on were never allowed to take root as a lived collective practice at any level of society. For reasons deeply embedded in English political traditions and class structure, the consensus, born during the social upheavals of World War II, quickly evolved into a highly contradictory experience, with paternalistic, elitist politicians and welfare-state bureaucrats administering socialist-inspired policies on behalf of people they insisted remain an aggregate of passive, isolated individuals. In short, the consensus was socialist in theory, yet profoundly individualistic in practice.

Since by definition the consensus consisted of a set of fixed national ideals soaring above class differences and partisan politics, any grass-roots collective acts of solidarity were either ignored or suppressed by those administering the consensus. Any less than national act of solidarity challenged and undermined the moral authority of the consensus from which the political parties and welfare-state bureaucracies ultimately derived their legitimacy. For those administering it, the consensus worked perfectly as long as people confined their political activity to a trip to a voting station during a national election. For those unwilling to limit themselves to such narrow parameters of political activity, it became increasingly clearer that the consensus was a destructive myth responsible for political paralysis and a stifling conservatism.

The massive burst of extra-parliamentary activism in Britain in the late 1960s and early 1970s testified to widespread feelings and convictions that were distinctly *un*consensual. David Marquand describes the mood of that period as "a growing suspicion of hierarchy, bureaucracy and complexity; a longing for the small-scale and the familiar; a growing demand for wider participation in decision-making . . ." (48). It is very easy of course to dismiss much of that activism—particularly the individualistic, anarchistic elements comprised of middle-class university students on their summer holidays—as totally irrelevant, yet few who do so press on to observe, as Robert Hewison does, that such irrelevance was not so much the result of political naiveté, psychological problems, or too many drugs, as it was of the ability of the consensus to marginalize and fragment radical politics. While explaining the impotence of various Trotskyist, Maoist, and socialist groups, Hewison writes: "Excluded by the consensus from influence on 'real' politics, these groups fought among themselves, further widening the gap between revolutionary ambition and achievement" (157).

When David Hare wrote *Knuckle* and *Teeth 'n' Smiles* in the early 1970s, the counter-cultural movement, if it could still be called that, had moved into a much more realistic and militant phase. Working-class industrial militancy increased dramatically. And as the pot-smoking, free-loving anarchists and hippies faded from the scene along with their utopian dreams of an alternative society, radical activists regrouped with renewed determination around single-issue campaigns fighting for, among other things, the rights of women, blacks, and gays. With all the progressive forces on the Left establishing their moral and political agendas on the basis of class, gender, race and region, it would have been problematic for anyone with strong socialist sympathies to reaffirm the consensual vision of a national/universal collection of classless, non-partisan individ-uals; yet, remarkably enough, this is precisely what Hare does in *Knuckle* and *Teeth 'n' Smiles*. That is, these plays assert the contradictory and self-destructive terms of the consensual political and moral framework in which solitary individuals believe in universalized socialist values.

The moral high ground in both plays is occupied by alienated, anguished young women possessed with a burning outrage at the loss of public morality, yet their moral authority is neither created nor sustained by any collective acts of solidarity. They simply partake of static, previously established moral standards by virtue of their highly receptive emotional faculties. Collective action is not only conspicuously absent from the experience of these painfully idealistic young women, it is explicitly attacked and trivialized, especially in *Teeth 'n' Smiles* in which class warfare and the pop culture of the late 1960s are presented as supremely irrelevant next to the more real and enduring values of Maggie, the moral centre of the play.

While *Teeth 'n' Smiles* endorses universal/national moral standards by undermining all partisan forms of solidarity, *Knuckle* does so by reenacting the traditional consensual relationship between the Labour Party and the Conservatives. As the natural guardians of the socialist ideals of the consensus, Labour had always been able to put the Tories on the defensive morally until the mid-1970s when Margaret Thatcher and Sir Keith Joseph began openly assaulting socialist assumptions. *Knuckle*, like the Labour Party, asserts a universal consensual morality with the assumption that everybody really knows that capitalism is bad and has to be modified with socialism. The surest sign that socialist assumptions retain authority in such a setup is the willingness of the capitalists to assume a defensive guilty posture. In *Knuckle* the entire effort of the plot is devoted to forcing Patrick Delafield, an investment banker who works in the financial district of London, to confess what he already knows: that capitalism is bad and that he has been corrupted by it.

This notion that everybody really knows what is right and wrong is clearly important to Hare's conception of how morality operates. It figures prominently, for example, in Hare's discussion of *Knuckle* in his interview with the editors of *Theatre Quarterly*:

> ... [*Knuckle* is] a play about knowing, about the fact that there are no excuses, and the fact that people who are damaged by the system know themselves to have been damaged, and are not ignorant of what they've done to themselves. And that is a large claim, because how you feel about capitalists—whether you believe them to be knaves or fools—determines everything you believe and think politically. (Itzin and Trussler 113)

Curly says much the same thing to Jenny in the play itself:

> Listen—sugar plum—the horror of the world. The horror of the world is there are no excuses left. There was a time when men who ruined other men could claim they were ignorant or simple or believed in God, or life was very hard, or we didn't know what we were doing, but now everybody knows the tricks, the same shabby hands have been played over and over, and men who persist in old ways of running their countries or their lives, those men now do it in the full knowledge of what they're doing. So that at last greed and selfishness and cruelty stand exposed in white neon: men are bad because they want to be. (71)

The claim that all capitalists "know" (the key word in both passages) and act with "full knowledge" assumes the existence of a previously established, universally recognized moral standard. The real moral battle against capitalism in *Knuckle* has already been won. Thus the play need not present genuine moral dilemmas or real political conflict which entail a confrontation between fundamentally different moral assumptions. The phrase "no excuses left" suggests that, instead of offering genuine disagreement, capitalists can only deflect the truth from themselves with "excuses" or unconvincing efforts to delude themselves and others. And people are considered bad not because they embrace radically different moral assumptions, but because "they want to be." In a world where the real moral struggle against capitalism has been won, the political activity of those who consider themselves at the moral cutting edge can shrivel to the passive task of extracting guilt from willful, self-deluding capitalists.

In the *Theatre Quarterly* interview, Hare calls *Knuckle* "an almost obscenely constructive play," and states that the claim that capitalists such as Patrick Delafield "know" themselves to have been damaged morally is a "huge claim" (Itzin and Trussler 113). However, the act of extracting guilt from capitalists is decidedly modest in the context of the early 1970s, and on the verge of becoming wholly implausible—modest because extracting guilt from capitalists was one of the traditional roles of the Labour Party, in the sense that they could always restrain the Conservatives by reminding them of their commitment to social equality and full employment. From 1945 to about 1975 the Conservatives "knew" that these twin pillars of the consensus represented the highest moral aspirations of their society. Edward Heath's famous U-turn in 1973–74, however, when he abandoned his new-Right economic and industrial policies, is the last time a Conservative government felt morally constrained by consensual ideals. Heath lost his nerve when unemployment rose to one million because, as Alan Sinfield says, "he would not risk the consequences of repudiating welfare-capitalism" (282). When Thatcher replaced Heath as leader of the Conservative Party in 1975 (the price Heath paid for his U-turn) and began her open assault on what she regarded as the corrupting collectivist morality of the consensus, it became no longer possible to claim that capitalists "knew" unrestrained capitalism was bad. Thatcher never forgave Heath for betraying free-market policies; when her turn came to confront the labour unions in the early 1980s, her fighting slogan—"this lady's not for turning"— pointedly repudiated the entire history of the Right's hedging concessions to the moral agenda of the Left. In the face of growing opposition to the consensus from both the Right and Left, then, Hare's assertion of a universal moral authority through confessions of guilt from capitalists resembles nothing so much as the beleaguered rearguard posture of the Labour Party establishment and welfare-state bureaucrats who remained the staunchest defenders of the consensus in the early 1970s.

Hare has commented that ". . . with *Knuckle* I particularly wanted to write a play which was available to everybody—it's about people for whom political rhetoric is no part of their lives. The characters aren't political—or intellectual—at all" (Itzin and Trussler 114). How can one write a play about the moral damage done to "capitalists" (a word implying genuine political differences between capitalists and non-capitalists) with characters who aren't political or intellectual? Well, by proceeding on the assumption that everybody knows capitalism is bad. If there is nothing anybody can learn about morality and there are ultimately no disagreements about what is right and wrong, then characters do not need to be political or intellectual.

Not surprisingly, since all is known to everybody in *Knuckle*, reactions to a fixed truth define characters rather than participation in a dialectic among beliefs or an active renegotiation of beliefs. There are basically two types of characters in *Knuckle*: those who admit capitalism is bad and those who don't. The "good" characters—Jenny Wilbur and Sarah Delafield— honestly face up to what they know, whereas the capitalists— Patrick Delafield and Mr. Malloy—are those who lie to themselves with varying degrees of success. To reduce capitalists to liars effectively depoliticizes and deintellectualizes discussion about them. (The detective/thriller format of *Knuckle* is admirably suited to Hare's scenario of exposing guilt and assigning blame in a world of fixed moral certainties. In the detective fiction of Ross Macdonald and Mickey Spillane, on which *Knuckle* is modeled, the job of the detective is to enforce an established morality, assign blame to villains who have always known the moral implications of their crimes, and bring about a clear, unambiguous resolution.)

The entire life of the chief villain Patrick Delafield, the investment banker, is presented as an elaborate lie, a series of delusions he creates to deflect guilt and convince himself of his integrity, thus rendering the moral case against capitalism a foregone conclusion. His lies take the form of an avid cultivation of literature and the arts: he reads symphonic sheet music and has undertaken an intensive study of Anglo-American literature; he praises the novels of Henry James for their "tremendous quality of civilization" (43). His Scottish housekeeper considers him "a very Christian man" (28) and stands in awe of his culture and learning. His son Curly both loathes and envies his "state of Zen" (47) which requires, as Patrick patiently explains to Curly at various times throughout the play, believing one's own propaganda and being grown-up, mature, and quiet.

Patrick's elaborate defenses against guilt and self-loathing would no doubt have remained impenetrable had his twenty-one-year-old daughter Sarah never discovered that he was tenuously linked to a sordid crime of blackmail perpetrated by property developers financed by Patrick's bank. Since Patrick never actually commits an illegal act (leaving aside the fact that he learned of the blackmail after it happened, bankers are not responsible for the illegal actions of legitimate clients), his only crime appears to be his complicity in the capitalist system per se, and the only evidence of this crime is the guilt betrayed by his overactive efforts to convince himself of his humanity and goodness. Nevertheless, Patrick's involvement at many removes from the crime gives his daughter Sarah an opportunity finally to break through his serene Zen-like pretense of integrity and force him to confess to being morally corrupted. Apparently her youth and innocence are intended to render plausible her assumption that Patrick's banking activity inevitably leads to blackmail.

As evidenced by her faked suicide/murder designed to implicate Patrick, a superabundance of feeling charges Sarah's hostility to her father's profession. Yet what is the moral basis of her feelings? What gives her the right to judge? The play provides absolutely no evidence of how her socialist moral perspective was formed. The same could be said of Jenny. In the absence of any collective practice or of social, historical realities that might have conditioned these idealistic young women, it appears that their moral authority rests entirely on their honesty—neither of them can be "bought." It is an honesty, however, that never goes beyond a passive state of mind (facing up to the self-evident moral facts) except insofar as they force Patrick to confess.

Sarah's letter from France, which Jenny reads at the close of the play, solves the mystery of her disappearance and suggests that, as far as Sarah is concerned, extracting guilt from Patrick fully justifies her moral standards and leaves her nothing more to do. She writes:

> Let us rejoice in the ugliness of the world. Strangely I am not upset. I am reassured. I think I left a finger pointing on the beach.
>
> Jenny, keep Pat on the flat of his back. On his knees, keep him confessing. Keep the wound fresh. . . . (86)

Sarah's absence ensures the maximum extraction of guilt from Patrick for it leaves him believing that he was very likely responsible for her suicide/murder. Thus, paradoxically, Sarah's moral authority is never more potent than when she wanders about France alone and destitute.

According to her powerful "fighting" phrases, Sarah believes she has morally overwhelmed and flattened her father with a stunning knockout punch—an image which appears a bit grandiose considering that all she has done is help force her father to confess what he already knows. The *real* knockout punch is the assumption that everybody already really knows what is right and wrong. Sarah's image of Patrick flat on his back presents in the starkest possible way the central contradiction of the play: how can a completely passive, solitary young woman be ascribed such massive moral power? How can Hare's "huge claim" about the existence of morality rest on a character who doesn't actually ever do anything? One answer, already proposed, is that if moral standards are universal and fixed, then there is no need to renegotiate them with any kind of practice.

Hare may have anticipated this question with some anxiety, for one of the dominant themes of the play is that action is next to impossible, thus rendering inaction much more acceptable. Hare's characterization of morality as all-powerful at one instant and then completely impotent in the next serves the contradictory terms of the consensus which depends on passive individuals upholding universal/national ideals. On the one hand, the power of morality has to be awesome and universal to extract guilt from the heart of even the toughest capitalists like Patrick and drive capitalists like Malloy, with weaker defenses against guilt, to suicide; on the other hand, in order to justify passive individuality whenever the issue of action is raised, morality needs to appear as a feeble and laughable force before the implacable facts of life.

Thus, while Jenny's unwavering idealism and indignation propel Curly's investigation forward, when the opportunity to *do* something arises at the end, her moral authority is suddenly not up to the task. In his last speech—a sort of postscript to the play—Curly says, "Jenny would go to the newspaper. They didn't believe her" (88). If she told the newspapers about Patrick's involvement, of course they wouldn't print her story, since it would be impossible to convict him for negotiating a bridging loan for property developers who later turned out to be unscrupulous: there is simply no story here. The only story Jenny could have told the press would have been about the blackmail that ultimately resulted in an elderly woman being forced from her home into a hospital for the insane. The question is, why didn't the newspapers believe this story for which Jenny had all the facts firsthand from the key witnesses? Newspapers thrive on stories of corruption and blackmail, especially if they can be proven. The answer seems to be that the implausible rejection of her story underscores the uselessness of action, thereby preserving the moral authority of passive individuals. Jenny's reputation as a woman of absolute integrity ("Jenny soars above us all" [41], one of her admirers comments) is allowed to remain intact.

Knuckle also pulls its punches in other ways suitable for the modest requirements of the consensus. Since Patrick is carefully kept at a safe remove from the crime of blackmail, it would seem that his real crime as a banker is his participation in the capitalist system. Yet in his pivotal confession scene, Patrick qualifies his confession so heavily that it becomes virtually meaningless. Patrick does not admit that capitalism is immoral or corrupting; the most he concedes is that it is sometimes dishonest: "The wide boys and the profiteers have sullied our reputation" (79)—with the further qualification that it became dishonest only in the last twenty years. To contrive a blander criticism of capitalism would be extremely difficult; plenty of room exists within even moderate consensual parameters to launch a much sharper attack. Patrick's confession cannot be read as just another of his face-saving, guilt-suppressing rationalizations because the play does not provide any critical perspective on what he says at this point. Curly, the only one to hear his confession, aspires to be a financier like his father, so naturally he does not point out that the nature of capitalism, not the integrity of those currently practicing it, should be the matter under discussion. And evidence suggests that no one else would have pointed this out either. Patrick's claim that Sarah "had never been able to fault him" (80) implies that she found capitalism more or less tolerable until she discovered that it was dishonest. The plot of *Knuckle* seems to bear this out: why does she wait until she uncovered the facts about the blackmail to attack her father?

The towering rage that drives Sarah to fake her suicide is arguably about more than the dishonesty of capitalism; after all, as Patrick says, she had always loathed his profession (29). Yet an investigation into the content of her loathing reveals how neatly consensual her convictions are. In one of her attempts to revive Curly's flagging interest in the investigation, Jenny bursts forth with this passionate testimony about Sarah's concern for the poor:

> JENNY: She was so naive. She used to tell Patrick your wealth is built on the suffering of the poor. And she expected an answer.
> CURLY: All right.
> JENNY: (*Screaming*) All right. . . .
> Always ready with an innocent question. Why don't you share what you've got? Why can't people run their own

lives? Why persist with a system you know to be wrong?
How can you bear to be rich when so many people are
poor? (56)

One's concern for the poor can be "naive" and "innocent" like
Sarah's provided a widespread public agreement exists about
the best way to help. It goes without saying that most people are
concerned about the poor; the issue becomes political, however,
as soon as people begin to disagree about how best to help them.
In 1972 it was still possible to say that most people in Britain
endorsed the socialist way of redistributing wealth through
social welfare programs. Sarah asserts this unspoken,
universalized public truth with her aggressive question, "Why
persist with a system you *know* to be wrong?" After a majority of
the voting public in 1979 elected a prime minister who
passionately believed that her free-market economic strategies
were the best means of helping the poor, it became no longer
credible for young people in their twenties to have a "naive,"
"innocent" concern for the poor.

In some ways *Teeth 'n' Smiles* affirms the contradictory
terms of the consensual experience more emphatically than
Knuckle. Maggie Frisby, the moral centre of the play, is even
more solitary, passive and alienated than her counterpart, Sarah
Delafield. While everybody really agrees with Sarah's moral
standards and therefore knows why she is outraged, nobody in
Teeth 'n' Smiles understands why Maggie is so full of rage and
seems intent on drinking herself to death. Only her ex-lover
Arthur gains a glimmer of understanding at the end of the play
when he realizes that she is unhappy not because, as he says,
"[s]he doesn't know how to be happy," but because "she's
frightened of being happy" (86). He learns, in other words, that
her unhappiness stems not from some personal psychological
problem, but from her feeling that it would be wrong to be
happy considering the moral decadence of society.

Explaining in an interview the thought process that led to
his play, Hare used the word "wrong," implying that he
intended Maggie's anger to have a moral basis:

> Suddenly I was very struck with the thought of somebody
> living a life in which they avoided all opportunities of

> being happy. It wasn't that they couldn't find themselves,
> or relate, or any of those boring things that people said in
> the fifties and sixties, it was because they were actually
> frightened of being happy because they felt it was wrong.
> (McFerran 15)

The moral values governing Maggie's sense of right and wrong
are soaring, universalized/national ones because, largely
through her, the play viciously lampoons and trivializes the
counter-cultural movement of the late 1960s along with working-
class solidarity. It also takes a swipe at homosexuals and blacks
by portraying Randolph, the gay rock singer, as a mindless
bimbo, and Nash, the black drummer, as a *"spaced-out"* drug
addict (12) (although all the musicians are stoned out of their
minds at some point). From her position of passive, totally
misunderstood alienation, Maggie possesses the only true moral
standards, against which nearly all possible forms of solidarity
hostile to the consensus are portrayed as completely devoid of
moral and political legitimacy.

Most of Maggie's rage, which she tries to numb with large
amounts of Johnny Walker, arises from the feeling that popular
culture is not a source of progressive social change—I say
"feeling," for, like Sarah, Maggie arrives at her morally superior
posture through a mixture of passion, intuition, honesty, and
innocence. In contrast, the rational approach of Arthur and
Anson, involving political and intellectual theories, blocks access
to true moral enlightenment. Arthur's misprision takes the form
of still believing in the counter-cultural revolution, which is why
Maggie finds him a bit pathetic and no longer loves him:

> You still want it to mean something, don't you? You can't
> get over that, can you? It's all gotta mean something . . .
> that's childish, Arthur. It don't mean anything. (52)

While attempting to interview Maggie for a university essay,
Anson, the young Cambridge student, manages to squeeze in
one question about the revolutionary role of popular music, to
which Maggie doesn't bother responding:

> Would you say the ideas expressed in popular music . . .
> have had the desired effect of changing . . . society in any
> way? (35)

If Anson were to apprehend this socio-political issue with his emotions like Maggie, instead of trying to understand and articulate some theory about it, he would see that the answer is obviously no. Anson's question is a legitimate one that has engaged many leading British and American sociologists, who contend that to some degree popular music did have a liberating and progressive impact on society in the late 1960s. It is clearly meant to sound foolish, however, in the context of this play, 90 percent of which is about the mindless backstage antics of a rock band far from the cutting edge of revolutionary social change (they actually play music during the other 10 percent).

The four members of the band (Wilson, Nash, Smegs, and Peyote) are portrayed as if it had never occurred to them that people like Anson (and formerly Maggie) thought they were supposed to be a force for social change—hence their bewilderment about Maggie's anger. Their total ignorance of the reasons for her rage and self-destructive behavior is the measure of their total irrelevance morally and politically. Although pointedly working-class (Wilson is introduced in the stage directions as "*a small, bearded cockney*" [12]), their music is not presented as a manifestation of class-consciousness. Hare further denies them their oppositional potential by making the pursuit of drugs and sex—the most notorious, overestimated and ephemeral part of the counter-cultural movement—the sum total of their ambition.

One may well wonder: how could Hare possibly be defending consensual ideals with an attack on the zonked-out acid heads of the late 1960s? How do dropouts like Peyote, Smegs, and Wilson pose a threat to the consensus? Further, if popular culture of the late 1960s were as stupid and mindless as Hare portrays it, then why bother attacking it? And why attack it in a play written in 1975, five to six years after the flakier elements had disappeared? Why kick a dead horse that everybody knows is dead? Regardless of what one may think of the impact of popular music on British society in the late 1960s, it is beyond debate that the acid-dreaming element of alternative culture that Hare chooses to focus on had pretty well burned itself out by the early 1970s.

Teeth 'n' Smiles appears pointless—little more than Hare's idiosyncratic expression of personal revenge on his own unsatisfactory undergraduate experience at Cambridge in the late 1960s—unless one considers Maggie and her band as representative of the counter-cultural movement, which, at its militant core, was undeniably consumed by rage at establishment values and class inequalities, and by a desire for social change in distinctly unconsensual ways. I suggest that Hare wrote about popular culture out of an anxiety to bolster the consensual moral framework that in 1975 was under more stress than ever before. *Teeth 'n' Smiles*, like *Knuckle* with its timorous claim that dishonest capitalism is bad, is a play that craves agreement because late 1960s popular culture, perhaps more than any other potential enemy of the consensus, provides an easy target to caricature and trivialize.

In light of the resurgence of working-class militancy in Britain in the early 1970s, it is not surprising that the other main target of Hare's hostility in *Teeth 'n' Smiles* is working-class solidarity. By portraying Saraffian, Maggie's manager, as a sleazy spiv, Hare reduces the class war to a series of petty crimes perpetrated against the rich. After Maggie has burned down the Mayball festivities tent, Saraffian enters in high spirits and says, "Bless you my dear. At a stroke the custard is crème brulée. You've totally restored my faith in the young" (81). Although it is not altogether clear why she burns the tent down (aside from fulfilling her puzzling desire to go to prison), she vehemently rejects Saraffian's interpretation of her gesture as an act of protest in the class war. The fire reminds him of a similar moment during the war thirty years earlier at the Café de Paris when he reaffirmed his lower-class origins in a political conversion that gave him a life-long faith in the class war. Yet his political epiphany, which he describes at length, involves nothing more than his watching low-life thieves loot the wealthy dead after two bombs destroyed the café, killing and injuring many of the clientele. Why contrive this nasty little story (the Café was actually bombed in the way described, but Saraffian's interpretation is Hare's creation entirely) that reduces the class war to spivvery and looting, except to demolish the legitimacy of working-class solidarity? What little we know of Saraffian's subsequent life indicates that he kept faith with his debased vision of the class war: he gleefully rips off his clients in the music business, and spends much of his time, while visiting his band at their Cambridge gig, stealing silver candlesticks and whatever else he can get his hands on.

Next to this travesty of working-class solidarity, it is not very difficult to assume, as Maggie does, a morally superior position:

> What a load of shit. You're full of shit, Saraffian. What a crucial insight, what a great moment in the Café de Paris. And what did you do the next *thirty years*?
> (*Pause.*)
> Well, I'm sure it gives you comfort, your nice little class war. It ties things up very nicely, of course, from the outside you look like any other clapped-out businessman, but inside, oh, inside you got it all worked out.
> (*Pause.*)
> This man has believed the same thing for thirty years. And it does not show. Is that going to happen to us? Fucking hell, somebody's got to keep on the move. (84)

This passionate denunciation of Saraffian provokes some of the same questions asked earlier of Jenny and Sarah in *Knuckle*. What is the basis of Maggie's moral superiority? What is it (aside from her aforementioned emotional aptitude) that prevents her from being blinded to the superior moral standards by some comforting and deluded theory of social progress? Surely her moral authority and insight rest on something more positive than a lack of falsely comforting beliefs. Is there an objective moral difference between burning someone's tent down and stealing jewellery from the dead and wounded? What has Maggie ever done or even thought of doing that gives her the right to demand of Saraffian "And what did you do the next thirty years? Somebody's got to keep on the move," she says— yet she says this just before she willingly goes to prison. With Maggie as a model, "moving on" evidently requires solitary, passive individuals who feel very strongly about the need to restore national ideals that float above petty, morally insignificant distractions like the class war and popular culture.

This individual/universal mode of "moving on" fits the contradictory terms of the consensus, yet the story Maggie tells Saraffian of a glorious childhood memory suggests that the taproots of her ideals are more impoverished and problematic than the consensus: identifying her moral authority as consensual is to some degree giving her the benefit of the doubt. Saraffian thinks her suffering and self-destructive behaviour have something to do with being a failed or unsatisfied artist. To assure him otherwise, she tells him a touching story that indicates her pain is not merely personal, but stems from the loss of a happiness she felt was somehow her birthright, a natural dispensation conferred on her by virtue of being English:

> . . . Saraffian. In Russia the peasants could not speak of the past without crying. What have we ever known?
> (*Pause.*)
> My aunt's garden led down to a river. . . . I was staying there, I was six, I think, I had a village there by the riverbank, doll village with village shop. . . . I took the local priest down there, I wanted him to consecrate the little doll church. The sun was shining and he took my head in his hands. He said, inside this skull the most beautiful piece of machinery that god ever made. He said, a fair-haired English child, you will think and feel the finest things in the world. The sun blazed and his hands enclosed my whole skull. (71–72)

Maggie says at the beginning of this speech that one human being is no more interesting than another, yet her romanticized pastoral vision of a small, fair-haired English child in a garden by the Thames being blessed by an Anglican priest has nothing to do with the experience of Saraffian or her working-class musicians. Who are the "we" in her question "What have we ever known?" How does her garden experience allow her to speak for what others have or have not known and to judge them?

This tableau of a child in an English garden evokes a myth of lost national unity and purpose more fraudulent than the consensus that was rooted, at least for a brief time during the war, in genuinely popular and collective action. Maggie's nostalgia for her aunt's garden, where she learned to expect to "think and feel the finest things in the world," fits into the tradition of "abstract upper-class kitsch" described by Tom Nairn in his discussion of English nationalism. This tradition, perfected in the poetry of A.E. Housman and echoed in less pleasing terms in the poetry of Enoch Powell, celebrates a synthetic "Old English" identity that, according to Nairn, floats off into a "rustic English limbo" redolent of a "Disney-like English world where the Saxon ploughs his fields and the sun sets to strains by Vaughan Williams" (261–62). And furthermore, the "finest things in the world" are effectively depoliticized, dehistoricized, and universalized with the assumption that the nature of the "finest things" would be self-evident to a naive, innocent child.

The tragedy of postwar Britain in *Knuckle* and *Teeth 'n' Smiles* is supposed to be that Jenny, Sarah, and Maggie never experienced the "finest things" because various regressive elements of society failed to keep faith with the nationally unifying socialist ideals formed during World War II. Yet their profoundly individualistic manner of lamenting the loss of collective national ideals dictates that Hare doesn't have a whisper of an idea why such ideals never materialized. The real tragedy of postwar Britain from a leftist perspective is that collective ideals never took root largely because of the individualistic way they were upheld and defended.

WORKS CITED

Griffiths, Trevor. *The Party*. London: Faber, 1974.

Hare, David. *Knuckle. The History Plays*. London: Faber, 1984.

———. *Teeth 'n' Smiles*. London: Faber, 1976.

Hewison, Robert. *Too Much: Art and Society in the Sixties 1960–75*. London: Methuen, 1986.

Itzin, Catherine and Simon Trussler. "From Portable Theatre to Joint Stock . . . via Shaftesbury Avenue." Interview with Hare. *Theatre Quarterly* 5.20 (1975–76): 108–15.

Marquand, David. *The Unprincipled Society: New Demands and Old Politics*. London: Fontana, 1988.

McFerran, Ann. "End of the Acid Era." *Time Out*. 29 Aug. 1975: 12–15.

Nairn, Tom. *The Break-Up of Britain: Crisis and Neo-Nationalism*. London: New Left Books, 1977.

Sinfield, Alan. *Literature, Politics and Culture in Postwar Britain*. Los Angeles: University of California Press, 1989.

Fanshen: Hare and Brecht

Janelle Reinelt

David Hare may be one of the more unlikely playwrights to be linked with Bertolt Brecht, both because he himself strenuously protests against any such link and because his great dramatic strength is the representation of personal and interpersonal crises, not something usually associated with epic theatre. Nevertheless, Hare has written the most exemplary epic play of his generation, *Fanshen*, and has also shown, in what I choose to call his "personal plays," how a modern appropriation of some epic techniques can produce a dramaturgy unique to the playwright and yet related to the Brechtian project, intentionally or not.

Hare absolutely rejects any suggestion that Brecht might be a positive influence on his work. Besides a distaste for Brecht as a human being—"he was a very objectionable man"[1]—he cites several areas of total disagreement with Brecht's views:

> I think his ideas about political theatre are really mistaken. The idea of the Alienation Effect seems to me absurd in that it is so clear that the purpose of the exercise is to involve the audience, so that to discuss *un*involving them seems to me a complete waste of time. It's incredibly hard to get people to go to the theatre; it's incredibly hard to move them when they are there. Your whole ambition is not that they should identify—I don't identify when I go to the theatre—but I do want to forget the passage of time. In particular, what theatre can do to time in the sense that you wake up and an hour's gone by, or that very short things seem very long, very long things seem very short—

all that which, if you like, is art—those things are
wonderful things and I can't see any point in destroying
them.

This major objection to Brecht's A-effect is based on Brecht's
mistrust of the audience's emotional experience, something
which Hare not only does not share, but, quite the opposite,
finds essential to theatrical representation. Most of his plays offer
the opportunity to understand how a character or group of
characters comes to make personal choices within a specific
social and historical context. The audience is asked to see and
understand the complexity of the situation and then to pass
judgment on it. While Brecht was afraid that identification with
the character's subjective state would serve to dull judgment, to
blur distinctions and thus leave the audience with a "culinary"
attitude, Hare believes that judgment comes from strongly
confronting the contradictions of the characters in moments of
personal crisis and that in "the act of judging the audience learns
something about its own values" ("A Note" 87).[2] Emotions and
mood facilitate this understanding rather than block it.

While Hare and Brecht hold opposing views of the value
of emotions in theatrical representation, these positions are
mediated by reference to their particular historical circumstances. Both men reacted to conditions in the theatre of their
times. When Brecht began writing plays, a deadly cult of
sentimentalism flourished of which he wanted no part: heavy
emotionalism was part of the ideological baggage of the German
theatre. The interruption of the habitual mode of representation
was essential if people were to think critically about what they
were seeing. For Hare, in a different time and place, the problem
of involving the spectators at all—of securing some personal
investment in the narrative—entails a set of English traditions of
theatrical representation which are, by contrast, "cooler," more
dispassionate: to provoke critical engagement, the audience must
be moved beyond detached speculation. The lethargy of
spectatorship is the enemy of both men, but the means of
combatting it are very different in incommensurable contexts.

Hare first became involved with theatre when he directed
some plays as an undergraduate at Cambridge. At the time he
did not know a great deal about the experimental theatre of the

day, had not seen an Edward Bond play, had never heard of La Mama, and was unaware of the visit to England of Brecht's Berliner Ensemble. When he and Tony Bicât started Portable Theatre in 1968, they were interested in establishing a direct relationship between actors and audiences in places where theatre normally didn't go. They shared a perception of mainstream theatre as "rhetorical, over-produced, lavish, saying nothing, conventional . . ." (Itzin and Trussler 109). When he started writing seriously, Hare became aware of a further area of dissent:

> When I began working, the theatre was largely psychological. It was a study of individuals and states of mind which were seen in isolation: plays were hermetic. It didn't seem to me that most of us lived isolated lives, and I didn't believe that life was absurd and all that lonely angst of the twentieth-century writer—I was drawn to the notion that people live their lives together and that, in fact, something could be done.

What Hare realized was that it was impossible to avoid being a part of social and political life, a dilemma which he incorporates in many of his plays and filmscripts, notably *A Map of the World* and *Wetherby*. He has worked three times on a projected screenplay of Joseph Conrad's novel *Victory*, unfortunately never produced, which he considers *the* story of the man who tries to escape from life only to find that he cannot, that life will come and get him. Hare finds that this view of the inescapable nature of social life lies "at the heart of my notion of politics. I'm not an ideological writer; I'm just saying that you're involved in [politics] whether you like it or not because it's to do with how people behave together." Often in Hare's work, a protagonist will attempt to set her/himself above or outside responsibility for what is happening in the present by referring to the past or by adopting a superior position of opposition: Susan in *Plenty*, Mehta in *A Map of the World*, and Maggie in *Teeth 'n' Smiles* come immediately to mind. This focus on the inevitable connection between personal behavior and its social and political consequences is one of the strongest themes in Hare's work and is remarkably similar to a major theme of Brecht's *Mother*

Courage and *Galileo*—namely the futility of trying to avoid the political consequences of personal action.

In writing for the theatre, Hare has encountered an aspect of theatre as dramatic genre which he detests, and which he concedes Brecht also loathed: a structural emphasis on bourgeois morality:

> It is a moral form, and two-thirds of the way through any play the audience expects to be told what it should do; there is something inexorable about the shape of the theatre. What Ibsen would call the obligation scene must be there—it tends to be the scene that hovers over the evening and for which the audience is waiting. I can see that Brecht hated that bourgeois preaching, that he's trying to say, "I'm drier, hipper, nastier than all you bourgeois moralists,"[3] and really it's a complaint about the theatre, that theatre is almost inevitably a bourgeois form, and it sort of is. . . . I know that if writers don't give the audience the sense of that scene, the audience feels disgruntled. . . . I can't bear all that. I just cringe the minute anybody tells me how I should live my life. . . . [Yet] it's very hard to avoid preachifying. There's absolutely no way to keep a serious moral theme from emerging in the theatre; I mean you can't stop it.

Serious moral themes are, of course, precisely what Hare writes about, and he will readily admit to a concern with such questions; it's the formulaic answer that he finds loathsome. In his work, therefore, one almost always encounters strategic ambiguity, a deliberate attempt to keep the audience from arriving at a pat answer to the questions of the evening. Whether by insisting on portraying characters in contradictory behavior, or by refusing to yield up any tidy or one-sided resolution, or, in the case of *A Map*, by a meta-technique whereby the dramatic genre itself is foregrounded and its conventions revealed, Hare confounds the thirst for the "obligation scene." Brecht's alienation techniques relative to character and his episodic structure had a similar purpose. In the contemporary theatre, dissatisfaction with Brecht's plays most often falls on those which, in the end, provide too much message and too formal closure (*The Caucasian Chalk Circle* and *The Good Woman of Setzuan*, for example).

In Hare's plays, however, alienation of the characters does not mean (as it does not mean in Brecht either) that one must never experience them sympathetically. It means, rather, that the reaction must be held up to question or fundamentally challenged by the changing circumstances of the social reference point or the internal contradictions of the character. No major character in a play by David Hare is allowed to claim sustained sympathy, or to be experienced apart from a shifting socio-historical background. "The personal is the political" is not a slogan exclusively for feminism: it is the basic political condition (although the attempt to separate the two has marked dominant bourgeois discourse, as has the tendency to occlude the political within the personal). Political theatre thus has a twofold task: to cut through representations of the dominant ideology which are usually "naturalized" to become a non-effect (that is, to pass by unnoticed), and then to discover and circumvent the ways in which the theatrical apparatus serves this ideology and automatically reinscribes it. Interrupting this hegemony may require various approaches in different historical/cultural contexts, but spectators must experience some discomfort, whether called *"Verfremdung"* or something else. *Fanshen* (1975)—in some ways the most atypical of Hare's work and at the same time the most obviously Brechtian—provides an excellent example of the structural and characterological techniques employed by Hare to accomplish these ends. Hare's pointed rejection of any connection to Brecht has organized the discussion so far; the following section reads Brecht intertextually with Hare's playscript, quite apart from the question of intention.

I

William Gaskill has remarked several times that he was rather surprised when Hare expressed interest in adapting William Hinton's 700–page book about the Chinese revolution in the village of Long Bow.[4] Hare cites the opportunity to write about an instance of positive change: "The excitement of *Fanshen* was to write about a society and to cover a period of time in which one felt that peoples' lives were being materially and spiritually improved, in a culture that was completely different to anything we knew about" (Itzin and Trussler 114). It became his first production with Joint Stock, a company which he helped found, and the only time he has worked with Gaskill and Max Stafford-Clark, the two directors of *Fanshen*, in the capacity of writer. The production came within the first year of the company's existence; the development and rehearsal procedures set the style and tone of the company's work for the next few years, and when the *Fanshen* model was no longer workable for Joint Stock, some of its original vitality and excellence waned. The key feature of the work was a workshop period for the actors, writer, and directors, who researched the source material and other aspects of Chinese life and acted out various scenes and fragments to experiment with ways of representing the material. After the workshop Hare went off by himself for four months and wrote an actual script, which Gaskill and Stafford-Clark then took into rehearsal.

The preparation period also involved a direct attempt to take on some of the political organization and ideas of the Long Bow community. From the beginning, the decision was made to decentralize authority and to work as equals, the directors and writer alongside the actors. As an exercise, they underwent a classification system similar to that in the play, where they told each other how much money they made from their theatre work. (Gaskill remarks on that as itself revolutionary, since English actors rarely talk about their salaries.) Actor Simon Callow notes that "the *form* of the Chinese revolution . . . seemed of direct relevance; the constant questioning and above all self-questioning seemed directly applicable to the rehearsal process" (76). At the end of each week, the company met in a session of self-criticism, similar to the "Gates" which the leaders of Long Bow underwent. Hare writes: "The adoption of a rehearsal process based on the Chinese political method of 'Self-Report, Public Appraisal' might, in other hands and with other material, have degenerated into a gimmick. But here it had weight and was surprisingly quick and effective. The self-criticism was real" (Ritchie 108). The actors developed a commitment to portray the truth of the historical situation, led by Gaskill's commitment to represent the sufferings of the Chinese peasants.

The production marked the most politically engaged work of Joint Stock; later the company struggled over its politics or lack of same. This way of working, where the actors control and invest in the meaning of their work, seems to Hare to be extremely political, and to make a perceptible difference in production: "It does alter the nature of the evening you see, it transforms it; if the actor means it, it makes a difference." Formally, this relationship between actors and material is represented in the opening of the play where the actors begin by presenting one piece of information about Long Bow to the audience and by introducing the characters they will play. However, since the company of nine plays over thirty parts, the actors invest in the narrative about Long Bow's people rather than in one particular character's point of view.

The introductory section of the play is only one of its formal Brechtian elements; Gaskill considers *Fanshen* the "most epic play" he's ever done: "The [Brechtian] theory was absolutely appropriate to the script." Some of *Fanshen*'s formal elements associated with Brecht's production style include legends and banners which clarify the action or provide organizing slogans ("Settling Accounts" [18], for example, or "Never Trust A Landlord, Never Protect A Landlord, There Is Only One Road And That Is To Struggle Against Them" [22]). The script calls for an epic aesthetic in design: no sets, no elaborate lighting, authentic props and costumes. Gaskill's interpretation of Brecht in England relies heavily on a direct relationship to objects as a means of establishing the social *gest* of the scenes;[5] Stafford-Clark's rehearsal diary records Gaskill's query to the actors as to what one prop they needed—they responded a hoe, a rifle, a pipe (Ritchie 114).

The approach of the company and the directors to the material and to Hare's script contributed to the integration of politics and aesthetics. For the workshop, actors improvised speeches denouncing something they were against or argued the values of Marxism. Actor Pauline Melville found this approach novel and valuable: "[I]t was an example of the beginning of a way of working that I had never come across in English theatre before, where instead of concentrating solely on character, individual motivation and so forth, we would undertake some sort of class analysis and look at the work from a political perspective" (Ritchie 117). Gaskill and Stafford-Clark shaped the episodes by identifying the political meaning of the scene. This was an established method for Gaskill; Stafford-Clark discovered it in rehearsal.[6] They worked simultaneously, sometimes in opposite corners of the room, and then showed each other their work; it was an exemplary collaboration. Gaskill cites this method of shaping scenes as something he took directly from Brecht—and also, as a principle of blocking, never to move anyone until something in the action changes. This has become an essential element in Hare's work, too—an element of composition which he compares to film: "The movement of a play is like the principle of film cutting—you must not cut until something has happened. That sense I do love in Brecht, even if you're an anti-Brechtian as I am; it is the one place I can stick."

Each of the sections in the play has a key action which illustrates some new lesson or event central to the struggle to *fanshen* in Long Bow. The word *"fanshen"* came out of the Chinese Revolution and meant "to turn the body" or "to turn over," in some way similar to the notion of turning over a new leaf, although of course a good deal more radical. Hare writes: *"To China's hundreds of millions of landless and land-poor peasants it meant to stand up, to throw off the landlord's yoke, to gain land, stock, implements and houses. But it meant much more than this. It meant to enter a new world"* (*Fanshen* 5). The play asks how this transformation was possible, and shows how it got started, how the community made progress with the help of the Communist Party leadership, and how it was necessary continually to appraise and revise the strategies for accomplishing *fanshen*. The play is an illustration of the Marxist concept of praxis: it shows theory developing and revising itself through practice in such a way that the distinction between the two terms is a false dichotomy.

From Hinton's lengthy book, Hare extracted his own version of the narrative. It begins at the point where the peasants are first asked to take responsibility for governing themselves by accusing and trying those who collaborated with the Japanese. In choosing this point of entry, Hare passed over 175 pages which describe the violence and cruelty of the landlords before the revolution. He says he was told that portraying this "would be very Brechtian," but, since he hated Brecht, he "chucked it out first thing." (Of course, such melodrama would not, as a rule, be Brechtian; on the contrary, *The Caucasian Chalk Circle* does not show the violence of pre-revolutionary Russia, nor does *Mother Courage* portray the carnage of the Thirty Years War. Brechtian narratives always begin with the social condition to be examined.) The various episodes which follow show the villagers becoming progressively able to take public, communal action, to organize themselves into the Peasants' Association, the Women's Association, the Village Government, the People's Militia, and, especially, to reason their way through to collective judgments concerning the affairs of Long Bow.

The script is very rich and manages to examine many aspects of Long Bow's revolution, but four major imperatives emerge from Hare's adaptation: (1) the necessity for assuming personal and collective responsibility; (2) the superiority of practical political solutions to abstract ideals; (3) the definition of good leadership as entailing self-criticism; and (4) the fact that personal vengeance is counter-productive. The second of these imperatives, the distinction between ideal and practical justice, became a major point of discussion between Hare and Hinton when Hare was revising the script for a BBC television version. Hare has commented several times about a particular line which, at Hinton's request, he removed.[7] Hare's account of this issue is worth quoting at length:

> The only way I could do *Fanshen* was through my own bourgeois morality; William Hinton is not a moralist, he's a Marxist. It's a play about how to structure justice, but it is not about fairness. There was a line, which was probably an absolutely terrible line: "people need justice like bread." Sometimes there's a line which may not seem to make very much difference, but to you [as playwright] it's the line you're working toward and which you're working away from. That is the way I wrote *Fanshen* and then when I took it to Hinton, he said, "And the line which I hate most in this play is. . . ." And of course when I took it out I saw that it didn't really matter.[8]

Hinton's problem was with the notion of justice as something abstract, ahistorical, absolute. The changes Hare made in the text clarify this distinction when Party Secretary Ch'en replies to Little Li's confusion:

> LITTLE LI: I thought it was justice, I thought we were interested in justice.
> CH'EN: Not as an abstract, as a practical thing. We've done what we can. From now on everyone's improvement must depend on production, on their new land, their new tools. If we'd gone on trying to equalize we'd have destroyed even that. (76)

These four lessons are not the only insights in Hare's version of Hinton's account of Long Bow's struggle to *fanshen*. They do illustrate, however, the social nature of the action portrayed and their practical applications in the staged representation. There are underlying, and perhaps "moral," assumptions in this text as well: that human beings will reward truth with trust, that reason is stronger than ignorance, that common struggle builds community. Even these truths, however, are seen to be historical in their specific meanings and subject to revision in the face of shifting conditions and contexts.

In 1988, the National Theatre mounted a revival of *Fanshen,* which, as part of the NT Education program, toured to various regional and school venues before opening in London at the Cottesloe. According to Hare, the production came about because of an interest in seeing how the ideas of the play applied in the 1980s, in light of the changes affecting China after the Cultural Revolution and England under Thatcherism. China's new policies of privatization of resources and relaxation of controls had been heralded in the West, especially in the press, as proof of the failure of the revolutionary ideals of collectivisation and as a validation of Western principles of mixed economy. The production affords an example of the shifting patterns of the reception of meaning which inevitably accompany theatrical representation. While for some the serious consideration of a revolutionary movement still seemed like leftist preaching,[9] for others—because of the conservative climate of Thatcherism and the passing of the revolutionary intellectual and artistic interests of the late 1960s—the balance of the play had shifted from an emphasis on the necessity for social justice to the necessity for increased production. Hare says that, to many, the people of Long Bow now appeared "to be wasting their time discussing when production is the first concern." Another factor affecting reception, Hare feels, was the age of the audience: "Older audiences who have seriously considered and rejected communism see it as an exploration of its assets and liabilities while young audiences have never even thought about communism seriously in the first place." Thus what audiences brought to the play in 1988 produced a less sympathetic response to the Chinese experiment than was possible in 1975.

The production itself contributed to this shift in meaning. Hare was not involved in the production until just before the London opening. He came in to rehearsal for one day at the request of the actors who had had a falling-out with their director, Les Waters. At issue were both the politics of the play and the politics of rehearsal. While Gaskill and Stafford-Clark had produced *Fanshen* in a democratic manner related to the subject matter of the play, Waters, Hare was told, had "approached the play as a set text, and rehearsed it with the notion of being 'dramatically effective.'" As the cast played the text on tour, especially to young audiences of high school students, they continued to search for a satisfactory way to portray the politics of the piece. They told Hare they "were good at playing doubt but not joy." He thought their self-analysis was correct and that "the turbo-charge of the early 1940s, of the joy of change, was needed in the early scenes." It seems that the actors, too, had been affected by history insofar as the experiential root of the possibility of revolutionary struggle is missing in contemporary life.

Looking back at his work, Hare is most pleased that the script held up, that it was "robust, indestructible," with a classical formal structure which some of his other work from the period lacked. He thinks that for a minority of people the play still has some importance politically, but he is also clear that he "can't assume responsibility for education when the whole spirit of the time is not to look and think at all politically. At least in this situation, the play requires people to *consider* rival claims of social justice and production. We don't ask those questions usually, or take social justice at all seriously."

Richard Cave, who considers Hare a consummate political writer, has traced the effect of *Fanshen* on Hare's subsequent writing, privileging chronological over thematic development. Seen from this vantage, Cave regards *Fanshen* as key to Hare's technical virtuosity:

> In retrospect, one begins to appreciate how crucial Hare's involvement in *Fanshen* has proved in helping him to find an individual style and technique. . . . *Fanshen* not only evoked a process of history, a turning-over and rebuilding of a community, it also showed how for each individual in that community a growth in consciousness, the creation of a self, had to accompany the larger social movement. Playing with an array of identities in order to shape acceptable private and social dimensions for the self has become the dominant preoccupation of Hare's more recent plays. (211–12)

Cave's perceptions help explain why important traces of epic structure and technique might still be apparent in Hare's work. (The austere control of form in *Fanshen* was still being identified as Brechtian by critics of the 1988 production.) The emphasis on social *gest* and its revelation of the relation between the individual and collective ideology links the peasants of Long Bow to Susan Traherne or even Victor Mehta. Historicization of the incidents has become an ever-present feature of Hare's work, whether he works in an overtly epic manner (*Plenty*) or in a seemingly realistic manner which, through juxtaposition, requires the audience to think historically (*The Bay at Nice* and its companion piece, *Wrecked Eggs*). The style which emerges from Hare's extensive work is *not* derivative Brecht; it is uniquely Hare's own. Seeing the Brechtian elements in Hare's plays, however, helps illuminate their structure, style, and dominant concerns—and, following Cave, provides one view of the unity underlying the rich diversity of David Hare's writing.

NOTES

1. Unless otherwise attributed, all quotations from David Hare are from two personal interviews conducted by the author, in July 1987 and July 1988.

2. This strategy of getting the audience to reflect on its own values and feelings is, at heart, Brechtian, in that it historicizes the incidents of the narrative and requires the characters' behavior to be examined as something which could have been otherwise.

3. Cf. Brecht: "People are used to seeing poets as unique and slightly unnatural beings who reveal with a truly godlike assurance things that other people can only recognize after much sweat and toil. It is naturally distasteful to have to admit that one does not belong to this select band" (73).

4. All quotations from Gaskill are from a personal interview conducted by the author, July 1987.

5. See Holland's perceptive comments on Gaskill's style of directing.

6. Stafford-Clark writes: ". . . I caught on to the dialectical method and was able to refocus whole scenes and characters by taking decisions based on the political line of the play—and not on how each actor thought his character would behave in a particular situation" (Ritchie 111).

7. Besides the interview cited in the text, Hare alludes to the line without quoting it in Ritchie (108) and in Itzin and Trussler (114).

8. Hare gave a paraphrase of the line to Stephen in *A Map of the World*: "We may say a people need ideals as they need bread" (211).

9. John Peter wrote in his review of the play: "I find Hare's play monstrously patronising. . . . Milan Kundera has written some unforgettable pages on totalitarian kitsch: this is the genuine article." *Sunday Times* 6 Mar. 1988: C9.

WORKS CITED

Brecht, Bertolt. "Theatre for Pleasure or Theatre for Instruction." *Brecht on Theatre: The Development of an Aesthetic.* Ed. and trans. John Willett. New York: Hill and Wang, 1964. 69–77.

Callow, Simon. *Being an Actor.* Harmondsworth: Penguin, 1985.

Cave, Richard Allen. *New British Drama in Performance on the London Stage: 1970–1985.* Gerrards Cross: Smythe, 1987.

Gaskill, William. Personal Interview. July 1987.

Hare, David. *Fanshen. The Asian Plays.* London: Faber, 1986.

———. *A Map of the World. The Asian Plays.* London: Faber, 1986.

———. "A Note on Performance." *Plenty.* Rev. ed. London: Faber, 1984. 87–88.

———. Personal Interview. July 1987.

———. Personal Interview. July 1988.

Holland, Peter. "Brecht, Bond, Gaskill, and the Practice of Political Theatre." *Theatre Quarterly* 8.30 (1978): 24–34.

Itzin, Catherine and Simon Trussler. "From Portable Theatre to Joint Stock . . . via Shaftesbury Avenue." Interview with Hare. *Theatre Quarterly* 5.20 (1975–76): 108–15.

Ritchie, Rob, ed. *The Joint Stock Book: The Making of a Theatre Collective.* London: Methuen, 1987.

Adapting the Model:
Plenty and *Licking Hitler*

John Bull

Of that generation of committed British playwrights whose earliest work dates from around 1968, David Hare is the most obviously still in public evidence as the 1980s years of the Thatcherite "new Right" slide into the 1990s and the Conservative administration of John Major. Where writers such as Trevor Griffiths have struggled, in the past thirteen years of severe economic retrenchment, to find theatres or television companies willing to take on drama that addresses current issues with a radical voice, Hare has had a steady stream of plays produced at London's National Theatre, and has also been successfully accepted as a film director. This is a measure not only of his continued enthusiasm and talent, but also of his peculiar relationship with the predominant models of mainstream theatre. He has, quite simply, proved both more willing and more able than his radical contemporaries to adapt the form of a particular play to the individual demands of its venue or its acting company. Although very capable, particularly in the early Portable Theatre years, of producing avant-garde theatre, of all the writers I considered in *New British Political Dramatists*[1] he alone consistently offers work that appears to adhere closely to the format of traditional West End theatre; that it does so in *manner* has misled many critics, including those of his most recent work, into believing that it therefore does so in *matter*.

If it was the epic model, with its opening out of the scale of political debate, that came increasingly to interest committed playwrights such as David Edgar and Howard Brenton through the 1970s and into the 1980s, the same cannot be said of Hare (*Fanshen* and his collaborations with Brenton excepted). Where Brenton saw his first commission by the National Theatre in 1976 as a challenge in terms of potential growth and territorial aggrandizement, Hare's recent succession of plays for the same theatre, dating from 1986, have remained consistently scaled-down in format, the action confined in rooms populated by small groups of people with tangled emotional relationships the likes of which are to be found only in Brenton's least characteristic play, *Sore Throats*.

Crudely, Brenton's characters are conceived from the outside, as embodiments of the various and conflicting strands of social reality. They are ideologically determined rather than psychologically explained, leading many critics, looking in vain for the conventionally peopled stage of the "well-made play," to talk absurdly of stereotypes. Curiously, it is just this tradition of the well-made play that is most frequently invoked in what scant critical attention Hare has received, his name being linked with that of Osborne and even Rattigan. Such a response is an attempt to assimilate the plays back into the mainstream by stressing their wit and polish, at the expense of attention to what it is that the characters are so articulate about. It ignores the deliberate sabotage that Hare deploys on the expectancies of the straight-line plot development—the status quo, disruption of the status quo by solvable moral dilemma, explication, and resolution of situation—of the standard model. As Ansorge has commented:

> In more conservative theatrical circles, which includes the vast majority of playgoers and critics, there has been much admiration expressed for the wit and bite of Hare's dialogue, . . . tempered with regret over his nagging refusal to lower the tone of his moral voice which is constantly to be heard wise-cracking away in the plays. (12)

In truth Hare is every bit as aware of and as interested in ideological conflict as Brenton, but, where the latter is concerned primarily with characterisation as a product of social reality,

Hare works from the inside. He is intensely interested in the particular individuality of the individual: most of his central characters are misfits, living out their disillusionment through the dismal unrolling of post-1939 British history. His characters do not embody the confusion of social reality but struggle against it, and it is in this clash that Hare seeks to define the arena of political debate. This raises particular problems because most of his plays are located almost symbolically in the camps of the enemy: an exclusive girls' school (*Slag*, 1970); the Hampstead home of a politically bankrupt Labour MP (*The Great Exhibition*, 1972); the City-commuter land of Surrey (*Knuckle*, 1974); Jesus College, Cambridge (*Teeth 'n' Smiles*, 1975); and an English country house (*Licking Hitler*, 1978). The debate, although occasionally interrupted by outside voices, is almost entirely contained within the precincts of what is clearly seen as the ruling class.

Hare's first direct involvement with the National Theatre came in 1976 when he directed Brenton's *Weapons of Happiness* as the opening production at the Lyttelton Theatre. Brenton saw the move to the large arena as a logical and inevitable progression for the kind of political theatre that interested contemporary socialist dramatists:

> These plays are big, in cast, staging, theme, and publicly declared ambition (they *do* want to change the world . . .). [T]hey are epic in that they are many scened, full of stories, ironic and argumentative, and deliberately written as "history plays for now." (Hay and Roberts 138)

Just as Hare had reacted brilliantly to the challenge of working with Joint Stock to produce the quasi-Brechtian *Fanshen* in 1975, so he clearly learnt much from the experience of working in the Lyttelton. Thus when, in 1978, the National Theatre put on the first of his plays, *Plenty*, he responded with, for him, a comparatively large-cast piece that allowed him, as both writer and director, to exploit the wide-open spaces of the same auditorium in a manner positively discouraged by the smaller intimacy of the commercial West End. The sophisticated resources of the Lyttelton allowed for the rapid changing of located scenes—so that, for instance, the stunning effect in the penultimate scene of *Weapons of Happiness* of the sudden

intrusion into the failed factory sit-in of the Russian tank through
a flood of white light finds its counterpoint in the equivalent
scene in *Plenty*, as Hare unexpectedly returns the action from
England in 1962 to France at the end of World War II in a way
that would have been impossible in the theatres of Shaftesbury
Avenue:

> LAZAR *opens the door of the room. At once music plays. Where
> you would expect a corridor you see the fields of France shining
> brilliantly in a fierce green square. The room scatters.* (205)

Although there is never the degree of complexity about the
staging of *Plenty* that there had been for *Weapons*, it is evident
that Hare realised the way in which access to the Lyttelton might
allow him to experiment with what was for him quite new
territory, territory that he was never again to attempt.

   Plenty is the nearest the playwright ever approached to the
contemporary epic style, moving him temporarily away from the
enclosed locations of institutions and domestic hearths; while the
result is a quite remarkable play, the deployment of the new
theatrical model caused problems that were never properly
resolved. The play jumped epic-style through postwar English
history in a way that was comparable to the Brenton/Hare
collaboration *Brassneck* of 1973—although characteristically it
laid far more emphasis on the disintegration of personal
relationships in the context of overall political decline, using
public events such as the Suez invasion and the 1951 Festival of
Britain as locatable benchmarks both publicly and privately.
And, as I will argue, it was this fusion that caused the most
problems for a playwright who had shown a detailed interest in
the workings of human relationships in a way that fellow writers
such as Brenton and Edgar eschewed.

   Interestingly, the same year that Hare had his first play
performed at the National the BBC screened his television play,
Licking Hitler, both plays with Kate Nelligan, to whom *Plenty* is
dedicated, as the lead female protagonist. Although produced
for two very different media, they were clearly intended as
companion plays, but the difference in "venues" gives a
fascinating insight into the playwright's ability to adapt to
changing dramatic demands, more particularly when we
compare the original stage version of *Plenty* to the later screen

adaptation starring Meryl Streep. These two plays represent a significant landmark in Hare's development as a playwright. They continue the theme of his earlier work from *Slag* onward, with an insistently empirical observation of despair as the only honest response to a bankrupt culture, but for the first time in his solo career he looks at the larger historical perspective (as he and Brenton had done in *Brassneck*), tracing the decline from the war years. It is an important move, and reinforces his claim to be fundamentally a history writer:

> ... [I]f you write about now, just today and nothing else, then you seem to be confronting only stasis; but if you begin to describe the movement of history, if you write plays that cover passages of time, then you begin to find a sense of movement, of social change, if you like; and the facile hopelessness that comes from confronting the day and only the day, the room and only the room, begins to disappear and in its place the writer can offer a record of movement and change. ("A Lecture" 66)

This sense of the "movement of history" is most obvious in *Plenty*, which covers, in a series of jumps, the period 1943–62. The play opens in a room in Knightsbridge in 1962. Susan Traherne is about to leave both house and husband. The first *"has been stripped bare,"* and the second lies naked and asleep (133). In packing cases are collected all the material goods that the couple has accumulated in the postwar years. The contrast is striking, the apparent "plenty" of the "never had it so good" years mocked by the real naked impoverishment of both individual and location. That the location is specifically England is stressed from the opening words of the play, delivered by Susan's friend, Alice: "I don't know why anybody lives in this country. . . . The wet. The cold. The flu. The food. The loveless English" (133). This is England before the alternative euphoria of the late 1960s and, more important, immediately before the Labour administration of which Hare had briefly entertained such hopes, an England still living in the aftermath of war. It is, furthermore, an England seen firmly from the perspective of the establishment rather than the shop floor, and the lives of all the characters are inextricably linked with the failure of English diplomacy either to succeed or to give way to change. Just as the lives of the characters are firmly rooted in the past, so are the explanations of continuity and decay.

The second scene takes Susan back to 1943, as an agent in occupied France, the only time in her history when she was able to believe that what she was doing had any point, that there was a cause worth fighting for. Her experiences in the war provide the only thing for her to hang on to, at first optimistically but finally in despair and a peculiarly refined English version of madness: "The most unlikely people. People I met only for an hour or two. Astonishing kindnesses. Bravery. The fact you could meet someone for an hour or two and see the very best of them and then move on" (158). Her work as an agent had of course been one of deception, and what Susan comes to experience subsequently is that in the business of government and commerce there is only deception, that the necessary lie does not conceal a greater truth. By 1952, working on copy for an advertising agency, she is well able to make the connection:

> In France . . . I told such glittering lies. But where's the fun in lying for a living? . . . To produce what my masters call good copy, it is simply a question of pitching my intelligence low enough. . . . This is all the future holds for any of us. We will spend the next twenty years of our lives pretending to be thick. (166)

If Susan's central discovery is the inadequacy of idealism, her husband, Brock, starts with fewer illusions. He is fascinated by her circle of literary and intellectual friends, but places all his hopes on inherited privilege and the accumulation of wealth. "I think everyone's going to be rich very soon," he tells Alice in 1947. "Once we've got over the effects of the war. It's going to be coming out of everyone's ears" (155). Postwar society, as conceived by all the characters, has nothing to do with the construction of the Welfare State and the early dreams engendered by the Labour administration in 1945. Even Brock's vision of wealth is set securely within the portals of the Diplomatic Service, in which he has made his career. Their world is that of the old England that will continue to administer a stranglehold over all attempts to change. One of Brock's colleagues in the Service, Darwin—described by Brock as "a modern Darwin who is in every aspect less advanced than the last" (145), an evolutionist too unsophisticated to be aware of the possibility of revolution—talks of building the new Europe. For him, it will be a programme along traditional paternalistic lines, about as wrong as it was possible to be about the new Europe. His imagery takes us steadily away from a present of road building, through the peasant fields of the Empire, to the inevitable and carefully placed tray of civilised drinks: "Massive work of reconstruction. Jobs. Ideals. Marvellous. Marvellous time to be alive in Europe. No end of it. Roads to be built. People to be educated. Land to be tilled. Lots to get on with. (*Pause.*) Have another gin" (149).

For Darwin in 1947, such an idealistic vision of what is essentially the continuation of Empire is still a possibility. Its public manifestation is the 1951 Festival of Britain, but Hare significantly uses the celebrations as a backdrop for the beginning of Susan's personal disintegration. Beneath the celebratory fireworks of the festival she negotiates the fathering of her child in exchange for a deal involving five hundred cheese-graters. But it is the Suez crisis of 1956 that is the personal and political breaking point. As a military manoeuvre it was misconceived and shambolic; Hare uses it to demonstrate the complete misreading of history, and in particular of Britain's role, in the postwar world, as exemplified by such as Darwin and the earnest representative from the once-ruled territories, M. Aung. At the height of the crisis Susan and Brock hold a dinner party for some of their fellow diplomats. A stage direction describes Susan as "*dangerously cheerful*" (172); the parallels between the Suez invasion and her own adventures in France are irresistible, and push her over into an excited madness. Aung puts forward a thesis about the American and English partnership—the Americans are the Romans, "power, armies, strength," and the English the Greeks, "ideas, civilisation, intellect" (171)—which is immediately undercut by the entrance of Darwin. The images of classic nostalgia collapse against Darwin's realisation that the whole campaign is a fraud, not the glorious cause that Susan would like it to be.

Darwin's crisis is that of the old ruling class. He had been against the campaign from the outset, but has subsequently discovered that the government had lied. Greeks and Romans give way in the new world to Hollywood stereotypes: "I would have defended it had it been honestly done. But this time we are cowboys and when the English are the cowboys, then in truth I fear for the future of the globe" (176). Darwin's notion of the traditional English code of fair dealing disintegrates around him faced with a final revelation of what had always been the political reality of deception, and the disintegration is mirrored dramatically by the breakup of the dinner party into shouting and abuse. As Darwin leaves to resign, Susan makes the connection between the parachute descents into occupied France, where "we were comparatively welcome" (178), and those into Egypt. Her final words before the interval now appear heavily ironic in their attempt to reconcile her and Brock's ideas of "plenty":

> Isn't this thrilling? Don't you think? Everything is up for grabs. At last. We will see some changes. Thank the Lord. Now, there was dinner. I made some more dinner. . . . A little ham. And chicken. And some pickles and tomato. And lettuce. And there are a couple of pheasants in the fridge. And I can get twelve bottles of claret from the cellar. Why not?
> There is plenty.
> Shall we eat again? (179)

The crazily expanding meal, the feast of expediency in the ruins of idealism, is a powerful manifestation of Susan's insanity. Throughout the second half of the play, her attempts to come to terms with a world of lies and deception provide a perfect image of the larger context of decay. Her efforts to advance her husband's career in the Service founder because of her refusal to lie, to understand that public life is simply a game with rules that may not be articulated. "[D]o you never find it in yourself to despise a profession in which nobody may speak their mind?" she asks Brock's superior, Sir Andrew Charleson. Sir Andrew replies:

> This is the nature of the service, Mrs Brock. It is called diplomacy. And in its practice the English lead the world. . . . As our power declines, the fight among us for access to that power becomes a little more urgent, a little

uglier perhaps. As our influence wanes, as our empire
collapses, there is little to believe in. Behaviour is all. (193)

Diplomacy is revealed not as compassion and tact, but as
duplicity and deception.

Susan has nothing with which to counter this. Her threat
to shoot herself is rightly seen as silly and in bad taste. The
elastic establishment will continue to preside over the final years
of plenty. Her closing words in the play, as she is transported
back into wartime France after a last impossible attempt at an
emotional relationship with Lazar, the man who has carried so
much of the symbolic weight of her idealism, underline the
irony. A brief moment of rapport has been established with a
French farmer, and she addresses him and the audience: "My
friend. . . . There will be days and days and days like this" (207).

Thus far I have stressed the way in which the audience is
carried intellectually through the play, but such an account does
Plenty less than justice, and avoids the potential pitfalls of the
piece. The burden of narrative unfolding falls largely on Susan—
her story, and her move towards disintegration, is also the story
of postwar England. Yet hers is not the only story to interest
Hare: in addition to the different but relatable despairs of Brock
and Darwin, there is the continuing presence of Susan's friend
Alice, who moves from bohemian rebel to provider of shelter for
unmarried mothers. This sense of different and opposing voices
is important in ways that move beyond the demands of
theatrical discourse; a sustained debate dominates the play, and
Hare's creation of characters who demand a complicated sense
of involvement from the audience means that the debate is never
merely an enclosed one. Ansorge talks of the ending in terms of
an illusion that the audience has already had shattered (16), but
this is to miss the point.[2] The irony derives not from the fact that
the audience has already had revealed to them that things did
not work out as hoped for—which is to reduce the play to the
level of simple exposition—but that it has been given the
opportunity to evaluate the essential falsity of Susan's vision. It
looks as though, on a narrative level, there is choice only
between the cynical manipulation of the establishment and
romantic idealism. The more subversive suggestion can be
drawn from the subtext of the play, the interaction between play

and audience that Hare talked of in his 1978 Cambridge lecture ("A Lecture" 63)—that there was a possibility of something else happening, that the presentation of English history is not only that of a pessimistic procession towards decline, but also there to be learned from.

Ultimately, however, it is the figure of Susan who dominates *Plenty*. A comparison with *Brassneck*, where Brenton and Hare also traced postwar history, is instructive. Here, the central figure, Bagley, is not presented as a psychologically realised figure, but simply as a product of his age, a logical embodiment of postwar capitalist enterprise; furthermore, not only is he a totally unsympathetic character, but he is killed off before the play reaches its climax. In contrast, Susan is a strongly realised character, both dominant and engaging, and it is her ironic declaration of belief in the future back in 1944 as the final words in the play that the audience retains. This juxtaposition of the public and the personal in *Plenty* is of course quite consciously problematic, and Hare is only too aware of a possible reading of the play that sees Susan's decline as an essentially personal affair:

> ... [T]he opposition to *Plenty* forms around the feeling that from the start Susan Traherne contains the seeds of her own destruction, and that the texture of the society in which she happens to live is merely irrelevant. ... I intend to show the struggle of a heroine against a deceitful and emotionally stultified class, yet some sections of the English audience miss this, for they see what Susan is up against as life itself. (Introduction 15)

It is in this sense that Susan chooses the wheeler-dealer Mick as the father of her child:

> SUSAN: I chose you because ... I don't see you very much. I barely ever see you. We live at opposite ends of town. Different worlds.
> MICK: Different class.
> SUSAN: That comes into it. (164)

But because, for all the articulation of other voices in the play, Susan so dominates the action, there is no doubt that Hare is setting any actress an extremely demanding task in resisting the temptation to turn the play into a merely personal tragedy. What helped greatly in the stage presentation was the deployment of time leaps, the effect of which is to make any consistent tragic development difficult and, more important, to force the audience to fill in gaps, creating time and space for larger questions to be asked.

Curiously, when Hare came to work on the screenplay the problem was actually made more acute. The proto-epic model was almost entirely abandoned in favour of a frequently uneasy naturalism, and the speech patterns were fitted into a more colloquial mode, though often at the expense of the political import of the words. The naturalistic demands of the film medium to present a straight-line story with a beginning, middle, and end were catered for by Hare's removal of the opening scene and the provision of a whole series of links that smoothed the chronological development of the narrative, filling in gaps where the stage play had relied on the jumps to disconnect the flow—so that, for example, we are given in the film Brock visiting Susan in the clinic during her breakdown, an event referred to only in passing in the play, a link that inevitably helps in the actually unwanted move towards empathy. Although the greater budget and the potential for far more varied scene locations allowed for a number of brief but telling glimpses at the ways of the ruling classes in postwar England, the overall effect was to place even more stress on *Plenty* as Susan's story rather than England's, in which carefully placed historical locations lost their ironic counterpoint and became simply nostalgic recreations. Even the added scene of Susan and Mick's first attempt at procreation to the accompaniment of the television broadcast of the 1953 Coronation—a memory, perhaps, of the Bagley wedding held against the background of the same television broadcast in *Brassneck*—lost any bite it might have had by its placement amidst scenes of street parties and the like.

Broadly speaking, what the film prevented, and what the stage play demanded, was the possibility of standing back from the action: it concentrated on close-ups—for instance, on the prone and drug-crumpled figure of Susan on the bed towards the end—where a more complicated confusion of objectivity and subjectivity is clearly needed. For this is a play that needs to fight hard against the urge for close-ups, and it is an urge that the cinema is particularly unable to resist. So, in the screen version of scene six when Susan opens her handbag, the camera reveals to us, unbidden by any original stage direction, that she still has the cuff links of Lazar, the English agent with whom she had a brief liaison in France at the beginning of the narrative. And, lo and behold, when the pair reunite briefly in the hotel room at the end of the story, Lazar discovers the cuff links still nestling in her bag. It is a small observation in itself, but what it does is to push a cinema audience away from the wider political analysis and provide it with material towards a glib reading of Susan's life as yet another unhappy love story—indeed, with Meryl Streep as Susan, as another French Lieutenant's Woman!

The film, then, far from solving the kind of problems raised by the original stage play, heightens them in the almost inevitable process of creating a suitable vehicle for a then rising star. The comparison with *Licking Hitler* is instructive. In this companion piece Hare demonstrated a masterly understanding of the possibilities and limitations of the television medium and, furthermore, provided a blueprint for the kind of direction his writing would take when he resumed writing for the National Theatre in the latter years of the 1980s. The television cameras make much use of close-ups, directing the audience towards the reception as well as the delivery of speech, thus stressing the sense of the play as open dialogue while, at the same time, reinforcing the claustrophobia of the location. Where *Plenty* had roamed abroad, *Licking Hitler* is confined to a single house, and where the former had jumped extravagantly through history, the latter confines itself to the events of a few days. This scaling-down is vital to its success.

Unlike *Plenty*, *Licking Hitler* is exclusively concerned with a version of the war far removed from dreams of glory. It is set in an English country house, requisitioned for use as a radio propaganda unit to broadcast, from supposedly German sources, a dialogue of lies and defamation to demoralise the enemy. A picture of Goebbels replaces the ancestral portraits, and a new meritocracy with its roots in the diplomatic world replaces the traditional landowner, Lord Minton, whose deafness and dumbness symbolise his ineffectualness and his inability to communicate with the new. Minton is ushered indirectly on his way by the man effectively running the broadcasts, Archie Maclean: "Tell him we appreciate his sacrifice. Having to spend the rest of the war in that squalid wee single end in Eaton Square" (95). The bitterness is important and places Archie apart from both the old and the new ruling class. He is, we learn, a Glaswegian from the Red Clyde, a journalist whose class and nationality cut off all contact with the continuity of the English status quo. His brilliance at his job stems from his absolute lack of belief in any lip service to the moral tenets of the class that he sees as the real enemy. In the country house, as in the Diplomatic Service in *Plenty*, the lie reigns supreme, but for Archie it is unencumbered by any sentimental attempts to pretend that there is a larger morality. He argues successfully that, instead of propagandising against the German invasion of Russia on the demoralising grounds of its evident stupidity, they should be aiding it because it *is* stupid.

The supremacy of the lie is stressed in the simple but masterly way in which Hare opens the play. We are presented with what is unquestionably an "English country house" exterior on a perfect summer day. The tranquillity is disturbed by the arrival of a convoy of military vehicles and then, without preparation, we are taken inside the house as a voice-over, Archie's as we discover, is heard elaborating a strange theory about Rudolf Hess's flight to Britain, a theory that concludes:

> Now what is frightening about Hess is not what he has done. It is the fact he once found his way so easily into Hitler's confidence. As loyal Germans we have to face the fact that Adolf Hitler chooses to surround himself with fools, arse-lickers, time-servers, traitors, megalomaniacs . . . and men who wish to rape their own mothers. (93)

Only then does the camera find the figure of Archie, who proceeds to conclude an increasingly outlandish attack on Hitler before finally acknowledging the dictating secretary: "Something like that" (94). The effect for the audience is one of initial bafflement at who is being addressed and why, before the essentially propagandist nature of the words is revealed. This working exercise once presented, the play then proceeds, after the event as it were, to fill in with narrative explanation.

Into this setting is introduced Anna, whose uncle is Second Sea Lord. Her total lack of contact with ordinary life has caused her to remain ignorant of the existence of electricity bills, and her efforts to make a pot of tea lead her to pour cold water over the entire week's rations. She represents very easily for Archie both the privilege and the helplessness of the old order he is really fighting. "I set myself the task," Archie tells her, ". . . [of getting] through the war":

> Just get through it, that's all. . . . This house is the war. And I'd rather be anywhere, I'd rather be in France, I'd rather be in the desert, I'd rather be in a Wellington over Berlin, anywhere but here with you and your people in this bloody awful English house. . . . (121)

Archie breaks into her room and substitutes himself in bed for her childhood teddy bear, and their relationship stays at the level of aggression. No communication occurs, and he has Anna removed from the project when the possibility of real emotion proves a threat to his careful world of lies.

Much of the strength of the play comes from the jagged nature of the relationship between Anna and Archie, two class enemies theoretically fighting on the same side. In contrast, Brock, in *Plenty*, offers no real dialectical opposition to Susan. Pushed in and out of the narrative in the original stage play, Susan's diplomat husband is transposed in the film into a nice but uncomprehending would-be father-figure who has sacrificed his life in the hope of helping his wife. Where the original quasi-epic model had struggled to contain the move of Susan towards the role of dominant heroine, the film fails to solve the problem by its overemphasis on the domestic menage. The carefully balanced characterisation of Anna and Archie, on the other hand, results in a convincing dialogue that stresses the impossibility of real communication across the class divide; in the converted "country house weekend" motif Hare had found a model that suited his needs more exactly, and without the problems, for him, of the epic model. In *Licking Hitler* Hare presented an apparent domesticity that is constantly undercut both by its changed function—English country house as Ministry of Lies—

and by the openly revealed hostility that prevails. This was the kind of territory that Hare was increasingly to claim as his own.

The point is reinforced when we realise how the playwright then subverts the expectancies of the model he is using. The overall narrative line of the play is left as deliberately unresolved as Anna and Archie's relationship. Hare has no interest whatever in the success or failure of the disinformation unit as a part of the war effort. The action is simply halted—carefully frustrating any audience expectation of a neat plot resolution, for nothing has been resolved politically—and the play ends in the present day with a perfect example of Hare's adaptation to the medium in which he is working. Using the technique of many 1970s quasi-documentary movies, a voice-over describes what has subsequently happened to the major characters. Archie moved into making evocative films of his working-class roots, but is now working in Hollywood—sentimentality giving way to the lie—and Anna went to work in an advertising agency, "increasingly distressed at the compromises forced on her by her profession. In 1956 she resigned and announced her intention to live an honest life" (126). The activities of the unit are shown to have been those which formed the basis of postwar society; the residents in the country house have spread through all positions of influence: "Many of the most brilliant men from the Propaganda and Intelligence Services went on to careers in public life, in Parliament, Fleet Street, the universities and the BBC" (125). The inference is that these were logical continuations of their profession of lies and propaganda, that they are perfect examples of a society founded on dishonesty.

The last words in the play are Anna's, reading from her final letter to Archie:

> . . . [W]hereas we knew exactly what we were fighting against, none of us had the whisper of an idea as to what we were fighting for. Over the years I have been watching the steady impoverishment of the people's ideals, their loss of faith, the lying, the daily inveterate lying, the thirty-year-old deep corrosive national habit of lying, and I have remembered you.[3] (128)

The country house in *Licking Hitler* was Hare's most successful historical location to date, linking the old with the new in an account of English history that is both disturbing and challenging. It offers not a programme for change, but rather a gauntlet thrown down, demanding an analysis that must be made before any thought of change is possible. As so often, it operates from within what is clearly seen as the camp of the enemy—the territory where Hare is always most incisively at his best. And, with the benefit of hindsight, it shows him for the first time, ironically on television, properly coming to terms with the kind of dramatically enclosed yet politically open theatre with which he would enliven the somewhat barren years of the late 1980s and early 1990s—the kind of theatre which, as Brecht once memorably declared, did not demand that an audience hang its brains up in the cloakroom along with its coat.[4]

NOTES

1. See John Bull, *New British Political Dramatists: Howard Brenton, David Hare, Trevor Griffiths and David Edgar,* 3rd ed. (London: Macmillan, 1991). Much of the material in this essay is drawn from chapter 3 of that book.

2. Although I take issue with Ansorge on this point, his essay is still the best introduction to Hare's work that I know.

3. Anna's words here—especially her reference to "the thirty-year-old deep corrosive national habit of lying"—are reminiscent of Maggie's confrontation with Saraffian in *Teeth 'n' Smiles* (1975): "What a load of shit. You're full of shit, Saraffian. What a crucial insight, what a great moment in the Café de Paris. And what did you do the next *thirty years?*" (84).

4. See Bertolt Brecht, "A Dialogue about Acting," *Brecht on Theatre: The Development of an Aesthetic,* ed. and trans. John Willett (New York: Hill and Wang, 1964), 27.

WORKS CITED

Ansorge, Peter. "David Hare: A War on Two Fronts." *Plays and Players* Apr. 1978: 12–16.

Brenton, Howard and David Hare. *Brassneck*. London: Methuen, 1974.

Hare, David. Introduction. *The History Plays*. London: Faber, 1984. 9–16.

———. "A Lecture Given at King's College, Cambridge, March 5 1978." *Licking Hitler*. London: Faber, 1978. 57–71.

———. *Licking Hitler*. *The History Plays*. London: Faber, 1984.

———. *Plenty*. *The History Plays*. London: Faber, 1984.

———. *Teeth 'n' Smiles*. London: Faber, 1976.

Hay, Malcolm and Philip Roberts. "Interview: Howard Brenton." *Performing Arts Journal* 3.3 (1979): 134–41.

Plenty. Dir. Fred Schepisi. Screenwriter David Hare. With Meryl Streep, Charles Dance, and Tracey Ullman. Twentieth Century Fox, 1985.

The Last Chopper Out:
Saigon: Year of the Cat

Toby Silverman Zinman

David Hare's television play, *Saigon: Year of the Cat* (1983), is a relatively minor work, but it is interesting in that it is an important political playwright's treatment of the most violent political issue of our times, the Vietnam War. Further, in the context of other Vietnam plays and films, it is distinguished as one of the few works by non-Americans. And it is further distinguished in that it is a Vietnam screenplay without jungle, "grunts," explosions, torching of villages, blood, gore, or dismemberment.

Since *Saigon* is included in the volume called *The Asian Plays*, it is, necessarily, seen in relation to Hare's two other dramatic works about the East, *Fanshen* and *A Map of the World*. Hare acknowledges that his attraction to Asia (there are Asian characters in *Plenty* and *Wetherby* as well) is a mystery to him; he has travelled in the East (he went to Saigon in 1973, when he "spent a very happy time . . . during the phoney peace which ran from the Paris agreement to the final collapse in 1975" [Introduction x]), but he admits a lack of expertise: "a little travel teaches you that the Westerner, however peripherally, must always be present in your view of things" (Introduction vii). His view in *Saigon* is almost wholly Western, unlike the view in *Fanshen*, which seems to be nearly wholly Eastern. *Map*, of course, is about the collision of the two.

Saigon is about the English and Americans living in Saigon at the end of 1974 and in early 1975. When a character says, "The

Year of the Tiger will soon be the Year of the Cat" (94), I think
we must assume that this is satiric political commentary on the
imminent loss of Western power—the reduction of the tiger to
cat—since there is no cat in the Chinese calendar, and since the
North Vietnamese regularly launched a major offensive attack at
the New Year; as the American Colonel says, it was as regular as
"the baseball season" (90). Although Hare makes us feel the
presence of the civilian Vietnamese population—the bank tellers,
the streetwalkers, the flower-sellers, the maids, the mass of city
dwellers—he does not attempt to provide their point of view;
instead he shows them to us either from a distance (often actual
long shots) or as something close to the clichéd "inscrutable," as
in the major character of Quoc, who is both moving and
dignified but whose responses to circumstances border on the
unfathomable.

For a political playwright writing about so political a
subject as the last days of the war, *Saigon* is surprisingly quiet.
We watch an affair begin and end between a middle-aged
Englishwoman and a young American man; she is the loan
officer of a large bank in downtown Saigon, and he is a CIA
operative who tried to hide from the draft in the government's
bureaucracy and was posted to Vietnam as a result of a
colleague's joke. Their affair is conveyed to us in short scenes, all
in a minor key: bits of conversation in bed, in the bathtub, on the
phone. Their compatibility seems to rest on their sexual
attraction and their shared language in this exotic and beautiful
city; they certainly do not see the political situation in Saigon
similarly, nor are their temperamental responses to crisis alike—
particularly in that Barbara seems incapable of urgency of any
sort. Finally, though, we feel that what they truly share is a self-
serving and therefore dangerous righteousness; both—in very
different ways, determined by national type—attempt to seize
the high moral ground of the play.

Barbara tells her lover, Bob Chesneau, that she left Bourne-
mouth because of the English "emotional cruelty. You feel
watched, disapproved of all the time. . . . Everyone spying on
everyone else" (104). She seems to see no irony in her having
escaped to a place of spies and spooks, apparently oblivious to
the elaborate network of disinformation and counterintelligence

which exists all around her, astonished to hear—after years of living in wartime Saigon—that prisoners are tortured. She never mentions the cruelties occurring daily in Vietnam, cruelties far more shocking than those of England's "little hedgerows squeezing you in" (104).

Her sympathies are passive and finally ineffectual. Her accusations that Bob has *"Done nothing.* And now you're inventing a fresh set of lies" (121) seem sanctimonious in that she has done nothing herself and freely makes use of the political help he provides. But everyone in this play is indicted: the sad and pathological Ambassador who sacrifices thousands of people to his nostalgic patriotism; Jack Ockham, the alcoholic CIA chief doublespeaker; Joan Mackintosh, a CIA analyst who carries a gun in her purse for a suicide pact; Mr. Haliwell, the head of the bank who complains about the labor unions in England causing chaos, so that "We can all be grateful we're living out here" (99), and who simply vanishes without a word from the bank one afternoon to take the last plane out; and so on. None of the Westerners is spared Hare's vituperative contempt, although interestingly the Vietnamese, even the informers, seem valorized by the play: they keep their word as the Americans do not, they are right when the CIA and Washington are wrong, they understand "blood scent."

I suspect Hare wants us to like Barbara rather more than I can manage, and finds her English reserve more elegant than blameworthy. When she says goodbye to Quoc, whom we gather she has worked with for years and whom she will never see again, there is this exchange:

> BARBARA: The bank will trade until the last moment.
> QUOC: Yes, of course.
> BARBARA: I needed to say . . .
> (*She stops, unable to express herself. She puts her hand suddenly over her mouth. QUOC seems simply to wait. She sees this and turns away.*)
> Well, I'm sorry, I shouldn't have disturbed you. (*She turns to go.*) Good night, Quoc. (127)

She later interprets this exchange as having "tried to say something affectionate to Quoc. Well, that's what you're left with. Gestures of affection. Which you then find mean nothing at all" (140). Her capacity for "gestures of affection" seems so truncated that her eroticism, her history of secret sexual liaisons, seems to spring from some impersonal desire, a kind of genetic propensity, rather than from warmth or eagerness for pleasure.

When, for instance, Henderson, a junior executive at the bank, declares his love for her, she reacts with frosty disdain for his feelings and embarrassment at his breach of etiquette:

> HENDERSON: Oh my God, Barbara, I can tell you despise me.
> BARBARA: Have I said anything?
> HENDERSON: No. Not at all. It's just . . . your general demeanour. You behave as if I'm doing something wrong. (BARBARA *looks down at him, as if a little surprised.*)
> I do have to tell you, I've been going crazy . . .
> BARBARA: Well, in that case it's best that you leave. Hong Kong is a good place to forget me. (*She smiles slightly, amused at the ludicrousness of the remark.*) So you'll be much happier there.
> (*She is looking at the floor.*)
> HENDERSON: I would like . . . I feel you disapprove of me.
> (*She does not answer.*)
> You feel I'm cowardly, that's right? (BARBARA *smiles, this time bitterly, at the inadequacy of what she will say.*)
> BARBARA: I think that we . . . who were not born here . . . should make sure we go with dignity. (106)

"Going with dignity" turns out to be harder than she thought. Her retrospective voice-over tells us, "Donald *did* leave with comparative dignity. . . . Compared with some of the rest of us, I mean" (107). We see *"the military and CIA scramble desperately out of the tiny exit door on the landing out to the waiting helicopter"* (150), while Haliwell is nearly trampled by the desperate crowd around the Embassy as he claims national privilege by screaming "English! English!" (142) and Barbara begs to forgo her place on the helicopter to stay with Chesneau—"Just the chance to be with you" (139)—who, of course, is not staying anywhere to be with anyone; our last image of her is of *"an old English spinster"* (144).

We see Bob Chesneau, already airborne, suddenly realize that he has committed the most stunning betrayal of the play. He remembers that he left the names of all his informants, thousands of names, on his desk in the Embassy, and has thus provided the North Vietnamese with an enormous list of their enemies. The subtly unstated realization creates a powerful concluding scene:

> *Inside the helicopter the group has settled, cheerful. A false exhilaration.* CHESNEAU *is sitting next to* JUDD, *on one side. Suddenly he remembers.*
> CHESNEAU: Shit.
> JUDD: What?
> CHESNEAU: I've remembered . . .
> (JUDD *puzzled.*)
> JUDD: What?
> (CHESNEAU *looks down, appalled, disturbed. Avoids the question.*)
> CHESNEAU: Something.
> JUDD: (*A joke*) Do you want to go back?
> (CHESNEAU *turns, looks back, the truth dawning on him of what he has done.*)
> CHESNEAU: (*Under his breath*) God forgive us.
> (*Suddenly the* PILOT *turns and yells back from the controls, as a can of Heineken is opened in front of him.*)
> PILOT: Hey, you guys. We're all going home!
> (*Fast fade.*) (151)

The word "all" may be the most painful word in the play, considering that they are on the last chopper out. For all the people still in Saigon—the Westerners, the South Vietnamese who worked for the Americans overtly or covertly—the options have closed down. But it is the unstatedness of this last scene, its passivity and flatness, that is so telling and true to both the character and the play. Chesneau's lack of affect has been matched by Barbara's, and thus the play seems to have a population of non-characters experiencing non-reactions. If Hare intended this lack of emotional capacity as a way of revealing their emptiness and therefore their culpable lack of humanity, he may have erred on the side of subtlety. The play—both on paper and on screen—feels as though it were written by the CIA: it gives away nothing, not its secrets or its passions, and one suspects, finally, it may have none to hide.

Interestingly, Hare resists the most ubiquitous and predictable of end-of-the-war images, that of the last chopper out; consider this passage from Joan Didion's novel, *Democracy*:

> [O]n the late March evening in 1975 . . . [they] sat in an empty off-limits bar across the bridge from Schofield Barracks and watched the evacuation on television of one or another capital in Southeast Asia. Conflicting reports, the anchorman said. Rapidly deteriorating situation. Scenes of panic and confusion. Down the tubes, the bartender said. Bye-bye Da Nang. On the screen above the bar the helicopter lifted again and again off the roof of the American mission. . . . (43)

The screenplay's final scene, the "freedom bird revelation scene," is a staple of Vietnam plays and movies. Consider this exchange near the end of *Casualties of War* (1990), for which American playwright David Rabe wrote the screenplay:

> ERIKSSON: I thought we were over there, you know, to help those people, man, not . . . not . . .
> EVANS: No, no, no. That ain't why we were over there, man. That was crazy what you did, but everybody was crazy in the Nam. Fuck it, man.
> ERIKSSON: Why were we over there?
> EVANS: The equipment, man. They had all this equipment, they needed to see if it worked. (120)

In an essay on this film, Martin Novelli's comment has considerable bearing here:

> Some day but certainly not some day soon, someone will make a Vietnam movie about "them"—the ones who had all the equipment to test, the ones for whom Vietnam was a laboratory for counter-insurgency, for "nation-building," for winning hearts and minds, for stopping the dominoes from falling, . . . [a movie about] the White House, the Pentagon, the State Department, the Think Tanks. (169–70)

Novelli cites the ultimate ironic/revelatory exchange from Robert Stone's Vietnam novel *Dog Soldiers*:

> "It's a funny place," Hicks said.

"Let smiles cease," Converse said. "Let laughter flee.
This is the place where everybody finds out who they
are."
Hicks shook his head. "What a bummer for the gooks."
(153)

It is, indeed, "a bummer," especially for the hundreds of
desperate people patiently waiting at their assigned places for
the evacuation helicopters to come as promised; naively, nobody
imagined they would be betrayed and abandoned so completely.
It will be even worse for the people attached to the names on
Chesneau's desk. What Hare has done is to write something like
the first Vietnam screenplay which indicts the "them"—those in
the world of diplomacy and secret intelligence, dependent on
word from a Washington more concerned with Congress's aid
allocations than with lives.

Saigon: Year of the Cat was produced for British television
and was first aired in 1983 in England; it has not been televised
in the United States or Canada,[1] although a video was released
recently. There is much that is disappointing about this
production—and lest we shift the blame, it is necessary to
acknowledge that Hare oversaw the filming (director Stephen
Frears had pneumonia) and persevered with Frederic Forrest
(who plays Bob Chesneau), despite Forrest's insistence on
inventing his own dialogue[2] and despite Hare's discovery that
"[m]y leading man did not truly believe that the Americans had
lost a war" (Introduction xii). There is a good deal else that
Forrest does to compromise the film. He is obviously too old for
the role—there is no visible age difference between him and Judi
Dench (who plays Barbara), despite the crucial fact that she is
supposed to be nearly twice his age; this, of course, vitiates the
supposed oddness of their public appearances as a couple.
Further, his style of acting is pure Old Hollywood and, next to
Dench's sophisticated professionalism, seems wooden and
corny. The inadvertent result of this is a political one:
Americanness seems indicted on grounds of crudeness and
ineptitude based on acting ability.

The television film does, however, create some interesting
effects with secretiveness; Barbara tells us right at the start that
"[i]t was never my intention my life should be secretive, it came

about by accident, I think . . ." (85). Thus, when she whispers to
Chesneau, we cannot hear what she says, and the long speech
the Ambassador makes at the airfield is kept a secret from us
since it is nearly inaudible, as are many of the CIA conversations
which we witness taking place behind plate glass. Barbara's
speech about feeling "watched" in England becomes more
interesting on the screen since we are watching her, and even her
swallowing sounds are so magnified that we have clearly
invaded her privacy. This is compounded by an excessive
number of extreme close-ups; thus, we become the British
television audience, peering and prying. That we never see
Barbara and Chesneau in the same frame except when they are
kissing or making love is a further effect of all the close-ups; this
foreshadows, cinematically, their lack of capacity for a
relationship.

In *David Hare: Theatricalizing Politics*, Oliva calls *Saigon*
Hare's "least effective work" (105): "the film is wanting because
no debate exists. . . . There is, in effect, no conflict to dramatize,
so events are scrutinized without the benefit of tension" (106). In
his review in the London *Times*, Michael Church called the script
"functional, intelligent and colourless. We are left with strictly
political thoughts—as we would have been had the lovers never
appeared." This is interesting in conjunction with Michael
Bloom's remark that the "romances Hare usually constructs are
distortions of true love in which the affair creates a terrible
imbalance. Romance destroys all sense of self and the outside
world . . ." (34). It is significant that the distortion created by
passionate, possessive love is missing here; the private story
which should particularize the familiar public story has so little
weight and strength because the characters feel so little for each
other, and thus the political plot is not adequately counter-
pointed. In an earlier interview Hare said, "We don't say, 'Oh,
during the 1968 Tet Offensive,' we say, 'In 1968, when I was with
that extraordinary woman'" (Harris 16). It is hard to imagine Bob
Chesneau saying, "In 1975, when I was with that extraordinary
woman in Saigon. . . ." He is much more likely to say, "In 1975,
when Saigon fell and I escaped on the last chopper out . . . ," so
that the "glamour and mystery and excitement of love between

men and women" Hare says he loves (Harris 16) is absent from *Saigon: Year of the Cat,* leaving it without half its subject.

Hare believes that tragedy "should be optimistic and stoical, and therefore reassuring":

> But the trouble is . . . showbusiness peddles the sentimental piety that you can always get over your problems. To go to the theatre and be told, "No, there are certain problems which you cannot get over—grief, separation, loss, aging, the need to part from people you love"—to go to a play where these things are faced seems to me to be a bracing way to spend an evening, not a depressing one. (Bloom 33)

Barbara's stolid departure from Saigon and from her lover, and Bob's quick assimilation of the horror he will cause—note his easy shift to the plural pronoun ("God forgive us") when he remembers the names he left on his desk—seem to preclude the "bracing" acknowledgment of grief and loss and waste and shame that *Saigon* might have provided. Vietnam seems to have defeated everyone, playwrights included.

NOTES

1. This information was provided by BBC Lionheart.

2. In a few instances this might not have been a bad idea, in that Hare now and then writes dialogue as no American would speak it—as when Chesneau is supposed to say, "But meanwhile the facts get pushed out the way" (103) or describes firecrackers as "Great lights in the night" (103); or when an American officer says, "Nothing for it. Let's go" (138); or when Chesneau tells Barbara, who is packing to leave, "Go your own speed" (139). This is all so clearly British in its phrasing (Americans do not omit prepositions or use "great" to mean "big") that no American actor could convincingly deliver these lines.

WORKS CITED

Bloom, Michael. "A Kinder, Gentler David Hare." *American Theatre* Nov. 1989: 30–34.

Church, Michael. Review of *Saigon: Year of the Cat*. *The Times* 1 Dec. 1983: 10.

Didion, Joan. *Democracy*. New York: Pocket Books, 1984.

Hare, David. Introduction. *The Asian Plays*. London: Faber, 1986. vii–xiv.

———. *Saigon: Year of the Cat*. *The Asian Plays*. London: Faber, 1986.

Harris, William. "Mapping the World of David Hare." *American Theatre* Dec. 1985: 12–17.

Novelli, Martin. "Spiking the Vietnam Film 'Canon.'" *David Rabe: A Casebook*. Ed. Toby Silverman Zinman. New York: Garland, 1991. 149–71.

Oliva, Judy Lee. *David Hare: Theatricalizing Politics*. Ann Arbor: UMI, 1990.

Rabe, David. "Casualties of War." Typescript of unpublished screenplay. 1990.

Living the Present: *The Bay at Nice* and *Wrecked Eggs*

Anthony Jenkins

> ... [A] play is what happens between the stage and the audience. A play is a performance. So if a play is to be a weapon in the class struggle, then that weapon is not going to be the things you are saying; it is the interaction of what you are saying and what the audience is thinking. The play is in the air.
>
> Hare, "A Lecture" 63

The Bay at Nice and *Wrecked Eggs* are conversation pieces. But what Hare's characters say, particularly in the first panel of that diptych, evaporates as they contradict themselves. The audience, sifting through those contradictions, listens and judges—without achieving distinct conclusions. "The play is in the air," somewhere between the auditorium and the stage. Reach out, and it breaks like a bubble or becomes as dead and ponderously academic as the painting *Iris and Morpheus* that looms from the rear wall in the *"airy and decaying gallery"* of *The Bay at Nice* (5). Critic beware! The talk moves in circles, studded with seemingly random anecdotes; yet most—though not all—of those stories have something in common: a search for happiness. That, too, is elusive: what might work for one character would not suit another, just as the decision arrived at by the end of the first play may perhaps be reversed in the second. Those choices have to take other people into account and, happy or not, must be lived with. To be numbed by nostalgia or to chase after rainbows

(Morpheus and Iris, again) erases the present. To seize the day—
heedlessly—makes it meaningless.

Hare's circular dialogue creates a series of present
moments which gather meaning as they accumulate. The first
play's bare set, a spacious white room with gilded ceiling and
parquet floor, concentrates our focus on the behaviour of its two
occupants. Their opening exchange doesn't sound like exposition: it establishes the women's manner and attitude—what
each of them stands for, now—and the peculiarly hermetic world
they move in. We know (from the programme) that the time is
1956, the place Leningrad, but, apart from a swipe at "socialist
realism," the dialogue happens now and here. The way the older
woman (Valentina) sits in her chair (aligned with other museum
furnishing against the back wall), her smart black clothes, her
"lively" talk—all convey her confidence. Despite an opening bid
for sympathy—"You don't want to leave an old woman" (5)—
she is obviously her own person. The younger woman (Sophia)
pales in comparison. Her clothes are colourless, her manner
diffident as she stands to the side, *looking anxiously out of the
door*," and worries that the gallery's Curator has somehow been
"offended" (5). Valentina claims centre stage, literally and
figuratively, and Hare underscored that by casting Irene Worth
in this role at the National Theatre. A "star" actress, whose cool
elegance and dark voice exudes authority, guaranteed the
character would charm despite her dismissive and peremptory
attitude. Such ambivalence is crucial since her words carry the
play's meaning yet, as *raisonneuse*, she seems from moment to
moment flawed, arrogant, prejudiced.

The opening sequence illustrates this when she dismisses
the gallery as "this graveyard" and its staff as "old idiots."
Insisting that she alone offended the Curator—"he was shabbily
dressed"—she refuses to view the new extension and the realists'
"whirlpools of mud"; though its walls at least are cleanly
painted, she has grown "tired of looking anyway." She
remembers Picasso whose ugly house dismayed his friends.
"You are all prisoners of taste," said the artist, kicking the walls
with his sandals. "They're solid. What more do you want?" (5)
The story makes Valentina's energetic independence attractive,
though not particularly likeable. Hare wants to detach her values

from her personality, so he punctures her assurance by making her ride roughshod over Sophia's reasonable suggestion that, if nothing is ugly, social realism must be beautiful:

> VALENTINA: Please. You know nothing of such things. Don't speak of them. Especially in front of other people. It's embarrassing. (VALENTINA *has got up from her seat and is walking to the other side of the room*.) What rubbish do they want me to look at?
> SOPHIA: They think they have a Matisse.
> (*There is a silence*. VALENTINA *shows no apparent reaction*.)
> (6)

Although it goes by rapidly, this exchange is worth examining as "a performance" and as a pattern for the rest of the play. Contradictory though she is, Valentina captures our interest and gives the lateral episodes a forward momentum. Through her we sense a clash between wisdom and egoism, and, in doubling back on itself, the sequence points intriguingly to Henri Matisse. As "a weapon," the action moves obliquely but stealthily to reveal the politics of living morally.

In the next segment, Valentina may at first seem merely willful. Impatient with Sophia's complaint about her lot as a woman ("It was so much more fun when I was young and you could just be a person" [6]), she is equally contemptuous of her only friends, the Troyanofskis, and of modern intellectuals: "Name anyone in Leningrad who's worth an hour. A full hour" (7). But if nothing in her life is as pleasing as it used to be, she presents that as a fact rather than as something to regret; she does not feel particularly sorry for herself. Past experience gives her a measure to live by, and she uses it discerningly. She knows she has terrorized the Curator, that her grandchildren had to be prompted to send their love, that her daughter Sophia means to talk of her unhappy marriage. Quite apart from that acuteness, Valentina's advice and judgment are essential to Sophia and the gallery's staff. Again the dialogue leads to Matisse, who painted every morning. By noon, if he was satisfied, he would sign his work; if not, he would throw it aside "like a dandy who throws white ties into the laundry basket until he ties one which pleases him. . . . Matisse was profligate" (8). Valentina's account reflects her own behaviour which seems profligate but, on closer scrutiny, proclaims her decisiveness. Her remark to Sophia underscores that distinction: "You think attitudes are all to do with whim. . . . Attitudes are all to do with character" (9).

What Hare means by character, as opposed to personality, emerges from the play's reflecting episodes which relate to each other thematically. To explain them in sequence falsifies the dialogue's thought-provoking opacity. Nonetheless, Valentina *has* been shaped by her youth in Paris. Outwardly bohemian, she had her own values even then. When urged to have an abortion—"You have a right to be happy. Get on with your painting, and realize yourself"—she saw that what her friends called a principle, living one's own life, was selfishness. Her views have hardened since then: "It's what's involved in facing up to being an adult. Sacrifice and discipline and giving yourself to others, not always thinking of yourself . . ." (20). Lest that sound didactic, Hare surrounds her in paradox. For most of that time she *was* "wayward": smoking too much, fussing about her hair, moving from man to man. Sophia's father might have lied about being called to war; Valentina didn't care then and hasn't since: "I knew him three weeks. . . . I never saw his battalion. . . . I've never checked" (28). She gave birth effortlessly in some *atelier*, helped by "a homosexual friend who delivered" Sophia (39). Yet, like Picasso in her story, she was never a prisoner, even of such incidentals as an invitation to meet Ford Madox Ford— "they said he was the least frequently washed of all modern novelists. So I didn't go"—or a fellow student's offer to pose for their life class (28). That context qualifies our reaction to her final account of her return to Russia in the 1920s:

> And then I thought—well, is this it? This lounging about?
> This thinking only of yourself? This—what word should I
> use—*freedom*? Having a child changed everything. I
> suddenly decided that Paris was meaningless. Indulgence
> only. I had a Russian daughter. I had to come home. (39)

Because of that experience, she understands the Count who, after years of exile, left the putative Matisse to the Soviet State. She knows his gift acknowledges his life's futility. A passionate horse-breeder and *bon viveur*, he must ultimately have felt himself "defined by an absence, by what is not happening, by where you can't be" (40). That same perception drove

Valentina back to Leningrad where, in the early years of the Revolution, she could paint. Her life has not been happy since the State decided what art should be. She hasn't exhibited for seventeen years, but exile would make her no happier, and so she lives by her decision knowingly: "Everyone here lives in the future. Or in the past. No one wants the present. What shall we do with the present? . . . Anything but here! Anything but now!" (44). Her life has become increasingly circumscribed; she is not free to do as she likes, yet her moral strength allows her to make decisions. By the end of the play, having railed against Sophia's need "to realize herself," she agrees without argument to give her the money for a divorce, and will sell her flat to raise that sum. Whether that will make either of them happy is beside the point. Valentina chooses to help her daughter because not to do so would set limits—"if I couldn't throw money away I'd really be tragic"—and might make life worse for her grandchildren: "I will speak to Grigor. No, not for you. Not to help you. But on behalf of the children, I will persuade him not to oppose you, so that it's quicker in the Regional Court" (45). This moment between mother and daughter is hedged with uncertainties. Sophia's future looks bleak; her children will probably hate her; her husband may lose credit with The Party. Valentina hovers between rage and love, insisting that her daughter "won't be happy. You'll die at forty" (46) yet succumbing, after protest, to her embrace. As she has said, there is no such thing as "right" action, and the episode is designed to make an audience puzzle over that. It *would* be wrong, though, if Sophia evaded the consequences of her second chance: "Whatever you do, this time you must live with it" (46).

Whether Sophia has sufficient character to do that remains uncertain; Valentina doubts it. Audiences, however, must push beyond their sympathy for someone so victimized by her mother, the school authorities she works for, and her domineering husband. Hare plays on those sympathies by drawing a self-sacrificing woman who works hard for her family after long days at school and, because she cares for others, must always do more. There's a good deal of truth in her description of the way marriage "casts" one partner as an adjunct of the other: "it's all got nothing to do with who you really are" (18).

Our response to that is coloured, too, by the fact that, as a non-communist, she can never be promoted, whereas Grigor, who so restricts her, has progressed with Party blessings to headmaster at thirty-seven. On the other hand, the man she wants to live with has no ambition, so she may have chosen him because he makes her strong—which, of course, casts her as the dominant partner. Valentina's "harsh" critique moves us behind the pathos of her daughter's situation and personality to the issues of happiness and freedom. Like a voice from the past, Sophia lays claim to the "principle" of living as she chooses; Valentina sees that as a convenient slogan, and later undermines her daughter's suffering: "In what way is she different from anyone in Russia? What is her complaint? That she is not *free*? . . . Well, who is free? Tell me, am I free?" (38). The answer is "no" and "yes." Like her mother, Sophia would be free once she stopped chasing happiness. Knowing that Peter's weakness could make her hate him, that his mannerisms might become insufferable, that their dreamed-of life together must be different once they achieve it, Sophia could be free to weigh good against bad. With Grigor, no effort of will would have won her that detachment, though it might have saved their marriage.

When Peter appears in the gallery, one expects to sound his character for clues as to the likelihood of Sophia's happiness. Resisting any such solution, Hare makes him imponderable. We first hear of him as "less of a challenge" than Grigor; he "works for the Sanitation Board" (19). Yet his entrance comes as a surprise: a man in his sixties, he is bald, anonymous, apologetic. Sophia leaps to defend him from Valentina's sneers: "It's called making a living, Mother, it involves silly names and unspeakable people . . . We scrabble about in the real world. Because we don't sit thinking all day about art" (22). Peter seems decent and "real," and he adores Sophia, but he is old enough to be her father and as weak as Valentina thought him. He is there to show there *is* no "right" way to live and, more pointedly, to link love's comedy to the illusory search for happiness. Hare has said that he writes "about romantic love, because it never goes away. And the view of the world it provides, the dislocation it offers, is the most intense experience that many people know on earth." Typically he then subverts himself: "such ideas as the one I have just uttered make me laugh" ("A Lecture" 69). Sophia emits pathos, which Hare then debunks; Peter takes on the comic aspects of love. Before they met, he puttered with his model airplanes, earned enough to support his ex-wife, had no plans for the future. Sophia disrupts all that. The thought of a future without her makes Peter suicidal; thinking about her past, before he knew her, makes him jealous; yet she is his "happiness." Whenever the two meet, they spend most of their time arranging their next meeting. Sophia sees that as a test of their endurance; in Valentina's view, life passes them by. Love makes them "raw" and supersensitive to every "nuance" of each other's feelings; were they ever to unite, what then? "—[N]ot a plateau. Oh no. Not safety. Not if it's love. Really love. Just as likely agony. Oh yes. A pure gambler's throw" (27). Yet, hopeless though it may seem, love has aroused Peter's sense of adventure: "At last something's happening. Even if . . . it's unbelievably uncomfortable. It uncovers feelings I didn't know I had" (35).

There can be no clear path through this tangle. Yet the play does seem to journey towards ultimate illumination because of Matisse. That Valentina has been asked to authenticate the Count's gift establishes that movement—a puzzle must be solved—and occasions continuous reminiscence of the man who, for a brief time, was her teacher. This image of Matisse, the consistent values behind his paradoxical persona, becomes a commentary on Valentina herself: a double thread that guides us through the maze. Both care about "rules" (29) but were never chained by them; both live a present that's attuned to the past: what is said of Matisse, "with him, everything belonged" (32), applies to Valentina. She also shares the artist's practicality: the sort of anecdote she remembers, like the one about the laurel wreath (32), points to both their characters and guards the play against artiness. Matisse's "one tiny denial" (32), the way he fought off love and would not absorb his daughter's suffering despite his deep affection, illumines Valentina's conflicting reactions to her daughter's final embrace. Then, in the play's last moments, she remembers how her mentor once sketched absently, while talking on the phone: "he said the result was truer and more beautiful than anything that came as an effort of will" (48). Through that we come to understand Valentina's contradictory response to self-discipline and feel the beauty of her spontaneous surrender to Sophia's divorce. Our sense of arrival strengthens as the room fades into blackness and we see the picture that was there with its back to us for most of the play: *"the stage is filled with the image of the bay at Nice"* (48).

The nature of that painting and its creator's methods correlate to Hare's own moral vision. Suspicious of strident ideology and aware of his own fallibility,[1] he explores the uncertainties that surround his characters' decisions. Hare's "message" rises from the total effect of his patterns. As with Matisse, "Each colour depends on what is placed next to it. . . . No line exists on its own. Only with its relation to another do you create volume" (30). Since theatre, particularly at the National, is so often reduced to a cultural event, just as "people only look at paintings when they are holding cubes of cheese on the end of toothpicks" (8), Hare seeks to move audiences towards that enigmatic space (in the air) in response to "the quality of feeling" (14) art creates. Though his theme is Marxist, he plays the tensions between an individual's happiness and the community's good in an involving way that cannot be measured by ordained creed: "You can't *see* with a caliper" (29). The interplay of light in an unsigned painting assures Valentina of its genuine worth: "The giveaway is the light through the shutters. . . . [Matisse] controlled the sun in his painting" (47). That same control stamps *The Bay at Nice* with Hare's own "handwriting" (33) and his decision, by the mid-1980s, to paint refracted light instead of direct politics: "The sun can't be painted" (13)—or, as Matisse insisted, "You can't paint a mountain. The scale is all wrong" (31). Yet the limits that preclude reference to the larger politics of 1956 (no Suez, no Hungary) focus in on the lives of individuals whose personalities dissolve so that we contemplate their ethics. In the same way that the play pushes past Valentina's charisma, the Matisse, which the Assistant Curator (a mere cataloguer) views as the first essay in a series, co-ordinates the pattern of balcony, sea, and sky: in this final version, Matisse "removed the woman. He sought to distil" (47). Then, with a postmodernist distrust of certainties, of linear cause and effect, Hare places his own picture beside a second. East confronts West as the scene shifts from

Leningrad to upstate New York. That movement invites an either/or reaction but, as we respond to the characters' insularity and see how that play, too, deconstructs the cult of personality, we are forced into a both/and acceptance of the limits that affect personal freedom in Russia *and* America.

As an isolated entity, *Wrecked Eggs* seems strangely flat. However, set beside the other play, its transparent texture, paper-thin characters, and jejune dialogue take on an increasing "volume." Hare's gambit is a risky one in that audiences might lose interest before the ideas click together in the last third of the action. He deliberately gives us three empty people, whom we can't feel attached to or moved by, so that we have to look at their lives rather than their likeability. Robbie, for instance, is a typical up-market consumer, a naive sophisticate, whose self-betraying dialogue makes him a stereotype of Western affluence. From the outset there's an air of parody about him, as the lights come up on a *"pleasant wooden living room"* to the sound of Nat King Cole's "Nature Boy." He is thirty-something, in *"check shirt and pressed slacks,"* a casually formal look that goes with his *"easy, slightly serious manner"* (53). Robbie cares about "quality" living, but to maintain his chosen style he *"has to run to stand still"* (56). With an apartment in Manhattan and this place in the country, he needs one hundred thousand dollars a year just to break even, so he works late at the office and brings legal papers out to his retreat on weekends in order to attain the "nut" that lets him enjoy his pool, his tennis court, and all the other accoutrements of success. Oblivious to the irony of that, he sees the pressure he is under as a badge of achievement like the good food and wine and the stylish comforts it wins him. His wife, Loelia, does think him funny—in an endearing, boyish way. It's a life they have both agreed on and, if she occasionally teases him about money—*"(Smiles)* Is it manly?"—Robbie never sees the point behind her humour:

> Sure money's manly. No question. I like it. It's there. We all understand it. It's universally accepted. You know what you've got. You want something? Right, then pay for it. . . . Money's good because it puts a value on things. (67)

Grace, a recent acquaintance, there for the weekend, can attack that "value," but her irony either puzzles him or sends him out to the pool he has built from a kit. "Hey, I earned this, I put in the work" (83). Such thoughts, as he swims naked and free, prove for him that, beyond money, his life "is something else. It's to do with good taste. And judgement. And there's relationships" (68).

Robbie seems so obvious a target that he's hardly worth knocking down. His "good taste" is what the glossy magazines have made fashionable and expensive. As for his "judgement," the way he offers ideas, food, ethics, and hospitality with indiscriminate earnestness condemns him. So it may look at first as though Hare does want to revile Western decadence by comparing it to the discomfort his Russians endure. But he intends much more than that. Robbie's moment-by-moment pleasures, which even Grace can't help but envy, stand in an interesting relationship to Valentina's determination to live for the present rather than turn back to the past or dream of a better future. What the first play implies becomes plain in the second: without social values one doesn't "live" at all. But, in creating that stance, *Wrecked Eggs* sometimes feels contrived. Even its title, which presumably describes the formless, extempore lives of its threesome, comes from a remark that seems "planted," since Grace's private metaphor begs for explanation (70). One catches Hare manipulating his shutters again when Robbie ponders the Japanese obsession with duty, politeness, custom and the funny "cylinders" in their business hotels (60–61). Robbie's inability to think beyond himself teeters into caricature at the idea of death: "Hey, that's pretty heavy. That's a pretty heavy thought. . . . It's very negative" (81). Yet, because all three characters tend to avoid issues, their world is as timeless as the Russians'. Hare has not moved us forward thirty years to show the increasing hedonism of Western history or to ask whether one set of characters behaves better or worse than the other. Instead, all the chat about bigamy, barbecued steaks, contraceptives, success, Diet Coke as spermicide, a bad actor as President, and New School cuisine leads ultimately to the surprising idea that, viewed from a particular angle, Russia and America are alike. Success in both societies is measured by an approved image: "America! Shit! . . . You know in this country there's meant to be freedom. . . . So why are we now all pretending to believe the same thing?" (90). Hare emphasized that lateral connection by having the same actor play the Assistant Curator (an obedient career communist) and Robbie (who thinks it "uncool" to question American ways).

So what began as a somewhat obvious sermonette turns paradoxical. And behind Robbie's all-American vacuity stands his father, Bill Dvořák, who believed "the two sides should be equal" (86) and delivered fairly low-level details about nuclear submarines to the Russians. That sheds new light on Robbie who has deliberately cultivated his accepting and acceptable persona in reaction to his father's principles: "Thinking gets you nowhere. So-called thinking people do the stupidest things. Because they live in their brains. Not in the real world" (87). Robbie has embraced Americana, a new surname, and conformity; his unthinking present fits him like a baseball glove, and, if forced to consider this, he wraps himself in national cliché: "That's why I love this country. The right to start again. . . . Cross out the past. Start over" (87). Interestingly, he refuses to argue the right or wrong of his father's actions. With the same sleight of mind that transmuted money into "quality of life," he claims he simply disliked the man "as a person" (86). That points straight to the centre of the play and to the way the strategy of the entire diptych aims to distinguish moral character from outward characteristics. In contemporary society image is everything. As Grace puts it, "The question is never 'Is this right or wrong?' . . . No, it's 'Do we like the guy who's doing this? Is he a nice guy?' Not even nice, is he good copy?" (77). But the marketing of politicians, pop stars, products, and preachers articulates an almost instinctive response to appearances. As the personal lives of all these figures show, it is only human to let emotion swamp judgement. People who do otherwise seem "harsh," like Valentina; that makes others angry and so, like Sophia, they twist moral principles into high-minded snobbery: "Down here below you, people are forced to be ridiculous. . . . We scrabble about in the real world" (22). In exactly the same vein, Robbie considers his father a "puritan," a "snob" whose "upright" views attack the lives of "ordinary people": "His contempt was astonishing" (76). Hare wants his audience to judge objectively but, at the same time, shows how difficult it is to do so.

Loelia exemplifies that entanglement. Liking her father-in-law, she can grant him "self-respect," but she also thinks him a "sad" figure: "He spends hours writing to his congressman about how his mail is steamed open. He's still so convinced of his 'personal integrity.' It's just ridiculous. As if anyone cared" (90–91). So she shrugs him off as a loser. But, naturally, she has a much more emotional investment in Robbie's "integrity" and has to cast him as a lovable "boy" in order to protect herself from admitting she's been married for ten years to "a man whose whole life is an attempt to pretend to be someone else" (90). Watching the way he needs to shape their son, Danny, into the desired American image, and knowing that she herself, in order to survive, must mold her own behaviour to that image ("I practically have to run the stars and stripes up the flagpole before I'm allowed to go to the john"), she feels "trapped" (90). Therapy, counselling, temporary separations have not resolved her unhappiness. In the pain and futility of the "prison-yard" in which "I've paced round his problems," Loelia feels compelled to shrug off Robbie, too: "Shit, I was born in Milton, Nebraska. They told me I'd be happy. . . . Am I allowed that? Aren't I entitled?" (92). But in the Land of the Free a person has no more right to happiness than in bureaucratic Russia. To walk away from the present or to live it pleasurably simply postpones the fact that, if we all "drive each other nuts" (91), there must be "something *more*," like "Loyalty. Courage. Perseverance"; "If you don't use them," Grace warns Loelia, "you're going to feel lousy" (93).

That appeal to Loelia's moral stamina sounds banal when separated from the ambience of the play's performance. Hare wants his critique to live in the world, where Marxist theory collides with human unpredictability. Loelia might take Grace's words to heart, but then again she might not, depending on what happens now that she has put off leaving until Tuesday. If she does decide to try again with Robbie, staying on would seem to be as "right" here as leaving was at the first play's dénouement. And, as spokesperson for communal values, Grace personifies life's contrariety.

Those contradictions begin when she talks of abortions: she has had them casually, "too often" (55), but they take their toll nonetheless. Somehow they connect with the cosmetic surface of American mores. To illustrate that, she searches her bag for a copy of the *New York Times* from which she has cut any mention of "success" (another contrivance) and which she exhibits *"like a conjuror's paper trick"* (58). As a publicity agent, Grace could not be more aware of her clients' need for public approval or of the fact that they pay her to project images which have nothing to do with what they are. Good at what she does, she disassociates herself from the shabby efficiency which gives her time to read what she likes. Although she can walk away from "absurdity," she sees the "luxury" of her apparent indifference: "I think it's too easy, that sort of attitude. . . . I've spent my life walking away from things" (66). Intelligent enough to know her most recent client's campaign to present himself as "complex" diverts attention from his commercial ambition, she has entangled herself emotionally with the man's son. Though he wants her to have their baby, she terminates that pregnancy: "do I really want a relationship that, in some form or other, will now have to last for the rest of my life?" (69). Unwilling to work at that, she sloughs off her hopelessness with jocular cynicism. But she will not give up entirely. A resistant part of her has found an outlet in "Amelia Grant." Knowing the sort of letter newspapers will print, what "the party line is" (75), she speaks her mind through a pseudonymous, acceptably eccentric writer-to-the-editor and so subverts convention: Amelia's "big thing is fantasy. Yeah. She attacks it. The idea that everyone can have what they want" (75). Grace sees around herself and consumers' fantasies, but the "Amelia Grant" in her responds to something in Loelia's character, a surrogate persistence which, despite the way things are, she must encourage: "I like the idea of people sticking together. . . . I hate this idea that we're all just sensation" (92–93).

Grace's disgust with herself and her public relations job recalls the self-loathing which drives Hare's earlier publicist, Susan Traherne, in *Plenty* (1978). With clockwork regularity, Grace becomes pregnant; Susan decides to conceive as impersonally as possible. Neither woman acknowledges her partner's feelings. That parallel illumines a change in Hare's perspective. Speaking in Cambridge in 1978, he had described "the extraordinary intensity of people's personal despair" ("A Lecture" 67) as socialist governments subscribed to the affluence of capitalism, and his plays of the 1970s mirrored that despair. But, in the same lecture, he detected a new generation who are cowed, who seem to have given up on the possibility of change, who seem to think that most of the experiments you could make with the human spirit are likely to be doomed or at any rate highly embarrassing (70). In the 1980s, Hare acknowledges that embarrassment by surrounding his characters' persistence with doubts that reflect his own unease with political dogma. The enigmatic determination which characterized Alice Park, and fascinated Susan Traherne, moves from the periphery of *Plenty* into the centre of these plays to become *character*. Both Sophia and Grace (played by the same actress) push against boundaries they cannot fracture. Yet they refuse to give up, despite their hesitance and the way marriage or male dominance marginalizes them. Like Valentina, who has overcome those disadvantages, these women seem to be the agents of integrity. *Dreams of Leaving* (1980) haunt them, as does the cowed bewilderment which infected Jean Travers and Stanley Pilborough (*Wetherby*, 1985). But here, somewhere "in the air," we are made to feel how the pursuit of individualism destroys the common good. Sophia must live with what she chooses, and Loelia, should she decide to stay, has to accept the present and learn that happiness has little to do with freedom: "Fuck you, Grace, you've ruined my weekend" (93).

NOTE

1. "I'm trying to push aside the business of being a teacher or a moralist because that is a trap for a writer," Hare has stated. "The longer I've been at it, the more I've felt it's silly telling people what to do. They've not taken any notice. And one's own life isn't so wonderful that one has the right to preach" (Billington).

WORKS CITED

Billington, Michael. "Broken Rules." *Radio Times* 12 Jan. 1980: 17.

Hare, David. *The Bay at Nice* and *Wrecked Eggs*. London: Faber, 1986.

———. "A Lecture Given at King's College, Cambridge, March 5 1978." *Licking Hitler*. London: Faber, 1978. 57–71.

Virtuous Women: Portraits of Goodness in *The Secret Rapture, Racing Demon,* and *Strapless*

Anne Nothof

> Thus grave these lessons on thy soul,—
> Hope, faith, and love; and thou shalt find
> Strength when life's surges rudest roll,
> Light when thou else wert blind!
>
> Schiller, *Hope, Faith, and Love*, Stanza 5

I

In two plays produced at London's National Theatre in 1988 and 1990 and in a film released in 1990, David Hare attempted an audacious experiment: to explore the nature of goodness in an era preoccupied with the malign energy of evil and with unscrupulous, deviant characters.[1] Although all of Hare's plays tackle contentious moral and social issues, dramatizing the search for ways of believing and living which transcend social habit and emphasizing the need for individual integrity, compassion, and courage, in *The Secret Rapture* (1988) he attempts to portray uncompromising goodness in terms of the essential character of a woman, and to show the effect of this character on others. Hare's next play, *Racing Demon* (1990), is another investigation of the power (or impotence) of goodness, this time in terms of institutionalized Christianity. Although the play is fundamentally dialectical, an extensive debate on the nature of Christian charity in a world fallen into moral decay and faithlessness, once again Hare embodies in a woman the spirit of selfless love, secular love providing a glimpse through a glass darkly of the liberating power of love as a force in society. In *Racing Demon*, Hare celebrates life's miracles—the possibilities of rebirth and renewal inherent in the world. *Strapless* (1990) is another celebration of faith, hope, and love—a portrait of a woman who learns just how liberating and strengthening love can be. In this film and in both plays, love is an operative principle of goodness in the world, whether couched in secular or carnal terms, which finds its clearest manifestation in a woman.

Hare's portraits of "good" women have been castigated by some critics as plaster saints, as minor variants of the Virgin Mary archetype, or as victim figures—the Desdemonas and Cordelias of modern British drama. Although he has been one of the few male playwrights of his generation to place women at the centre of his works, as in *Teeth 'n' Smiles*, *Plenty*, and *Wetherby*, these characters have been dismissed as convenient and simplistic dramatic devices:

> Essentially Hare does not write about women at all but rather as blanks on which he can imprint an external, male pressure; and to such pressure they respond only with pain or madness, or, if they are secondary characters, with baffled dismay. They exist without any personal form; they have neither history nor any specific individual comment. They are a formal expression of what Hare sees as the only human response to the nature of society, an expression of the detachment which seems to be his recipe for survival. Men have to assume some kind of presence in his plays that alters what they find around them; the women exist as vacuums. (Chambers and Prior 186)

Griffiths and Woddis also dismiss Hare's main female characters as ciphers:

> Despite its popularity, *Pravda* confirmed a general unease among female critics about Hare's handling of female characterisation. As in *Plenty*, the leading female character carries the play's moral force, but remains an unreal, one-

dimensional figure, on the periphery of the main action—
more of a cipher than a fully-rounded character. (157)

Similar criticism has been levelled against *The Secret Rapture*, in
which all of the main roles are given to women, one of whom
again functions as the "moral force" of the play against whom all
the other characters are pitted and measured. This protagonist,
Isobel Glass, is dismissed by Maureen Paton in her review as
"one of those irritating doormats who brings out the sadist in all
of us. Saints tend not to make interesting drama since they spend
their whole life denying their humanity" (1386). Others are more
puzzled about the significance of Isobel. In his review of *The
Secret Rapture*, Michael Billington moots several possibilities:
"Does she embody a supine English tolerance that allows itself to
be exploited? Is she a shining example of integrity? Or is she a
born martyr half in love with easeful death?" Finally he hazards
an interpretation:

> Under Hare the sharp satirist I suspect there lurks a
> romantic who sees suffering and pain as proof of the
> validity of existence and who wants us to celebrate the
> idea of Isobel as a secular bride of Christ . . . , [the]
> transcendental assumption that goodness can only
> triumph through death. (1388)

The Secret Rapture is Hare's theatrical complement to an
earlier film which portrays the destructiveness of a selfish
pursuit of personal and political power—*Paris by Night*, shot in
1987. In this film, Hare undertakes a portrait of the social and
personal consequences of the predatory philosophy of
Thatcherism: "No more having to think. Not wasting your life in
uncertainty and guilt. Do what you want to. . . . That's the basis
of freedom" (16). The protagonist of *Paris by Night*, Clara Paige,
is a hard-nosed politician working for the European Parliament
who compromises all of her personal relationships for her career.
Driven by the values of her society, her essentially loving and
compassionate nature has been repressed by her need to achieve
status and recognition. At the end, she is shot by the husband
she has debilitated and betrayed.

Hare provides another portrait of a Thatcherite woman in
The Secret Rapture—Marion French, an ambitious politician who
ruthlessly pushes her way up the echelons of power. In contrast,

he provides a portrait of the "good" woman in her sister Isobel. As the play begins, both sisters are present for the funeral of their father, and their radically different responses to his death establish their values immediately: Isobel sits quietly in the dark by his bedside, in a vigil which suggests her respect and deep sense of loss. Typically, she watches over him, and even claims to have seen his spirit leave his body. Marion, on the other hand, sneaks into the room to retrieve a ring which she had given her father, cognizant more of material loss than of the human one. The third major female character in the play is the sisters' stepmother, a young woman who has recently married their father and whose anarchic behaviour proves a trial for each of them. Isobel, against the best interests of her business, tries to help Katherine, and, as she begins to realize just how hopeless Katherine is, commits her life to caring for her, with the result that her relationship with her partner in business and in love is destroyed. The play ends as it began, with the death of a good person—first the father, then the daughter, both victims of human limitations: the inability of others to accept kindness without interpreting it as a judgement of their own inadequacies.

The Christian correspondences are quite clear, although Hare satirizes dogmatic belief in the person of Tom, Marion's born-again husband. Isobel has many of the characteristics of a saint or Christian martyr: she takes a vow to commit herself to caring for Katherine; she is betrayed by those closest to her; and she is finally murdered when she will not recant. In the penultimate scene she is dressed in a large blue raincoat—blue being the iconographic colour for Hope and for the Virgin Mary—and her feet are bare. She is also financially impoverished, having decided to buy back the ancestral home which Katherine has thoughtlessly sold. Significantly, the last scene returns to her father's house, where the family has gathered for her funeral. Although the repentant and distraught Marion calls for her to return, it is quite clear that she is present in the lives of those she has left behind: her death is accepted in a way that her life was not. In the National Theatre production of *The Secret Rapture*, the figure of Isobel appeared in the garden at the end of the play; the effect of her spiritual immanence was achieved by placing her in the backstage area which was opened out to the mainstage. The text does not specify this overt manifestation of Isobel, but suggests that Isobel has joined her father in his house of many mansions, having gone to prepare a place for others (John 14.2).

The programme notes for the National Theatre production reinforce this conception of Isobel as a saint-figure with an extensive quotation from the writing of St. Teresa of Avila, who describes her own "secret rapture": her experience of the presence of the holy spirit. As many have pointed out, St. Teresa's description bears many similarities to sexual orgasm, an interpretation which is also suggested by Bernini's statue of the Ecstasy of St. Teresa. The close association of carnal and spiritual love so prevalent in medieval and renaissance poetry is also alluded to in *The Secret Rapture*: it is Isobel's lover Irwin who shoots her, and the propinquity of love and death is suggested several times in the play. For Isobel, love must be a free giving of hearts and minds: "The great thing is to love. If you're loved back then it's a bonus" (5). Once trust and confidence have been betrayed by the lover, however, love cannot be forced; as she explains to Irwin:

> Force me. You can force me if you like. Why not? You can take me here. On the bed. On the floor. You can fuck me till the morning. You can fuck me all tomorrow. Then the whole week. At the end you can shoot me and hold my heart in your hand. You still won't have what you want. *(Her gaze does not wander.)* The bit that you want I'm not giving you. You can make me say or do anything you like. Sure, I'll do it. Sure, I'll say it. But you'll never have the bit that you need. It isn't yours. (75)

The "secret rapture" usually refers to the moment of death—in Hare's words, "the moment at which a nun will be reunited with the risen Christ. The secret rapture is that for which a nun lives" (Lustig 15). This suggests that only in death can Isobel's goodness triumph and her essential nature be recognized by those who have so wilfully misunderstood her in order to justify their own more selfish ways of thinking and behaving. There are strong indications in *The Secret Rapture* that Isobel is a personification of "good," refusing to compromise her integrity even while she wishes only to help others. She commits herself to doing what her "father" would have wished—that is, caring for the weakest among them, Katherine. In effect, she engages herself in a struggle with evil, as Katherine embodies all those traits which are antithetical to Isobel's character: she is manipulative, irresponsible, destructive, selfish—chaos personified. Thus in many important respects *The Secret Rapture* is a modern morality play, portraying the reality of good and evil in a society where moral distinctions are at best vague. Fearing for her safety, Irwin warns Isobel of Katherine's evil nature, that she is as determined to destroy Isobel as Isobel is to help her. Significantly, it is Katherine who opens the door to her apartment against Isobel's admonitions to admit the one who will kill her— who is also, tragically, the one who loves her. On one level, then, evil triumphs, although in the wider context of the battle for souls it is Isobel who triumphs, as her goodness is finally recognized, valued, and emulated.

The Secret Rapture is more complex than a simple morality play, however. It shows that goodness for most individuals is a variable concept, interpreted according to their own needs. Katherine accuses Isobel of hypocrisy, since her "kindness and tolerance and decency" are without any practical demonstration (15). But even operative goodness does not necessarily have positive results in a world characterized by compromise and doubt. Isobel's kindness to others is in many respects completely ineffectual, as she herself recognizes, and she discovers that her reluctance to hurt others results only in her own suffering. When she finally makes a decision to follow one course—to cut through the complexities of feelings with which she cannot cope and adopt a more monastic way of life with Katherine—the result is even more suffering and inevitable violence. Katherine's surprising and accurate assessment that other-worldliness must be paid for (28) takes on a terrible irony. As Marion protests at the conclusion of the play, life is indeed very complex; it is impossible to reduce it to simple alternatives of good and evil:

> . . . I've stood at the side. Just watching. It's made me angry. I've been angry all my life. Because people's passions seem so out of control. (*She shakes her head slightly*.) You either say, "Right, OK, I don't understand anything, I'll take some simple point of view, just in the

hope of getting things done. Just achieve something, by
pretending things are simpler than they are." Or else you
say, "I will try to understand everything." (*She smiles.*)
Then I think you go mad. (81)

Isobel's kindness is initially seen by Marion as a weakness, an
inability to take a stand or make a hard decision which will
cause pain to others. But she also thinks that she sees in her
sister's smile and extended hand tactics to disarm.

Katherine's anarchic energy, in contrast, may be seen as
being more fully alive, feeling intensely and acting impulsively.
Certainly there was some reason why Isobel's father was so
attracted to her; perhaps she seemed "free." Yet it remains in
doubt whether marriage to Katherine brought him a fuller life or
a premature death. When she is confined by Isobel's goodness in
a small, bare apartment, Katherine accuses her of being more
dead than alive, and Isobel does take on an ascetic appearance
just before her death, as the stage directions indicate and as was
obvious in performance: "(ISOBEL *has appeared in the other
doorway. She is also changed. She wears a long dark blue overcoat and
thin glasses. Her hair is swept back on her head. She appears tense,
thin, but also strangely cheerful)*" (64). The play's epigraph by
Rebecca West ("Only half of us is sane. . . . The other half of us is
nearly mad . . .") suggests that Isobel and Katherine are opposite
impulses in one psyche—the ego and the id; the yin and the
yang; the one desiring peace and order, the other disruption and
disorder. Perhaps Isobel becomes obsessed by Katherine
precisely because she embodies just those passionate, uncon-
trolled instincts which she lacks or will not permit, just as the
highly disciplined Marion is attracted to the sexually permissive
Rhonda, another disruptive presence in the play. But Hare is not
writing a psychological or sociological analysis; he is attempting,
rather, an investigation of how the impulses of good and evil are
operational within both the individual and society.

Goodness is finally reasserted in *The Secret Rapture*, but its
nature remains somewhat obscure and its manifestation in the
person of Isobel is not without ambiguity. The implication is that
principles cannot be embodied in people or operate without
ambivalence in a "postmodern" world which questions or
undermines all systems of faith or belief. In the midst of this

confusion Hare offers a positive image of hope in the person of Isobel, the "one certain source of good" (62). As Isobel has contended, however, it is impossible to be saved through another person (77). Isobel's goodness is continuously subject to interpretation; *The Secret Rapture* is a process of investigation, not a definitive moral treatise. Hare's method is dialectical, and no one character has the answers, although she may afford some insights.

II

In his next play, *Racing Demon*, Hare again explores the possibilities of goodness in a materialistic, competitive, and violent society; the play shows, according to Hare, "the persistence of private goodness in Thatcherite Britain" (Nightingale). His concern is again more with affairs of the heart and spirit than with sociological issues, but this time the debate is waged in terms of the theology and politics of the Church of England: six "men of God" attempt to interpret the appropriate role of the Church in modern society, each according to his character and faith (or lack of faith). And again it is in the character of a woman, Frances Parnell, who much like Isobel Glass subscribes to no organized system of belief, that Hare places the clarity of vision which cuts through intellectual argument to the more human dimensions of faith and love.

The play begins with a plea to God by the Reverend Lionel Espy to manifest Himself in a world which badly needs help and which has lost faith in divine beneficence, as has Lionel himself. His vocation has become that of a social worker, seeking to alleviate the suffering of his parishioners, even though he knows that his efforts are for the most part ineffectual. Like Shaw's Andrew Undershaft, he believes that the bodies of men and women must be tended to before their souls can be saved, but his Bishop argues that his ministry has become too secular and that he is disregarding the rituals which are the mainstay of the Church. Lionel's curate, Tony Ferris, takes an evangelical view of religion, that people can be saved only through complete commitment to God. His friend, "Streaky" Bacon, has a more beneficent and liberal attitude completely devoid of convoluted theology—simply to love each other, and to love life. In the debate among these clerics, Hare accurately reflects the diversity of "beliefs" and the secularization process in the Church of England. As Hare demonstrates in the play, the Church has become preoccupied with such social matters as abortion and divorce, and is torn by the debate over the ordination of women and homosexuals.

In contrast to the doubt and debate is the calm certainty of Frances in respect to what is of value in life. She first appears naked under a sheet, having just made love to Tony. While he justifies to himself this act of carnal love outside of marriage and rationalizes his guilt, Frances simply explains that she made love because she wanted him. For her the important considerations are honesty with herself and with others, trust, and the freedom to express herself without the necessity of accounting to someone else's set of values—much like the values of Lionel, who believes in acting from the heart, "in a way that is unforced and that suits you . . ." (19). Frances is still recovering from a childhood in which her parents' commitment to a mission, a higher good, has deprived her of the emotional intimacy of a family; she recognizes in Lionel's wife, Heather, another woman whose life has been starved because of Lionel's total involvement in his vocation. Yet Lionel's goodness is regarded by his superiors, and by himself, as being ineffectual. The crux of the play is a discussion between Frances—an agnostic—and Lionel—an atheist—over a game of chess. Lionel's frustration over his inability to change things is countered by Frances's determination that he not allow himself to be a sacrificial victim to the system for which he has worked so hard; she even goes so far as to change his moves on the chessboard to prevent his defeat.

Despite his basic goodness and kindness, however, Lionel has been undermined by his unbelief. In the programme for the first production of *Racing Demon* at the Cottesloe appeared a quotation from Browning's "Bishop Blougram's Apology" which quite aptly applies to this scene:

All we have gained by our unbelief
Is a life of doubt diversified by faith,

> For one of faith diversified by doubt:
> We called the chess-board white,—we call it black. (209–
> 12)

In a cogent interpretation of *Racing Demon*, Richard Harries, Bishop of Oxford, takes a more positive view of this scene, which he sees as the "soul" of the play:

> Both characters are in touch not only with one another, but with a realty they sense cannot easily, perhaps not at all, be put into words. . . . There is a deliberate link between the apparent absence of God disclosed in the [initial] prayer and the sense of something beyond our conceiving or imagining, apprehended in the quiet personal disclosures of Lionel and Frances. . . . So the play is not, as some have seen it, simply about the tension between social commitment and brash religion. Lionel, for all his hesitancy and diffidence, is also struggling to explore and convey the divine mystery.

But Lionel is defeated by the different view of the "good" people in his own Church, and by his refusal to defend himself, trusting too much in the good faith of others; he is forced to confront his professional and personal failure. Frances is more resilient, less trammelled by the compulsion to define her values according to a dogmatic Christianity or a coherent theology, although she too is hurt by the betrayal of Tony when he denies that their love has any lasting significance or value. For Frances, values can have significance only in terms of life on this earth, since that is all humanity can really experience: "It's here. We live here. On this earth. That's where we have to love one another" (68). But she also feels that her countrymen lack the courage and imagination to change, and so she decides to leave a country which appears to be almost hopelessly compromised by social, economic and moral divisions, in order to help in the Third World, "where things have value. Because life is so hard" (59). It is Frances who experiences the joy and miracle of living in terms of an ascent from earth towards the sun, while Lionel and Tony remain earthbound in darkness. In performance at the Cottesloe on a traverse stage in the shape of a cross, the light of the sun blazed through the turned slats of a billboard which advertised the world's preoccupation with money and sex and was unmistakably associated with Frances's hope. Given, however, her earlier address to an absent God in an empty church, where she contends that the sun coming up over the mountains is insufficient proof for the existence of God (34), the blazing light could hardly be taken for divine revelation. Perhaps the most one can hope for is a clear recognition of the values by which one chooses to live, and the courage to live them. In Hare's plays, these values are quite clearly the three virtues of faith, hope, and charity, traditionally represented in Christian iconography as women.

III

In *Strapless*, Hare once more explores the mysteries of the human heart and shows how an assertion of faith in life and in love can enable a personal salvation:

> . . . I've found myself in *Wetherby*, in *Paris by Night*, in *The Secret Rapture* and in *Strapless* drawn more and more to feeling that there's something which isn't just what we're conditioned by. More and more I find myself believing things which I don't sense are believed by the rest of my class and background. I'm not interested in what current sociological movements think about things. It just bores me. I find people being defined by what comes out of their mouths incredibly depressing. (Lustig 18)

In the female protagonist of *Strapless*, Hare traces a gradual realization of the emotional strength and freedom which grow from a total surrender to love. Although love is dramatized in a highly romanticized way, the film suggests visually and verbally that strong mutual attraction between a man and a woman, and the surrender of both totally to their feelings for each other, are dark reflections of the kind of love on which Christianity is founded. Significantly, *Strapless* begins with images of a European Renaissance cathedral, immediately establishing a context of value in terms of art, culture, and religion even though, as the scenic directions indicate, these values may be slowly crumbling away with the architecture: *"The texture of crumbling façades, stucco, sky-blue walls and pink plaster. Wooded hillsides, dying blooms, mists in the mountains. Parapets and water"* (1). The setting also evokes the countryside of Robert Browning's intensely romantic poetry, which suggests that the love between men and women is but one piece of the radiant dome of many colours—love as a universal principle.[2] Love for Browning, as for Hare, is the principle of operative goodness in the world. Even if for individuals it may be elusive, barely possible, it provides value and meaning to life. Significantly, Hare quotes the opening lines of Browning's "Cristina" as the epigraph for *Strapless*: "She should never have looked at me / If she meant I should not love her!" Also evident in the opening scene is a statue of a woman *"holding up her dress with a single hand held over her breast"* (1), suggesting vulnerability, apprehension, but also perhaps a capacity for living and loving.

The scene then moves into the cathedral, with a close-up of the face of the suffering Christ: *"His head is at an angle, looking down"* (1), suggesting selfless compassion for those below. In front of this statue of Christ, guidebook in hand, stands Lillian Hempel, an American physician in her mid-thirties, working for the National Health in London and holidaying in Europe. She accidentally drops her handkerchief, which is retrieved by Raymond Forbes, a mysterious, gallant gentleman with impeccable taste. Both are struck by the beauty of the statue, but more particularly by the roses which have been placed in Christ's wound where the blood should flow. The image of roses is of course a transmogrification of suffering into ecstasy and beauty, and it becomes a kind of stigmata for Raymond, who draws a rose on the envelope of each letter he sends to Lillian in his untiring pursuit of her. Lillian, whose name suggests the virginal purity of another Christian icon, the lily, evades Raymond's passionate pursuit and returns to England with her feelings almost intact. Despite her American origins, she has the more stereotypically English trait of emotional restraint, and thinks that she prefers being left alone to the attention of a stranger. But her goodness is evident in her devotion to her work—caring for the sick and dying in a cancer ward—and in her patiently enduring her younger sister's anarchic love life.

According to Hare's value system, however, goodness is a matter of feelings more than of willed behaviour or even action. Love must be freely and wholly given, and freely received; it can sustain no compromises or precautions. A suggestion of Lillian's emotional possibilities are evident in her flat, which is furnished in a *"very wild, romantic, nineteenth-century style"* (10), but it is in the portrait of Lillian's sister, Amy, that a telling contrast of lifestyles is made. As in *The Secret Rapture*, Hare sets in opposition two women with radically different values, and establishes a psychological dialectic which is observed more in action than in debate. Amy loves almost compulsively, and opens herself to whatever new experience comes her way; like Katherine in *The Secret Rapture*, she is almost totally irresponsible, although without the destructive impulses. Lillian, on the other hand, is consumed by her responsibilities. She is almost incapable of a free act, of anything that will jeopardize her emotional security, and that includes sticking her neck out by helping to organize a hospital protest against government cutbacks. Although she gives to the point of physical and mental exhaustion in the care of her patients, she is careful not to become too emotionally involved in their lives, to spare herself the pain of their deaths. In a moment of frustration, Amy accuses Lillian of being the "kind" one of the family: "So patient. So tolerant. And in that kindness . . . there is such condescension" (44). Lillian's "goodness," like Isobel's, is almost intolerable for others because they feel judged by it: it requires more from them than they are capable of giving.

As Lillian gradually learns, however, the mysterious Raymond is a very generous giver—of gifts, and of himself. He surprises her at her home with the gift of a horse, suitably named "Heartfree," which Lillian at first refuses but then much appreciates after an exhilarating ride in the country. Raymond is convinced of the importance of knowing what is of value in life, of knowing what you want and going after it, whereas Lillian has been afraid of risk. She comes to appreciate that valuable human relationships are based on trust; even though relationships may end, in extending that trust—in experiencing the love that trust has made possible—she has acquired the strength to act more freely, even if alone. The image of the strapless gown, one that holds up without visible means of support, may be slightly tacky—and certainly misleading in the advertisements for the film, which feature the actresses Blair Brown and Bridget Fonda in glamorous black strapless gowns and sexy smiles—but Hare makes its significance quite specific in the dialogue.

After Raymond's sudden and unexpected departure from Lillian's life, she undergoes a midnight of the soul: she loses her belief in herself and in her work, and wonders when, after years of giving to others, she will get something back. The response of the emotionally constrained hospital administrator, who attempts to persuade her to leave the cupboard to which she has retreated in her misery, is that she has done "good" work and has brought comfort (60), a true enough statement, if an undemonstrative one. The quality of her virtue has been in selfless giving of her time and talent, but she has yet to learn the value of giving herself emotionally and of accepting freely what a lover has given her. In her search for the elusive Raymond, she learns that others have benefitted from his unusual capacity for giving, especially his rare gift for loving women. There are subtle suggestions that Raymond has Christ-like attributes of selfless love and devotion, which may be misunderstood by many, such as his stepfather, but which are valued by a few, especially the women in his life—his stepmother and his first wife. Losing belief in this kind of goodness represents a fundamental loss of faith, not just in human nature, but in a value system which may provide an underpinning for meaning in life—as has happened to Raymond's stepfather, a schoolmaster at a boys' public school. Lillian first meets him in a Gothic chapel, looking up in rapt contemplation at the figure of Christ in a stained-glass window. He explains to her that he is "enjoying a reminder" of his lost faith (67), a scenario strongly reminiscent of the first scene of *Racing Demon*, in which Lionel attempts to talk with the absent God. Lillian comes to appreciate, however, that, even though Raymond is absent, he is essentially with her, since nothing can negate their shared love. And it is this free act of love which will continue to inform her life.

Thus Lillian can finally accept the wish of a young cancer patient to be taken off the drugs and allowed to die as himself.

Her question to Raymond in the Portuguese cathedral in front of Christ's statue about the significance of the death of Christ, whether "just by dying in some way he would make everyone's life better" (2), is in part answered: there can be a form of redemption in dying. And she can rejoice in a new birth—Amy's daughter. She recognizes as Amy has done that no one is exempt: "You have certain feelings. And then you must pick up the bill" (79). But she also knows that her faith in Raymond has been repaid.

In David Hare's *The Secret Rapture, Racing Demon,* and *Strapless,* faith, hope, and charity do abide, and of these three the greatest is charity, which is seen through a glass darkly and known only in part. But the daunting task of realizing through character such unfashionable virtues has to some extent sapped the vitality of the virtuous women in the two plays. Moreover, their final posture as victims of male emotional insecurities partially undermines their credibility as positive images. In *Strapless,* however, perhaps because of the emotional intimacy of the film, achieved through lush detail of setting, a rich musical score, and the sensitivity of the acting, Hare's portrait of goodness is incontrovertible.

NOTES

1. In an interview with Anne Busby in the National Theatre programme for *The Secret Rapture,* Hare cites Christopher Hampton's *Les Liaisons dangereuses* and Caryl Churchill's *Serious Money* as examples of this "celebration of malign energy" in the drama of the 1980s.

2. Browning's "Two in the Campagna," for example, a poem included in his 1855 collection *Men and Women,* evokes the same kind of heightened physical and spiritual ecstasy as Hare attempts to dramatize in *Strapless.*

WORKS CITED

Billington, Michael. Review of *The Secret Rapture*. *The Guardian* 5 Oct. 1988. Rpt. in *London Theatre Record* 8 (1988): 1387–88.

Browning, Robert. "Bishop Blougram's Apology." *Men and Women*. 1855. *Selected Poetry of Robert Browning*. Ed. and intro. Kenneth L. Knickerbocker. New York: Random House, 1951. 317–42.

———. "Cristina." *Dramatic Lyrics*. 1842. *Selected Poetry of Robert Browning*, 79–81.

Chambers, Colin and Mike Prior. *Playwrights' Progress: Patterns of Postwar British Drama*. Oxford: Amber Lane, 1987.

Griffiths, Trevor R. and Carole Woddis. *Bloomsbury Theatre Guide*. 2nd ed. London: Bloomsbury, 1991.

Hare, David. *Paris by Night*. London: Faber, 1988.

———. *Racing Demon*. Rev. ed. London: Faber, 1991.

———. *The Secret Rapture*. Rev. ed. London: Faber, 1989.

———. *Strapless*. London: Faber, 1989.

Harries, Richard. "Finding the Soul in Hare's New Drama." *The Times* 19 Feb. 1990: 16.

Lustig, Vera. "Soul Searching." *Drama* 170 (1988): 15–18.

Nightingale, Benedict. "An Outsider's Flawed Vision." *The Times* 9 Feb. 1990: 16.

Paton, Maureen. Review of *The Secret Rapture*. *Daily Express* 6 Oct. 1988. Rpt. in *London Theatre Record* 8 (1988): 1385–86.

"Our Father": The Profession of Faith in *Racing Demon*

Ann Wilson

Racing Demon, the first play in David Hare's trilogy dealing with British social institutions in the aftermath of Thatcherism, focuses on four Church of England clergymen who are attempting to minister to an economically and racially mixed parish in the diocese of Southwark. The disparity within the parish forces the team to negotiate between the seemingly irreconcilable demands of their middle-class parishioners, who want theology divorced from politics, and their working-class parishioners who, in the wake of government cuts to social services, need a Church which serves as their advocate. The Church can accommodate these differences only through theological vagueness, with the result that faith becomes a matter of individual conscience. *Racing Demon* suggests that the despair and hardship brought to England by Thatcherism pose particular challenges to Christians who must find their way without the spiritual guidance of the Church. Faced with this void, individuals must rely on each other; but if personal friendship, and not the profession of faith, characterizes contemporary Christianity, then the Church has no sense of itself as a corporate body and hence cannot be an agent of social change.

Racing Demon opens with Lionel Espy, the leader of the parish team, in a prayer which is both troubled and troubling because it appeals to God to make his presence known to the faithful who feel that they have been abandoned:

> God. Where are you? I wish you would talk to me. . . . You
> see, I tell you, it's this perpetual absence—yes?—this not
> being here—it's that—I mean, let's be honest—it's just
> beginning to get some of us down. (1)

In prayer, Lionel is tentative, unable to find the words with
which to address God; but as he struggles to express himself, his
petition is to a deity of whose existence he is uncertain. Without
a sign of God's existence, Lionel's faith wavers; yet he nevertheless appeals to God, an indication that, whatever his doubts,
he wants to believe. Indeed, as a cleric, Lionel has a professional
responsibility to believe—or at least to appear to believe—if he is
to minister to his congregation. This point is forcibly made to
him in the next scene when his ministry is challenged by his
bishop, Southwark, who says, "There is an element in your
parish which is unsure of you. They've begun to doubt you.
Maybe question the power of your convictions" (2).

Lionel responds to this criticism by pointing out that his
parishioners are mainly working-class, although he does
acknowledge that the congregation has a "small middle-class
rump. . . . And since the poor are not given to visiting bishops'
palaces, I assume the complaint is from them?" (2–3). These
comments reveal the difficulties facing the Church as it attempts
to reconcile the diverse needs of these two groups. The middle-
class communicants value the liturgical, and particularly
sacramental, aspects of worship which Lionel sees as irrelevant
to the lives of most of those living within the parish because their
focus is on trying "to make a life at all" (3). The two men's
discussion of the conflicting demands of these segments within
the parish initially seems innocuous. The meeting ends with
Southwark's commenting "That's your opinion," and then
advising Lionel to hold his parish together by serving the needs
not only of the working people but of those from the middle
class. He then blithely calls to his wife, informing her that he and
Lionel are ready to sit down to their lunch (4). But in this benign
exchange, the terms of the conflict which propels the dramatic
action of *Racing Demon* begin to emerge.

Southwark's advice to Lionel that he administer the Communion with greater care is an appeal to appease the middle-
class worshippers who are part of what he describes as "a very

loose church" (3), "a disparate body held together by a common liturgy" (4). "Only one thing unites us," he explains. "The administration of the sacrament. (*Pauses a moment.*) Finally that's what you're there for. As a priest you have only one duty. That's to put on a show" (3). For Lionel, the issue is faith and the problem is how a Christian witnesses effectively: "Charlie, to me, Christ is in our actions" (4). Southwark initially responds by denying that class is a factor in the Church's ministry—"I don't call them any class. I call them believers"—and then by advising Lionel to "fulfil your job description. Keep everyone happy" (4). The scene establishes several axes of tension: between needs of the middle and the working classes, between the Bishop and his priest, between Southwark's view of the ministry as a job and Lionel's that it is a vocation. The civility of the conversation seems a matter of rhetorical style which belies the high stakes of their debate because, beneath the veneer of politeness, the conflict between Lionel Espy and Charlie Allen, the Bishop of Southwark, is a conflict over the relation between the Church and state. This debate is not original to Hare's play but was the focus of public attention in Britain during the Thatcher years.

During the 1970s, the Church of England, like all other established denominations in Britain, suffered a staggering drop in the number of adherents. Between 1970 and 1985, there was a marked decline in the number of worshippers attending Sunday services, from 3.3 percent of the population to 2.5 percent (Martin 331). Yet despite this decline, the profile of the Church as a force in the social and political life of the country was particularly high. Perhaps, as the Bishop of Winchester suggested, this was a consequence of the disarray of the Labour Party which necessitated that opposition to Thatcher's government be assumed by liberal forces outside parliament (Martin 337). Leaders from all denominations were empowered by their belief that churches had a moral prerogative to provide leadership on issues of social injustice. As John Baker, Bishop of Salisbury, explained in an address at the University of Manchester:

> The prophets and sages of the Old Testament were constantly concerned with political and social issues. . . . To them international affairs were central to revelation

and ethics, and the right conduct of rulers was at the heart
of religious teaching and reflection. (Moyser 13)

We should remember that the Church of England has an
institutionalized authority within England marked, for example,
by the fact that, on state occasions requiring ecclesiastical
participation, the representative of the Church of England is
always the principal officiating cleric (Moyser 7). Given this
institutional prominence, its leader, the Archbishop of Canterbury, speaks with particular authority. In 1983, Robert Runcie,
then Archbishop of Canterbury, established a Commis-sion to
"examine the strength, insights, problems and needs of the
Church's life and mission in the Urban Priority Areas" (Gould
70) which published its recommendations in *Faith in the City*. The
report, because it was a document of the Church, received a
great deal of attention—and indeed stirred controversy because
it criticizes Thatcher's government for creating economic
conditions (including cuts to social services) which contribute to
the poverty of inner cities. Rather predictably, it calls for the
government to reform its social policies and to create programs
which will lead to urban renewal. In this context, it grapples
with the responsibilities of the Church, citing the imperative of
St. Paul that we must "remember the poor" (47).

But how? The report formulates the problem of whether
Christian action "should be confined to personal charity or
whether it can legitimately take the form of social and political
actions aimed at altering the circumstances which appear to
create poverty and distress . . ." (48). Hare, considering some of
the same issues raised by *Faith in the City*, implies that the
consequence of the Church's having lost its theological base is
that it now models itself on secular corporations, the very
institutions which perpetuate social disparity.

Throughout *Racing Demon* there are indications that those
on the upper levels of ecclesiastical government, particularly the
bishops, conceive of themselves as executives in a business.
Southwark's seemingly offhand comment to Lionel that he fulfil
his "job description" seems less than a casual comment when
Frances Parnell, the woman from a "big church-going family,"
recounts a conversation among four bishops which she has

overheard at her family's home: "They were moaning, as bishops do. Chester said if they were running any other kind of business, they could make rational decisions" (29).[1] In this context, the chat between Lionel and Southwark is only superficially about approaches to the ministry. In the revised edition of the text, the conversation is about Lionel's inefficiency, but in the first edition Lionel sees the problem as more clearly political: "Is that the problem? Is that what they're saying? That I've bought what they call the whole inner-city package?" (1990: 32).

If the Church is a corporate business with bishops as its chief executive officers, its efficacy as a force opposing Thatcher's policies of promoting free-market capitalism is dubious; rather, it must be seen as implicitly supporting these policies. As Frances suggests, the ads which the Church is placing to attract new members, like all ads, are designed to expand the Church's market and so increase its revenues. Hare presents the upper levels of Church government as divided: some segments want to address social injustice while others are conciliatory towards the government. He alludes to the latter when two members of Lionel's pastoral team, Harry Henderson and "Streaky" Bacon, approach Gilbert Heffernan, the Bishop of Kingston and Southwark's suffragan bishop, to alert him to Southwark's intention of dismissing their leader. Streaky reminds Kingston that an important Tory minister is a member of Lionel's congregation and has heard his sermons denouncing government policies which have created a "divided nation," a phrase recurring in *Faith in the City* and used by Hare (41). Harry continues Streaky's conjecture: "The minister is on the Ecclesiastical Committee of the House of Commons. You're not telling me he hasn't had a word with Southwark" (42). The political implications of Lionel's conflict with Southwark are evident in Kingston's reply: "[T]he tensions are impossible. Ever since we failed to confer on the Falklands expedition the theological status of a holy war. Church and State are held together by a single thread" (42)—a reference to Runcie's antagonizing Mrs. Thatcher during the service of reconciliation after the Falklands War when he "failed to strike a sufficiently triumphal note" (Hastings and Jenkins 315). It is clear that, at its highest levels, the Church of England is indeed "a very loose church" which, consequently, cannot formulate effective social policies. The absence of a clearly defined theology to serve as a spiritual guide creates the problem of how adherents to the Church of England profess their faith. The social turmoil of England would seem to beg for the moral leadership of the Church which is finally incapable of offering such leadership. Without the guidance of the Church, each person must individually negotiate his or her witnessing of faith.

In the course of *Racing Demon*, a number of the characters, including each member of the parish team, offer individual prayers to God, questioning what it is to be a Christian. Tony, the team's youngest member, meditates on the problem of ministry: "Christ didn't come to sit on a committee. He didn't come to do social work. He came to preach repentance. And to offer everyone the chance of redemption" (20). In his prayer, Streaky tells God: "The whole thing's so clear. You're there. In people's happiness. Tonight, in the taste of that drink. Or the love of my friends. The whole thing's so simple. Infinitely loving" (56). For Harry, "There is people as they are. And there is people as they could be. The priest's job is to try and yank the two a little bit closer" (63). For each of the priests, the effective realization of vocation is a personal negotiation between himself and God. This is particularly problematic for Lionel who, because his faith is wavering, is not as confident as Tony that his ministry expresses God's will. In contrast, Tony acts with absolute certainty of his faith and of his mission. But this certainty, the absence of which Hare seems to suggest is problematic because it leads to inaction, is not an unconditionally good thing. As it is manifest in Tony, for example, it results in self-righteousness which blinds him to the needs of others. Because he cannot tolerate others' doubt, which he reads as failure, and because he believes that he has a privileged knowledge of the truth, he becomes an extremely dangerous person who acts with the full confidence that he is realizing God's will (66–67).

In the course of the play, Tony twice betrays others in ways which are extremely damaging to them. Early in *Racing Demon*, he arrives for a meeting of the parish team and finds Lionel counselling a young black woman who has terminated her pregnancy because her husband does not want to have children. The woman, named Stella, is left vulnerable and needy by the experience. Physically weakened because she needed two procedures before she aborted, Stella feels guilt about the decision which she made out of fear that if she didn't accede to the wishes of her husband, he would beat her. Lionel listens to her and offers her comfort: "I don't know if God'll help you. But now you do have a friend. You have me. This house is always open. Whenever you're lonely" (12). To Tony, this pastoral care is inadequate because Lionel does not witness to her. ". . . [I]sn't this the perfect moment to tell her about Christ?" (13), Tony asks. Lionel believes that such proselytizing would endanger her:

> If I give her a Bible, her husband will find it. . . . If he finds out she's been to see me, he'll get even more hostile. The marriage is in trouble already. We don't want to make it worse by making him feel the do-gooders are all ganging up on him. (13)

Convinced of the inadequacy of Lionel's care, Tony goes to see Stella after hearing that her face has been severely scalded. In the first edition of *Racing Demon*, he meets her husband as he is returning home and demands to see Stella, but her husband, Jabbai, refuses. Tony accuses him of abusing his wife: "Remember, she came to us for help. I have come to see both of you. I want to stop such a thing happening again." When Jabbai still refuses to allow Tony to see his wife, the curate, "*los[ing] control completely*," rushes the husband and tries to throw a punch at him: "You think I can do nothing? Yes? Because this is round my neck? (*Gestures at his collar.*) Well, you're wrong" (1990: 28).

In the second edition of the play, the scene has been rewritten and now is between Stella and Tony, who asks her how she scalded her face. She claims that she spilt a saucepan of boiling water, an explanation which Tony doesn't accept. Tony ascribes feelings to her, insisting, despite her denials, that she is frightened. Finally she counters,

> I'm not scared. I din' come to you. I come to the other man. I wouldn'a' come if I'd known you'd come back. (*Looks at him fiercely.*) All I want is to try and get over it.

> You say you want to help. Well you can. I tell you how
> you help. You help me by staying away. (25–26)

Despite her refusal of help, Tony insists that he will act to protect
her by going to the police. The next scene provides an account by
Frances of the confrontation and ensuing fight between Tony
and Stella's husband. What emerges in the second edition is the
extent to which Tony's sense of his own moral authority blinds
him to the needs of others. In the revised edition, Hare has Tony
arrange for the police to remove Stella from her home and for
her to become a char in the church, for which she is paid very
low wages. She prays:

> I din' want this. I din' want any of it. He lost 'is temper. . . .
> You ask me what's Christian? I thought the Christian
> thing was to forgive.
>   But I'm not allowed to. I 'ad to leave. They said, you're
> livin' with a dangerous man. And I keep sayin', yes, 'e's
> dangerous now, 'cos 'e's so frightened. Jus' leave us alone.
> And that way, we'll 'ave a chance. (71)

The scene is problematic inasmuch as Stella bears the
marks of her abuse, both physically—the scars on her face—and
psychologically—her unwillingness to leave a relationship in
which she is in danger. Hare does not allow that Stella might be
part of a community of black women which would offer her
support; strikingly, Hare never allows that Stella might not need
to turn to the white community for support.[2] Indeed, in both the
first and second editions, his focus seems to be the male
characters, particularly Tony whose need to act—in effect, to be a
hero—involves his sense of himself as a man. As is characteristic
of heroic narratives, the function of the woman is to facilitate the
man's realizing of his heroism. And in this instance, a racial
politic is mapped onto the gender politic of the heroic narrative:
a *black* woman is saved by a *white* man. Hare's vindication of
Lionel's response to Stella and, by implication, his criticism of
Tony occur at the expense of Stella who, in some sense, is not a
fully realized character but a device to forward the plot. While
the play seems to criticize Tony for being utterly unaware of how
his actions meet his own needs and not those of Stella, questions
are raised by this situation which remain unanswered: should
Stella, despite her protests, remain in a relationship where she is

battered? Surely Lionel's response to her was equally ineffectual, as he himself admits when confronted by Tony: "I can call the social services. You know the mess they're in" (13). Earlier in the play, it would seem that Stella is betrayed by the social system or, more specifically, the British government which has so severely cut services that there is no agency which can provide the support for women like her who are in need. By the second act, questions of Christian action in the context of Thatcherism are abandoned as the focus shifts to individuals.

Hare consolidates this shift through Tony's second act of betrayal, his dinner with the Bishops of Southwark and Kingston at the Savoy Hotel. As Tony arrives at the hotel for dinner, he is intercepted by Streaky and Harry who take him to the bar to try and warn him of the implications of speaking with the Bishops about Lionel's performance:

> HARRY: And you think a man should be sacked for the expression on his face? . . . It's a very long way from saying he looks miserable, he's ineffective, and in your view, which is extremely partial, he may be theologically unsound . . . it's a very big step to talk of these things to his bishop. (49)

Despite his counsel to Tony that he modify his assessment of Lionel, Harry fails to persuade his colleague, who complains that he has experienced "this feeling of utter powerlessness. The Church can do nothing in our parish except witness to suffering. . . . I think it's vital we now do something positive. . . . I think we come out with what we believe" (49). What Tony believes is that Lionel is ineffective; when he acts on his belief and complains to the Bishops, he provides Southwark with the justification for dismissing Lionel from the parish team.

In Act Two, scene eight, Lionel confronts Southwark, asking for an explanation of his dismissal. As the conversation progresses, Southwark initially describes the dismissal as political, claiming that the left-leaning faction of the clergy is destroying the Church: "You've politicized everything. . . . Everything turned into an issue. Everyone belonging to a faction. The church has been turned into a ghastly parody of government" (77). Lionel refuses to accept that political differences account for the vehemence with which Southwark presses his dismissal, insisting that the Bishop tell him why he has been singled out. Finally Southwark, losing his temper, explodes:

> All right, very well, you want to know my reason. Why I chose you. Because you alone would dare to tell me I can do nothing about incompetence. What, I'm to be blackmailed because I'm too frightened to *fight*? . . . Yes, I chose you. Because you are the reason the whole church is dying. Immobile. Wracked. Turned inward. Caught in a cycle of decline. Your personal integrity your only concern. Incapable of reaching out. A great vacillating pea-green half-set jelly. (79)

For Southwark, Lionel personifies his fear of an ineffectual priesthood. By dismissing Lionel, he not only rids his diocese of the man whom he perceives to be symptomatic of the Church's decay and powerlessness, but he *acts*, thereby proving to himself that he is not ineffectual. In that way, Southwark and Tony are alike: both are plagued by a sense that they are ineffective; both need to act in order to prove to themselves that they can be effective; both mask their motives, which seem largely governed by self-interest, through claims of acting with integrity and in ways which are consistent with Christian theology, although eventually Southwark admits his hatred of Lionel is personal.

The combination of righteousness and wrongness—the act of betrayal—certainly allows that either of these men might be identified as a "racing demon." But they are not the only characters in the play who betray others. Harry, who is homosexual, betrays his lover, a young Scottish actor named Ewan. When Ewan visits Harry in his flat in Lambeth, he leaves photographs of himself with another man in an attempt to provoke Harry's jealousy, hoping that he will declare his love. Ewan is increasingly frustrated with Harry who won't be seen publicly with him because he fears he will alienate homophobic parishioners. Harry justifies his concern for maintaining appearances by claiming ". . . if I upset my communicants in any way, then the focus is moved. From the Lord Jesus. On to his minister" (23). Although Ewan is hurt by Harry's rationalization of his fear, he apparently remains loyal even when he has an opportunity of betraying his lover. While sitting in a bar he is approached by Tommy Adair, a reporter with one of the British tabloids. Adair makes not very veiled references to Ewan's relationship with Harry, offering him large sums of money for the details. Even though he is unemployed and presumably in financial straits, Ewan refuses to violate his relationship with Harry:

> You'll never get me, you know? You won't get anyone. I'll tell you why. Because life in this country is such a bloody sewer. But what people still have . . . which is theirs . . . which belongs to them . . . which is precious . . . is what happens in private. (36)

While Harry's betrayal of Ewan is inaction—his failure to act and to declare his feelings—Lionel's betrayal of his wife Heather is neglect. We first see Heather in the scene where the parish team is meeting. She interrupts the discussion to get money from Lionel to pay a bill which he has forgotten; "Oh Lord," say Lionel, "I haven't had time to go to the bank" (17). Nor, it appears, does Lionel have time for much concerning his family. Heather reminds him of his son's concert, asking him to go: "You won't let him down?" Lionel replies: "I may let him down. But I'm not yet admitting it. . . . Please, I shall try. Thank you, darling" (18).

We are given a full sense of Lionel's neglect of his family life when Heather has a mild stroke. Released from the hospital on the same day she had been admitted, she is brought home by Lionel for whom her illness intimates mortality and what has been lost between them. He feels alone and so calls on Frances who comes to sit with him. He confesses to her that Heather lay on the floor for half an hour before he realized that she had collapsed: "You see I was in my study, working on my sermon. It's on this terrible poll tax thing. It's very intricate. And it's important I get it right. . . . She fell in the kitchen. I heard nothing. It was so typical" (57). While the initial betrayal is Lionel's self-absorption in his work, what is horrifying is that his admission of guilt, in its focus on *his* failing, does not rupture but perpetuates his self-absorption: his account of Heather's illness focuses on *his* failure, an apparent, although perhaps unconscious, appeal for Frances's sympathy. Indeed, Frances's presence as his comfort is not entirely innocent because, after confiding in her, "*[h]e reaches out and for a moment it looks as if he will touch her cheek. But he stops just short"* (58). Heather's illness is an occasion for Lionel to feel self-pity and to seek solace for himself, without regard for Heather who, still disoriented after the stroke, wanders into the living room and, finding Frances with Lionel, is upset. Lionel takes his ill wife back to her bed and then returns to Frances and to the pleasure of their mild flirtation, but she refuses him, insisting that he return to his wife. It falls to Frances to be the pastor's guide to moral behaviour, to direct him to act charitably.

This is the second occasion on which Frances has been a friend to Lionel, acting without self-interest for his well-being. The first instance is when she comes to Lionel's home to recount the conversation about Lionel's dismissal which she overheard at her parents' home. There are several other occasions in *Racing Demon* when characters behave with generosity towards others: Lionel's counselling Stella which ends in his offering her friendship; Ewan's refusal to grant Adair an interview about Harry; Harry and Streaky speaking first to the Bishop of Kingston and then to Tony. In *Racing Demon*, these gestures come to define true Christian action, even if they are committed by people who, like Ewan and Frances, don't identify themselves as Christians. Indeed, Hare is explicit that Christian action is characterized by the generosity of friendship. In the scene where the parish team is discussing its work for the next week, Tony pushes Lionel to articulate what holds the team together. Not satisfied by Lionel's claim that the team is united by its desire to help others and a belief in the Trinity, he asks "But does anything else hold us together?":

> LIONEL: Of course. I'd have thought that was obvious.
> TONY: Not to me.
> (LIONEL *smiles again,* STREAKY *looking down as if he knew the answer.*)
> LIONEL: Why, Tony, surely the fact that we're friends?
> (20)

But viewing someone as a friend, although having a certain appeal to "gentlemanly" virtues, is not always politically sagacious. When Frances tells Lionel that "Southwark's out to get you" (32), he responds by telling her that he doesn't have full confidence in the Bishop and took measures to protect himself.

He went to Kingston and asked if the new system of parish teams would be used as a way to dismiss people from their charges. He was assured by the Bishop that it would not be: "He gave me a promise. There's no problem. Gilbert gave me his word" (32). We see a similar premium placed on friendship by Southwark when he greets Harry at the Savoy: "How are you, Harry? It's so long since I saw you. I miss you, you know." Harry replies, "Well, thank you, Charlie. I miss you too. (*They . . . embrace, full of fondness, looking into each other's eyes with real warmth)*" (54).

The importance of these moments of friendship and loyalty which transcend political differences is explicated fully in the first version of the text when Lionel nostalgically tells Frances of the Church he once knew:

> It's funny, I think I must have been thirty years in gardens. It seemed like for ever. . . . Because that's where the churches were. Behind trellises. Singing plainsong, stuck away in the shires. But meanwhile the people had all moved to the cities. So the old Church had died. So had its values. We were slow to realize. . . . And the new Church is having its troubles being born. . . . (1990: 32)

The speech, although sentimental in its romanticization of the country as the site of older and truer values, suggests that the Church once was based on an ethos which included loyalty as a mark of human decency. But this ethos has ceased to have currency in the new Church of the inner cities: Kingston's word has no value; Southwark may greet Harry with warmth, but whatever feelings he has for Harry are superseded by his need to act and so he ruthlessly dismisses Harry's friend.

Hare's privileging of friendship, particularly his inscription of Frances as the paragon of friendship, is problematic. First, she seems to epitomize virtue: she is morally upright, tries to address injustice when she sees it, and seems not only sympathetic and understanding but also wise. She is also selfless; by the end of the play, she plans to leave England to work abroad: "I want to work abroad. I'm from a missionary family. It just happens I don't have the faith" (59). In Frances, Hare may be trying to create the secular "Christian" but, whatever his intention, she embodies the maternal virtues commonly ascribed by male writers to "good" women, including representing them only in relation to men. Beyond my discomfort with Hare's depiction of Frances, which is the fulfillment of a masculine fantasy of woman, I have other difficulties with *Racing Demon*. The shift in focus from a social and political system to the personal, from the failure of the Church and state to the failure of friends, is important because it forecloses the possibility of political change. Neither Lionel nor Tony can help Stella because, as individuals, they do not have the resources to take on a social system which is being eroded by the policies of the Thatcher government. Their actions, while in Lionel's case providing some measure of comfort, do not begin to address the problems which are the consequence of a social system which is bankrupt. In every instance, the acts of friendship do not make the slightest difference: Stella loses a relationship which she values and is offered nothing in its place; Adair finds out about Harry and publishes the story; Lionel is moved from the parish. While people's behaving kindly towards one another makes the world a more pleasant place to live, these acts would seem ultimately inconsequential when pitted against the deteriorating social conditions in contemporary Britain. Hare seems to offer no particular hope for the future, apparently unable to envision the terms of political change. His represent-ation of the Church is particularly interesting in this context. Although he alludes to the left-wing elements of the Church through his implied reference to *Faith in the City*, and more directly through references to Runcie's stand on the Falklands War and the ordination of homosexuals and women as priests, he seems reluctant to see the Church as a catalyst of social change. Perhaps this is because he sees the Church as operating like a large corporation which consequently is ideologically complicit in the very issues of social injustice which it wants to address. That is, however, only a partial explanation.

Racing Demon, although dealing with a "team" ministry, never gives a sense that the team functions effectively. Tony's observation that the team is ineffective because it has no clear objectives in its ministry except to "help people" (19) has a certain credibility because the team seems to be a microcosm of the Church of England, loosely held together with no articulated common philosophy. As Southwark explains, "Start talking to our members and you'll find we hold a thousand different views" (3). The plurality of the contemporary Church precludes action because the Church cannot easily take and implement a position without alienating some of its communicants. The failure of the Church to constitute itself as a corporate body is strikingly illustrated through the various prayers in the play. Throughout *Racing Demon*, Hare shows a number of characters in private prayer, but only once shows adherents praying together: in the penultimate scene of Act One, the session of the Synod begins with the recitation of "Our Father." Given that earlier in the scene we see Gilbert Heffernan dressed in the formal robes of the Bishop, that the *"doors throughout the hall are thrown open. Clergy and laity flock in to take their places. Men in legal wigs and gowns assemble at the central table"* (44), the prayer seems a matter of formality, a ritual which marks a continuity with tradition but which has no other effect. But the recitation of "Our Father" is, within Protestant theology, a collective prayer and so, in the context of *Racing Demon*, alludes to another possibility which Hare does not explore. Christian faith is not simply a private matter between God and the believer; it has a corporate aspect which theologically is marked through the collectivity of public worship and, more particularly, through partaking of the sacrament of communion. While I would be reluctant to suggest that political reform can come from the Church because Christian theology historically has reinforced the hegemony, nevertheless it is clear from *Racing Demon* that individuals, acting alone, cannot be effective agents of social change. Change occurs when individuals act collectively, even if finding the terms of that collective action may be problematic.[3]

NOTES

1. The first published edition of the text provides further evidence that the bishops conceive of the Church as a business—and one which is in a slump. They argue that the Church must undertake an ad campaign because it "needs exposure. It needs money" (1990: 31).

2. Interestingly, Hare refers to the black community in Streaky's prayer, in which the Jamaican members of the congregation are described as a "blissful people" given to enjoying rum and curried goat (56).

3. Thanks to Giles Croft for a lively discussion of *Racing Demon* which drew my attention to aspects of Hare's work which I might not otherwise have noticed.

WORKS CITED

The Archbishop of Canterbury's Commission on Urban Priority Areas. *Faith in the City: A Call for Action by Church and Nation.* London: Church House, 1985.

Gould, Julius. "Theologians in the Political Mêlée: On 'Relevant' Churchmen." *Encounter* June 1986: 70–76.

Hare, David. *Racing Demon.* London: Faber, 1990.

———. *Racing Demon.* Rev. ed. London: Faber, 1991.

Hastings, Max and Simon Jenkins. *The Battle for the Falklands.* New York: Norton, 1983.

Martin, David. "The Churches: Pink Bishops and the Iron Lady." *The Thatcher Effect: A Decade of Change.* Ed. Dennis Kavanagh and Anthony Seldon. Oxford: Clarendon, 1989. 330–41.

Moyser, George. "The Church of England and Politics: Patterns and Trends." *Church and Politics Today: Essays on the Role of the Church of England in Contemporary Politics.* Ed. George Moyser. Edinburgh: Clark, 1985. 1–24.

Playwright of Popular Dissent: David Hare and the Trilogy

Lane A. Glenn

As one of Britain's most successful playwright-polemicists, David Hare has been lauded for his ability to attract largely mainstream, middle-class audiences to productions that often tear at the very fabric of bourgeois English life. For the last fifteen years he has been assisted in his efforts by the Royal National Theatre of Great Britain, where he is an associate director: since 1978, Hare has launched nine plays from the National's three stages, including *Plenty*, *A Map of the World*, *Pravda* (written with Howard Brenton), *The Bay at Nice* and *Wrecked Eggs*, and *The Secret Rapture*. His most ambitious work to date, however, involves not just one play but an entire trilogy examining British institutions. What Hare and Brenton began with their 1985 satire of the Fleet Street press, *Pravda*, has been continued in the halls of Britain's National Theatre with Hare's solo efforts: *Racing Demon*, *Murmuring Judges*, and *The Absence of War*. The plays examine the Church of England, the British legal system, and English party politics respectively, and they provide a revealing look at the evolution of a creative process involving a playwright, director, and theatre—David Hare, Richard Eyre, and the National's Olivier stage.

The man critics have labeled Britain's leading dissident playwright did not set out to create a dramatic investigation of such an epic sweep. It all began with a single play: the genesis of the trilogy lies in Hare's curiosity about and gentle prodding of the venerable Church of England, an institution some feel is

217

mired in dogma and hopelessly behind the times, stuck performing mundane social work while longing to provide spiritual fulfillment. His friend of more than twenty years, Director of the National Theatre Richard Eyre, then set him along the path that led to *Racing Demon*. "I was able to put him in contact with a vicar who had been fired from his church," Eyre has stated. "It was something that was making the news quite a bit at the time." The substance of this meeting became one of the central issues of the play: the function of the individual conscience within the Church, and the Church's role in a decidedly secular community. As Hare has noted, he then "put the research on one side and wrote a work of pure fiction."[1] The result was a triumph for both Hare and the National Theatre: *Racing Demon*, a tale of four London clergymen battling faith, bureaucracy, hierarchy, and tradition, garnered four Best Play awards, as well as Best Actor and Best Supporting Actor recognitions for two of its company. It entered the repertoire of the Cottesloe Theatre on 8 February 1990, transferred to the larger Olivier stage in August of that year, and returned the following autumn to the Lyttelton before touring the United Kingdom—possibly the only production in the National's history to perform on all three of its stages.

Hare did not have to wait for critical kudos to realize he had come upon a formula for success: "I had the idea, during the rehearsals of *Racing Demon*, that we should try and do three plays rather than just one. I wanted eventually to put three plays together in one day—the Church, the Law and the State." After a very public fracas with Frank Rich of the *New York Times* over his directorial skill in the American production of *The Secret Rapture*, however, Hare was hesitant to oversee such a project himself; this was the reason he turned to Richard Eyre as the director for *Racing Demon*, and continued the alliance for the next two plays. For his part, Eyre was ready to rise to the challenge. "Both of us enjoyed working on *Racing Demon*," the director has commented, "and we felt strongly the value of an ensemble and continuity. At the same time I was keen to find a project that was very ambitious—a grand folly—and this seemed to be the idea. If you run a theatre you need those landmarks in your life and in the life of the theatre. This challenges everyone involved." Thus the David Hare Trilogy was conceived.

Theatrical works on this grand scale are rare in modern drama. Wagner's *Ring* cycle, Ibsen's *Peer Gynt* and Peter Brook's *Mahabharata* rival Hare's trilogy in terms of epic length, a quality the playwright praises. "I love long days in the theatre," he has said. "When they work, they do make you more open and receptive. There is a wonderful stage you go through at about the seventh or eighth hour at which all your critical faculties are gone and all your resistance is gone and you become more open and you simply accept." And August Wilson's chronicle of African-American experience in different decades of the twentieth century—*Ma Rainey's Black Bottom, Fences, Joe Turner's Come and Gone, The Piano Lesson,* and *Two Trains Running*—compares in terms of extended narratives around a broad central theme. None of these works, however, assumes the authority in wide-ranging subjects that Hare's plays do.

On a socio-political level, *Racing Demon* found its admirers and detractors among the London press, clergy, and theatre-going public. Few refute the despairing statistics offered by the play—English clergy are largely overworked and underpaid, parish church attendance on most Sundays is less than 1 percent, and the Church finds itself desperately behind the times, clinging to doctrines that are often irrelevant and ineffective in their present environment. Some, however, argue that there are important facets to the crisis-of-faith issue within the Church that Hare has not presented. A few even point to what seems an obvious agnostic bias on Hare's part as a barrier to effective judgement of religious issues. At the human level, though, *Racing Demon* is one of Hare's most effective plays to date. It combines humor with pathos while doing what Hare does best: exploring vital public issues in intensely personal realms. He had created for himself a hard act to follow.

The second play in the trilogy, *Murmuring Judges*, was not greeted as warmly when it first appeared at the National's Olivier Theatre in October of 1991. Taking to task English law—the prisons, the bar and bench, and the police—Hare attempts to prove the futility of a system that actually treats less than 2 percent of the crimes in Britain, convicts even fewer criminals, then recycles them in jails that prove training grounds for further misdeeds. The intertwining plots of *Murmuring Judges* reflect the three levels of the law as Hare perceives them. At the constabulary level are DC Barry Hopper, a semi-corrupt officer who will stop at nothing to nab his culprits, including planting false evidence, and PC Sandra Bingham, his sometime lover caught in a moral dilemma: whether to reveal the truth about her rising-star detective boyfriend or observe *esprit de corps* and turn a blind eye. At the bar and bench are Sir Peter Edgecombe QC, head of a law firm and prone to taking on attractive female barristers fresh from law school to handle his criminal cases and act as dinner and opera escorts, and Justice Cuddeford, a career judge enamored of the roast venison and fine wines in the dining halls of the Inns of Court but averse to actual contact with the public or the prison system he administers. As is common in many of Hare's plays, the voice of goodness and moral indignation belongs to a woman: balancing these unscrupulous characters is Irina Platt, Sir Peter's most recent acquisition. A native Antiguan, Irina is an outsider to her profession in terms of both her gender and race, facts which do not prevent her from becoming a cunning legal crusader and ostensibly the play's hero.

Running the gamut through the police, the courts, and into the prisons is Gerard McKinnon. Born and raised in Northern Ireland, McKinnon is a product of hard times; desperate to support his family (which includes a handicapped child), he agrees to accompany a pair of more seasoned criminals on a heist and is caught after his first larcenous act. He is given an extremely harsh sentence (presumably because he is Irish) and sent to prison where, because of overcrowding, he is housed in the wing for serious offenders. The main dramatic action of the play focuses on the obstacles Irina faces in her attempts to secure a lighter sentence for McKinnon, obstacles erected by an over-burdened, uncaring, sometimes corrupt legal system.

In addition to being chronologically the center of the trilogy, *Murmuring Judges* may be seen as a kind of fulcrum for the entire project, balancing what came before, *Racing Demon*, and what was to follow, *The Absence of War*. This involves both benefits and drawbacks. While the script itself is flawed in many respects compared to its companions, the production style literally set the stage for the future production of the entire trilogy. Structurally, *Murmuring Judges* is the weakest of the three plays. Initial complaints from London critics focused on Hare's overabundance of research and overzealous lecturing in unfolding his story line. A few were plainly (and somewhat comically) puzzled. "We know from *Pravda* that critics are dolts with drinking problems," wrote Benedict Nightingale, "but when we are found in a tiny cluster after curtain-down, debating the plot's essentials, something needs clarifying" ("Hare Brained"). The difficulty Hare seemingly encountered in *Murmuring Judges* was balancing the issues of the play with a well-constructed, compelling plot and believable, empathetic characters, something *Racing Demon* had done so well. Instead of a Shavian weighing of ideas against a backdrop of personal turmoil, the play provides iconographic mouthpieces and dialogue that occasionally seem more akin to agit-prop drama than Hare's usual brand of contemporary realism.

In *Racing Demon*, Lionel Espy and Harry Henderson, the persecuted vicars, are fully-fleshed human beings, likeable in their earnestness but not without their faults. One of them has difficulty caring for his wife the way he cares for himself and others, and experiences a crisis in faith so severe that many of his parishioners feel he is unable to lead them; the other is a withdrawn homosexual, reticent about admitting his sexual orientation and publicly recognizing his lover. Even their conservative adversary, Tony Ferris, an upstart curate of missionary zeal, is given equitable treatment: behind his evangelical religious fervor lie a tragic childhood and the guilt of a recent love affair.

No such balance is struck, however, with the characters in *Murmuring Judges*. Though the crises they encounter are rarely obvious black-and-white ones, the forces of good and evil represented by the police, lawyers, judges, prison wardens, and criminals are clearly aligned, with little gray area between them. Sir Peter, for example, takes advantage of women, prefers high-paying and exciting civil court cases to standard-fare, run-of-the-mill criminal ones, and cares little for the truth. "You know what's so boring about criminal law?" he asks barrister Irina

Platt. ". . . [Y]ou have to establish the facts. . . . That's why I also like libel cases. Because so often they're a matter of opinion. You're arguing about things which no one can prove. You're juggling with air, pure and simple" (85). At an Inns of Court dinner, Justice Cuddeford, a minor but important character representing the judiciary, is equally unconcerned and malicious. He avoids discussing with the Home Secretary the practical dilemmas of convicting and sentencing criminals, preferring instead to dwell on the fine menu for the evening and some of the more archaic customs of the Inns. When he is finally cornered he reveals what Hare presumably thinks is one of the larger failings of the judiciary. "[I]f for one single moment, when I'm at work in my court," Cuddeford tells his companion, "if I begin to consider . . . if I ever consider what prison is now like . . . then I cannot fairly administer justice. Because my head is full of what we may call failings of society. . . . Which are truly not my concern" (57).

The crusading lawyer Irina Platt, on the other hand, certainly has the forces of right and reason on her side. Her client, McKinnon, is guilty, but he was apprehended improperly and punished too severely by a prejudiced, unsympathetic court; her appeal for leniency is justifiable. Finally, however, her unceasing idealism and wholesomeness seem somewhat naive. In her climactic confrontation with Sir Peter, she attacks his apathy toward the downtrodden and his interest in personal gain. "All this behaviour, the honours, the huge sums of money, the buildings, the absurd dressing-up. They do have a purpose," she tells him. "It's anaesthetic. It's to render you incapable of imagining life the other way round" (91). While her feeling is sincere and her point valid, the issue is one that already has been raised in the play several times; thus, rather than startling the audience, it seems merely redundant.

Other characters in the play have the similar problem of establishing three-dimensional identities beyond their roles as informers or moralizers. The problem is especially acute in scenes involving the police, who seem to have extraordinary memories for abysmal job-related statistics. DC Barry Hopper, frustrated at the amount of paperwork necessary to charge someone with abstracting electricity, "the most boring crime of all time," tells his charge room cohorts: "I read this statistic. If you take all the crime, all of it, every single bit, in money it doesn't add up to what's lost every year in tax evasion. . . . And yet look at us! . . . One hundred and thirty thousand policemen. Twenty-eight thousand in London alone. . . . To collect a sum of money—at incredible expense—which is actually less than the government happily lets rich bastards get up and walk away with every year" (66).

Manufacturing scenes for relaying this kind of information is something Hare did not need to do in *Racing Demon*. The real-life problems reflected in the play are better integrated with the action of the plot, and characters who may reveal important facts and statistics are motivated to do so for more personal reasons. For Barry, tax dollars and thousands of uniformed police across London are things he has merely read about; alarming news seems somehow more urgent when it more immediately involves the characters. For example, in *Racing Demon* Tony tells his fellow clergymen: "We feel we've had a good Sunday if between us we attract one per cent. One per cent of our whole catchment area. . . . I want a full church. Is that so disgraceful?" (16). And rather than simply throwing out poverty statistics, the playwright allows the experience of the characters to tell the tale; thus Lionel explains his dual role as minister and social worker by saying, "I don't think anyone from the outside quite understands what the job is. Mostly it's just listening to the anger. One reason or another. Lately it's the change in the DSS rules. If you're young, setting up home, you can no longer get a loan for a stove, unless you can prove you'll be able to pay the money back. I've had three couples in the last week. They need somewhere to go to express their frustration. Everyone does" (31). Instead of being told what the extent of the problem is, the audience is presented with one small piece of it—a handful of concerned but confused vicars. From this it must extrapolate the larger societal concerns.

The problems *Murmuring Judges* has with realistic character and theme development seem to stem from Hare's working method on the project. After thoroughly investigating his subject, rather than laying aside his research to "write a pure work of fiction," as he did with *Racing Demon*, he frequently allowed his findings to take precedence over literary technique. What the play lacks on the page, however, it attempts to compensate for in production. While its forerunner began on a bare, crucifix-shaped stage in the much smaller Cottesloe Theatre and only later transferred to the cavernous Olivier, *Murmuring Judges* was written with the 1,100–seat grand stage in mind. According to both the playwright and the director, writing for the Olivier carries with it a certain weight of responsibility, and requires particular qualities from the play that is to be performed there. First of all, the play must hold a large sense of importance for the audience. As Hare has stated: "The audience know that it would be wrong to have something called the 'National Theatre' and then present new plays only in the smaller auditoria. It seems to me important to put big public subjects on this stage, which reflect the audience's own lives."

Additionally, the Olivier space is not conducive to an intimately styled play. While some smaller-cast plays can pull it off (*Racing Demon* contains only eleven speaking parts), larger ones are the more usual bill of fare (*Murmuring Judges* has a cast of nearly thirty, plus extras, while *The Absence of War* uses a company of at least twenty-six). "The production has to have a bit of muscularity to it," according to Richard Eyre. "It's got to be robust. [The Olivier] can't take fragile writing—you have to make bold statements. They can be complex but they have to be bold—visually and in their acting as well. And, of course, it's got to have a public face to it. A theatre where people are sat in a 130 degree arc—the acting has to turn out, not in. Plays with direct address work better in there." A big public subject, robustness, and a strong visual flair, no matter the flatness of some characters and a few script problems, are certainly things *Murmuring Judges* has going for it. Almost to a reviewer London critics responded favorably to Richard Eyre's staging and Bob Crowley's design for the play, which proved to be the inspiration for the whole trilogy when it was remounted.

Of course, the production team had to work from the playwright's model, and in this respect Hare's fifteen years as an occasional film director and screenwriter profited him. *Murmuring Judges*, like many of Hare's plays, prescribes certain visual elements and production techniques. There is a cinematic structure to the play—close-up, crowd scene, montage, fade-out—that translates into a varied and compelling stage presentation. Hare describes the first scene of the play this way: *"An empty stage. Then suddenly from nowhere they're all there—the judge, the jury, the battery of lawyers in wigs, the public, the police, the press, the ushers, the guards, and at the centre of the forward-facing court, the defendants. The entire company of the law has appeared in the blinking of an eye"* (1). Such theatre magic is facilitated by the Olivier: with its enormous upstage and wing space, and rows of vomitoriums leading through the audience to the stage, a large company can be assembled in a matter of seconds. Once the characters are onstage, the fluidity of their movements and the film-like qualities of the production continue. A spotlight separates the defendant, McKinnon, from the courtroom as his thoughts are presented simultaneously with the reading of the verdict. When the court disbands, the setting is immediately replaced by a new one. *"The court at once melds into the incoming scene,"* Hare directs, *"led by the defence counsel, who walk from the court towards us"* (3). The effect is that of a rapid dissolve, one image replaced by another.

This technique, which continues throughout the play, was assisted in production by a triptych of enormous screens, onto which were flashed slide-projection images appropriate to each setting. In the charge room, images of fingerprint sheets, a giant wall of clipboards, and mile-high piles of file baskets stretched from the stage floor up into the fly gallery. Exterior scenes were accompanied by cloudless skies or leafy trees, while the barristers' offices sat in front of immense library shelves, crammed with legal briefs and texts. The tri-screen approach also allowed the stage to be split into separate, alternating scenes, the live equivalent of a series of cinematic dissolves into different locales. Hare employs this effect to its fullest at the close of Act 1: onstage are Barry Hopper and his partner in the darkened police station, McKinnon in his prison cell, and Irina and Sir Peter at the Royal Opera House. The juxtaposition of images and characters—the policemen leaving for a drink at the end of a long day, the criminal stewing in his cold steel cell, and the upper-crust lawyers out on the town—speaks volumes more than some of the play's antiseptic statistics. As Mozart's *The*

Magic Flute crashes into life and the prison warders call "Lights
out!" (49), the play becomes truly thought-provoking and
meaningful.

A further benefit of the rear-wall projections was that they
allowed for a relatively uncluttered floor plan. This served the
first play in the trilogy especially well: clearing the stage of
unnecessary settings and props focused attention on the actors
and the text. Comparisons were made between *Racing Demon*
and some of Bertolt Brecht's works, particularly *Galileo*. One
reviewer was prompted to write: "Richard Eyre's production
makes such skillful use of the symbolic possibilities of a
cruciform open stage that one wonders why anyone bothered to
invent the proscenium arch" (Hebblethwaite). Of course, this
effect was easier to manage in a smaller theatre. As Eyre has
pointed out, "*Racing Demon* started in the Cottesloe. It was very
intimate. The audience sat around a cruciform stage and no one
was further than ten feet from the actors. The problem has been
trying to preserve the virtues of the production, the delicacy of
the acting. It's been amplified and technically adapted to the new
space [at the Olivier] and to the trilogy. The idea we followed
throughout, though, remains a minimalist one. Nothing appears
on stage that is decorative or gratuitous, nothing that is not
functional and necessary." In order to revive *Racing Demon* as
part of the trilogy, this meant taking a few cues from *Murmuring
Judges* and enhancing the visual elements. What began as a bare
horizontal crucifix laid across the stage now stretched vertically
as well, in a mirror-like image toward the rear of the acting area.
The center of the upright cross became the projection screen for
this play, still a simpler effect than the giant images flashed on
the walls in the next two productions, but enough to provide
visual unity.

Murmuring Judges, then, borrowed research techniques,
thematic ideas and, of course, impetus from its predecessor
while returning visual flair. *Racing Demon*, with its understated
lessons and simple concurrent plots all revolving around a small
coterie of churchfolk, carries more weight than its more
complicated and didactic follower. It seems, finally, far more
universal and enduring, much more likely to withstand what

Hare has referred to as "the ten-year test," being equally accessible a decade from now.

The final play in the trilogy, *The Absence of War*, is an attempt to combine the best elements of the first two. Visually as grand and cinematic as *Murmuring Judges*, it nonetheless maintains a simple, single plot line, reminiscent of *Racing Demon*. Hare was somewhat evasive while planning the trilogy's concluding play. During a discussion with Eyre following a production of *Murmuring Judges*, the writer was asked if his next play would be about politicians. "Yes," he responded. "In Western democracies, politicians and those around them are currently held in such low regard that I was fascinated by the prospect of trying to look at the world from their point of view. More than that, at the moment, I don't want to say." The playwright's hesitation may be quite understandable given the task he had chosen. *The Absence of War* is not just a play about politicians in Britain. More specifically, it is about the Labour Party and its attempt to win power in the general election of 1992. While his research for *Racing Demon* and *Murmuring Judges* involved shadowing and interviewing parish vicars, policemen, lawyers, and judges, his subjects were mostly low-profile professionals whose personalities, even if duplicated on the stage, were not likely to be recognized or slandered. An up-to-the-minute description of the Labour Party's inner workings, however, would likely produce events and characters immediately recognizable to a politically conscious theatre-going public.

In actuality, there was some friction. Hare has been a supporter, albeit a critical one, of the Labour Party for years, and even developed a friendship with then Labour Leader Neil Kinnock. In the early writing stages of the play, Kinnock gave Hare access to his campaign team and made him privy to behind-the-scenes meetings. He was allowed to conduct interviews with important Labour figures and record all that he saw and heard. It wasn't until the play was announced, along with publication of a book by Hare that chronicles his research methods, *Asking Around*, that Labourites became suspicious and defensive. Suddenly there was concern that the Party's support for the project might be withdrawn, a prospect that, while not damning for Hare the playwright and his artistic creation, could be messy for a heavily subsidized theatre and a company made up largely of Labour supporters. The *Evening Standard* reported one Party insider as saying, "I knew he was researching a play but I didn't know he was going to repeat whole conversations in a book. He would not have been allowed that sort of access from the start if we had known about the book" (Hooberman and Robertshaw). The issue was apparently resolved when the playwright presented his work to Kinnock, not for censoring but for reassurance. "David has battled with the Labour Party all summer," his publisher was quoted as saying, "but Neil Kinnock likes the play, and everything seems to be hunky-dory now with the high command" (De Jongh).

While the play does bear many similarities to recent political events in Britain, and certainly aims its share of broadsides at both leading political parties, it still generally transcends simple immediacy. Certainly Hare's depiction of a struggling Labour Party, inches away from capturing the top seat in government during a drastic financial crisis only to fumble once again and cede to Conservative sensibilities, is familiar to anyone who voted in the last British election. But the play is also about larger issues: *The Absence of War* raises perennial and universal questions about the relationship between the governors and the governed, the ethics of politicking, the integrity of belief, and more. What Hare hopes the play offers that no others before have offered is an honest look at the people who legislate our lives. Rather than devoting itself exclusively to celebrating or satirizing a particular figure or group of people, it attempts a balanced assessment of the pros and cons of politics. And, indeed, most of the characters in *The Absence of War* are much better defined than the legal caricatures of *Murmuring Judges*; they are at least as dimensional as the clergy in *Racing Demon*.

While both Hare's earlier attempts involved three or more simultaneous stories, this one revolves around a single person and a single event: the Right Honorable George Jones MP, leader of the opposition Labour Party, and his attempt to become Prime Minister. The other characters of the play—Labour Party officials, campaign workers, reporters, and political adversaries—all contribute somehow to the saga of the rise and fall of Jones's ambition. The beginning of the play finds them all sharing an emotional moment during a ritual sure to engage immediately the minds of British audiences: the Memorial Day ceremony at the Cenotaph. The leaders of the major political parties, along with their retinues, have gathered at the monument to pay their respects to their countrymen who have fallen in battle. A reverent narrator conducts the service as the men lay wreaths in memory of Britain's heroes. The scene allows for some quick exposition. While the observance proceeds in the background, Andrew Buchan, Jones's assistant, explains to the audience the hectic nature of politicians' work and the significance of the play's title:

> Why these hours? Why these ridiculous schedules? Up and out of our beds at six every day. Read the papers. When you know already what the papers will say. . . . [T]hen the first meeting of the day. Seven o'clock and I'm there. And outside that meeting another meeting, already beating, bulging, pressing against the door. . . . What is this for? This madness? . . . I have a theory. People of my age, we did not fight in a war. If you fight in a war, you have some sense of personal worth. So now we seek it by keeping busy. We work and hope we will feel we do good.
> (2)

Mingled in Andrew's speech are Hare's grudging acknowledgement of the way war can mold lives and a sort of existential longing to fill a void in one's sense of self-worth. Within the first few lines of the play a character with human contradictions, needs, and motivations has already been established.

The technique of rapid scene changing and character/ action montage that Hare employed in *Murmuring Judges* is duplicated in *The Absence of War*: characters move from one locale to the next in an artfully flowing liaison of scenes. The Cenotaph ceremony quickly dissolves into the House of Commons lobby, represented by rear projections of marbled statuary and long corridors and a few carefully chosen set pieces. A meeting of the House provides a convenient way to introduce the other personalities of the play as well as establish a rhythm for the production. Jones's office staff arrive one at a time to await their eccentric leader's late appearance. Gwenda Aaron, Jones's diary secretary, and Mary Housego, his press secretary, frantically scour the halls searching for their missing leader while the Members of Parliament, including Jones's Shadow Chancellor, Malcolm Pryce, begin to assemble. A hasty meeting is conducted between Andrew and Lindsay Fontaine, a public relations guru who hopes to become the Labour Party's new imagemaker.

The excitement and confusion prior to Jones's actual arrival lend a sense of anticipation to the moment: when he finally appears (though he feigns an air of unassuming innocence), his importance is obvious. Hare has managed to create in Jones a unique (fictional) political figure. He is not a man of straw, designed to be propped up and knocked down for his ideological bent, nor is he a mythological hero, lionized like Churchill or Lord Nelson, but rather a multi-faceted human being. Very quickly Jones's political convictions are presented in a speech to the House of Commons. From his position on the floor the Leader harangues his Conservative opposition, accusing them of running down the country with ineffective policy and taking advantage of their constituencies. Yet his rhetoric reveals a politician with a sense of humor and human foibles. He compares the Tories to "a lonely drunk wandering through the streets at four-thirty in the morning, muttering to itself, blaming its misfortunes on others and desperately searching, scrabbling through the early morning trashcans for any political ideas it might still be able to lift" (11). Jones's colorful dialogue and fanciful ideas are a product of his upbringing and affiliation: like many Labour Party members, he comes from a working-class background. He reveals that it was his father, a laborer and unionist, who helped produce his rhetorical skill, encouraging him to "speak, just speak from the heart" (93). It is Jones's sincerity, his ability to "speak from the heart," that catapulted him to his preeminent position.

The Leader's laurel is not one he wears comfortably, however. He continues to indulge in activities that seem frivolous given his position, being especially fond of unaccompanied walks in the park where he can admire the lives of "ordinary" people, and trips to the theatre, where he derives inspiration for his life and career. When Oliver Dix, his political consultant, fears that Jones may be losing his nerve, the Leader responds:

> GEORGE: Go to the theatre, I keep telling you. Brutus has qualms.
> OLIVER: What does that mean?
> GEORGE: There's a scene in a tent. Before battle. All leaders have them. In plays, the leader always has a quiet crisis.
> OLIVER: Then? Then what happens?
> GEORGE: Oh then. . . .
> OLIVER: Come on, tell me. I didn't read English. . . .
> GEORGE: It's all right, Oliver. Then they always murder their doubts.
> OLIVER: Thank God for that. (18–19)

George Jones's blend of charisma, creativity, and simple straightforwardness gains him a minor cult following among Labour insiders; the Old Guard and many of the young idealists revere him for his idealism and leadership ability. His popularity with the public, however, is lukewarm, and some of the moderate Labourites and career politicians fear that, while the party gains momentum, Jones might slow them down. Foremost among the dissenters is Jones's second-in-command, Malcolm Pryce. Pryce's Iagoesque characteristics are noticeable almost immediately. While the Leader is given to taking walks in the park and sneaking out for cigarettes unattended, visiting the theatre religiously and kibitzing with his constituency, all the while keeping his staff on pins and needles, Malcolm is constantly accompanied by Bruce, his "minder." His days are ordered, he meets with the right people, dresses for the occasion, and is ever mindful of the Party line—in short, the "perfect" politician. Bound to support his superior, he is nevertheless inexorably drawn by his ambition.

Lindsay Fontaine, Jones's new PR agent, becomes one of the most important secondary figures in the play. Like nearly all of Hare's female characters, Lindsay is a self-made, savvy professional who poses some of the play's trickiest questions and often seems to act as the audience's representative on the stage, seeking answers that have troubled us all. She becomes involved with Jones's campaign seemingly out of occupational interest; he poses a challenge to her. As she explains to Andrew, "[Y]ou meet George, you think: 'this man is dynamite.' So then you ask the next question. Why on earth does this never quite come across?" (4). It is Lindsay who, at the time of the most severe crisis in Jones's campaign, suggests a return to his roots as a remedy. After being humiliated on national television, thanks in part to information leaked by Pryce, Jones and his party begin to falter in the polls. The hopeful politician is scheduled to address a large Labour convention and his remarks will be carried to the entire country. Rather than stick to a prepared, carefully edited speech, Lindsay encourages Jones to follow his father's advice and speak from the heart.

The following scenes are the most dramatic in the play. The MP steels himself, steps to the lectern, and launches into what begins as an inspiring speech, reminiscent of his younger days. "It is said to me: there is no longer hope in our future," he addresses the attentive crowd. "No sense of potential. No sense of possibility. In our own lifetime, a whole generation has been effectively abandoned and dispossessed. They have been told to fend for themselves. . . . Comrades, my socialism is the socialism that says these people must not be let go" (95). It is not long, though, before the orator falters, his eloquence escaping him, and he must rely on his adequate, if less passionate, prepared speech. Following the convention debacle, as Jones and his staff are beginning to realize the election is lost, he fumes about the way politics has made him impotent. In a passage designed to show the playwright's contempt for the homogeneity of politics, the Leader rants:

> I got up there, I thought all the things I truly care about . . .
> Northern Ireland. What can you say? You can't say
> anything. Not publicly. The whole bloody country's been
> bleeding for years. . . . It's been dying and we can't speak,
> we can't say anything, you're not allowed to say
> *anything.* . . . I thought, you know, out there I was
> thinking, Northern Ireland, it's "above politics." That's
> what we say. Well what sort of politics is it which says
> that certain things are too important to be spoken of? . . .
> We can't speak of history, you can't say Britain happens to
> be trapped in historical decline. You can't even say that.

> But it's true. . . . Defence! Abandoning nuclear weapons,
> which everyone knows we should do, I could make a great
> speech about that. My God! If only I could! But of course if
> I say it, that's fifty thousand jobs. . . . (98–99)

In the end the election is lost and there is genuine pity for
George Jones and his supporters. His hubris was his idealism—
believing fervently that his goals and the goals of his party were
what the country needed and wanted, while ignoring some of
the realities of modern politics. Unlike the idealism of Irina in
Murmuring Judges, however, which seems childishly naive,
Jones's convictions seem more plausible because they are given a
chance to become reality. Additionally, Hare uses Jones's failure
as a model for politicians and a message for the voting public.
During the campaign Jones could have distanced himself from
Pryce and the damage he was causing, perhaps even ejected him
from the Leader's office. Such a response, though, would have
caused a rift in the Party at a time when Labour's popularity was
at its highest peak in many years. Instead, he sacrificed personal
pursuits for the good of the Party and its ideals, preparing his
followers to be led by the very man who had betrayed him. It is a
sacrifice that Hare and presumably all conscientious voters
expect their leaders to make if the time comes, yet one which is
quite rare in modern politics.

Though it follows the Labour Party so attentively, *The
Absence of War* is not a liberally biased play. Perhaps
surprisingly, considering some of Hare's earlier works, there is
little discussion of the merits of any particular party. Crusading
would, of course, detract from more important issues. For
England, some of those issues are: What does it mean to be a
socialist? How has the definition changed over time? What are
the dangers of an ostensibly multi-party system combining into a
like mind? On an even larger scale, the play suggests dangers
inherent in "the age of communication," when the media control
so many parts of public life and truth is held captive by image.
As the culmination of Hare's efforts, then, *The Absence of War*
draws effectively on its predecessors, continuing the production
style trend set by *Murmuring Judges* while reaching back to
Racing Demon for depth of character and theme.

But what of the trilogy as a whole? The plays were never meant to function like Aeschylus's *Oresteia*: they don't tell a single story. Their importance may lie rather in their very existence. As London critics indicated, Hare may be the only playwright of his time able, or at least willing, to attempt to place his fingers on the pulse of his nation in this way. Admirers and detractors of Hare's past work seemed to share a healthy respect for his enthusiasm about the project. In his review for *The Times*, Benedict Nightingale, who expressed certain reservations about the individual plays, nevertheless admitted that "the overall achievement is considerable. What other dramatist is inspecting the inner workings of our country at all, let alone doing so in such a determined, systematic way?" ("Dogged Hare's").

Furthermore, though many of its criticisms are harsh and simple solutions don't seem easy to come by, Hare's trilogy may provide some hope for Britain's ailing institutions. The playwright does not suggest that trends are irreversible and crises unmanageable; the tradition of socialist writing, of which Hare is a part, believes otherwise. As D. Keith Peacock has pointed out: "Typically, bourgeois history may perhaps best be represented in terms of discrete historical moments which are held forever in amber. . . . Marxist and Socialist history, on the other hand, is primarily concerned with change. For both Socialist historians and writers, history—even when it has involved set-backs for the working class—is viewed as fundamentally a record of a long journey towards an inevitable utopia" (15). Perhaps Hare had in mind such a utopia when he delivered his speech at King's College, Cambridge, nearly fifteen years before the trilogy was produced. In that 1978 lecture, the man who was to become Britain's leading playwright of popular dissent said: "[I]f you write about now, just today and nothing else, then you seem to be confronting only stasis; but if you begin to describe the movement of history, if you write plays that cover passages of time, then you begin to find a sense of movement, of social change, if you like; and the facile hopelessness that comes from confronting the day and only the day, the room and only the room, begins to disappear and in its place the writer can offer a record of movement and change" (66).

NOTE

1. Unless otherwise attributed, all quotations from David Hare are from the Platform Discussion at the National Theatre, London, 1 Oct. 1991.

WORKS CITED

De Jongh, Nicholas. "An Outsider Looks In." *Evening Standard* 9 Sept. 1993: 31.

Eyre, Richard. Personal Interview. 22 Sept. 1993.

Hare, David. *The Absence of War*. London: Faber, 1993.

———. "A Lecture Given at King's College, Cambridge, March 5 1978." *Licking Hitler*. London: Faber, 1978. 57–71.

———. *Murmuring Judges*. Rev. ed. London: Faber, 1993.

———. Platform Discussion at the National Theatre, London. 1 Oct. 1991.

———. *Racing Demon*. Rev. ed. London: Faber, 1991.

Hebblethwaite, Peter. "Pastoral Problems." *Times Literary Supplement* 16 Feb. 1990: 172.

Hooberman, Matthew and Emma Robertshaw. "Lefties v. Luvvies." *Evening Standard* 13 Sept. 1993: 11.

Nightingale, Benedict. "Dogged Hare's Anatomy of Britain." *The Times* 4 Oct. 1993: 33.

———. "Hare Brained Confusion." *The Times* 11 Oct. 1991: 12.

Peacock, D. Keith. *Radical Stages: Alternative History in Modern British Drama*. Westport: Greenwood, 1991.

Selected Bibliography

Primary Sources

Plays

The Absence of War. London: Faber, 1993.

The Asian Plays. London: Faber, 1986. Contains *Fanshen, Saigon: Year of the Cat*, the revised text of *A Map of the World*, and an introduction by Hare.

The Bay at Nice and *Wrecked Eggs.* London: Faber, 1986.

Deathshead. Unpublished. Performed 1971.

The Early Plays. London: Faber, 1992. Contains *Slag, The Great Exhibition, Teeth 'n' Smiles*, and an introduction by Hare ("On Political Theatre"), a reprint of "A Lecture Given at King's College, Cambridge, March 5 1978," originally published in *Licking Hitler*.

Fanshen. Based on the book by William Hinton. *Plays and Players* Sept. 1975: 41–50 [Act 1]; Oct. 1975: 43–50 [Act 2]. London: Faber, 1976. Contains a preface by Hare.

The Great Exhibition. Plays and Players May 1972: 63–81. London: Faber, 1972.

The History Plays. London: Faber, 1984. Contains a revised text of *Knuckle, Licking Hitler*, a revised text of *Plenty*, and an introduction by Hare.

How Brophy Made Good. Gambit 5.17 (1971): 83–125.

Knuckle. London: Faber, 1974.

A Map of the World. London: Faber, 1982. Rev. ed. 1983.

Murmuring Judges. London: Faber, 1991. Rev. ed. 1993.

Plenty. London: Faber, 1978.

Plenty. New York: NAL, 1983. A revised text prepared for the American stage production. Contains "A Note on Performance," appended after 1984 to reprints of the play in the Faber edition.

Racing Demon. London: Faber, 1990. Rev. ed. 1991.

The Secret Rapture. London: Faber, 1988. Rev. ed. 1989.

Slag. *Plays and Players* June 1970: 61–77. London: Faber, 1971.

Teeth 'n' Smiles. London: Faber, 1976.

What Happened to Blake. Unpublished. Performed 1970.

Collaborations

Brassneck. Written with Howard Brenton. *Plays and Players* Oct. 1973: I–XVI. London: Methuen, 1974.

Deeds. Written with Howard Brenton, Ken Campbell, and Trevor Griffiths. *Plays and Players* May 1978: 41–50 [Act 1]; June 1978: 43–50 [Act 2].

England's Ireland. Written with Tony Bicât, Howard Brenton, Brian Clark, David Edgar, Francis Fuchs, and Snoo Wilson. Unpublished. Performed 1972.

Inside Out. Written with Tony Bicât. Adaptation of Kafka's *Diaries*. Unpublished. Performed 1969.

The Knife. A musical/opera with lyrics by Tim Rose Price and music by Nick Bicât. Unpublished. Performed 1987.

Lay By. Written with Howard Brenton, Brian Clark, Trevor Griffiths, Stephen Poliakoff, Hugh Stoddart, and Snoo Wilson. *Plays and Players* Nov. 1971: 65–75. London: Calder, 1972.

Pravda: A Fleet Street Comedy. Written with Howard Brenton. London: Methuen, 1985. Rev. ed. 1986.

The Rules of the Game. Written with Robert Rietty. An English version of Pirandello's play. Unpublished. Performed 1971.

Screenplays (Film and Television)

Damage. Based on the novel by Josephine Hart. Dir. Louis Malle. Unpublished. Released 1992.

Dreams of Leaving. London: Faber, 1980.

Heading Home. Heading Home, Wetherby and *Dreams of Leaving*. London: Faber, 1991.

Licking Hitler. London: Faber, 1978. Contains "A Lecture Given at King's College, Cambridge, March 5 1978."

Man above Men. Dir. Alan Clarke. Unpublished. Televised 1973.

Paris by Night. London: Faber, 1988. Contains an introduction by Hare.

Plenty. Dir. Fred Schepisi. Unpublished. Released 1985.

Saigon: Year of the Cat. Dir. Stephen Frears. London: Faber, 1983.

The Secret Rapture. Dir. Howard Davies. Unpublished. Released 1994.

Strapless. London: Faber, 1989.

Wetherby. London: Faber, 1985.

Prose (Selected)

Asking Around: Background to the David Hare Trilogy. Ed. Lyn Haill. London: Faber, 1993. Interviews conducted by Hare while researching his recent theatre trilogy.

"Green Room." *Plays and Players* Oct. 1981: 49–50.

"I Still Have an Unfashionable Belief." *The Guardian* 3 Feb. 1983: 12. [On *A Map of the World* and theatre critics.]

"Nicaragua: An Appeal." *Granta* 16 (1985): 232–36.

"Why I Shall Vote Labour." *The Spectator* 23 May 1987: 14.

Writing Left-Handed. London: Faber, 1991. Contains an introduction by Hare. Reprints 11 previously published prose pieces (the introductions to *The Asian Plays* [titled "Why Pick On Us?"], *The History Plays* [titled "Now Think This Time"] and *Paris by Night* [titled "A Bit of Luck"]; "Cycles of Hope: A Memoir of Raymond Williams"; "A Lecture" [retitled "The Play is in the Air: On Political Theatre"]; "Time of Unease: At the Royal Court Theatre"; "The Awkward Squad: About Joint Stock"; "Ah! Mischief: On Public Broadcasting"; "A Stint at Notre Dame: On Literary Fame"; "Writers and the Cinema: On *Wetherby*"; "Sailing Downwind: On *Pravda*") and 5 previously unpublished pieces: "Looking Foolish: On Taking Risks" [the text of a speech delivered at the Cheltenham Festival, 1990]; "The Dead Heart: A Production Log of *A Map of the World*"; "An Unacceptable Form: On *The Knife*"; "Oh! Goodness: On *The Secret Rapture*"; and "Four

Actors" [an appreciation of Vanessa Redgrave, Blair Brown, Charlotte Rampling, and Anthony Hopkins].

Secondary Sources (Selected)

Interviews and Interview Profiles

"After *Fanshen:* A Discussion." *Performance and Politics in Popular Drama: Aspects of Popular Entertainment in Theatre, Film and Television 1800–1976.* Ed. David Bradby et al. Cambridge: Cambridge University Press, 1980. 297–314.

Ansorge, Peter. "Current Concerns: Trevor Griffiths and David Hare Outline the Problems of Two Contemporary Playwrights." *Plays and Players* July 1974: 18–22.

———. "Underground Explorations No. 1: Portable Playwrights. David Hare." *Plays and Players* Feb. 1972: 18–20.

Billington, Michael. "Broken Rules." *Radio Times* 12 Jan. 1980: 17.

———. "What Excites Me About *Pravda.*" *The Guardian* 2 Mar. 1985: 12.

Bloom, Michael. "A Kinder, Gentler David Hare." *American Theatre* Nov. 1989: 30–34.

Busby, Anne. Interview. National Theatre programme for *The Secret Rapture.* 1988.

Coveney, Michael. "Impure Meditations on Ideas of Goodness." *The Observer* 4 Feb. 1990: 55.

Crew, Robert. "Playwright Hare Feels the Sting of Controversy." *The Toronto Star* 11 Feb. 1989: F3.

Dempsey, Judy. Interview. *Literary Review* 22 Aug. 1980: 35–36.

Dugdale, John. "Love, Death and Edwina." *The Listener* 15 Sept. 1988: 38–39.

Ford, John. "Getting the Carp Out of the Mud." *Plays and Players* Nov. 1971: 20+. [Interview with Howard Brenton and Snoo Wilson, in addition to Hare.]

Gaston, Georg. "Interview: David Hare." *Theatre Journal* 45 (1993): 213–25.

Grant, Steve. "Peace and Plenty." *Time Out* 7 Apr. 1978: 15.

Gussow, Mel. "David Hare: Playwright as Provocateur." *New York Times Magazine* 29 Sept. 1985: 42+.

Harris, William. "Mapping the World of David Hare." *American Theatre* Dec. 1985: 12–17.

Itzin, Catherine and Simon Trussler. "From Portable Theatre to Joint Stock . . . via Shaftesbury Avenue." *Theatre Quarterly* 5.20 (1975–76): 108–15. Excerpted in Trussler 110–20.

Lawson, Steve. "Hare Apparent." *Film Comment* Sept.–Oct. 1985: 18–22.

Lewis, Peter. Interview. National Theatre programme for *A Map of the World*. 1983.

Lustig, Vera. "Soul Searching." *Drama* 170 (1988): 15–18.

McFerran, Ann. "End of the Acid Era." *Time Out* 29 Aug. 1975: 12–15.

Mortimer, John. "On the Left Side of the Law." *Sunday Times* 6 Oct. 1991: 10–11.

Nightingale, Benedict. "An Angry Young Man of the Eighties Brings His Play to New York." *New York Times* 17 Oct. 1982, sec. 2: 1.

———. "David Hare Captures His Muse on Stage." *New York Times* 22 Oct. 1989: H5+.

Raymond, Gerard. *"The Secret Rapture:* David Hare's X-Ray of the Soul." *TheaterWeek* 30 Oct. 1989: 16–21.

Tynan, Kathleen. "Dramatically Speaking." *Interview* Feb. 1989: 80+.

Wyver, John. "Brenton and Hare." *City Limits* 3 May 1985: 85–86.

Yakir, Dan. "A Hare's-breadth Away from Controversy." *Globe and Mail* [Toronto] 30 Aug. 1985: E5.

———. "Hare Style." *Horizon* Dec. 1985: 45–47.

Criticism/Background

Ansorge, Peter. "David Hare: A War on Two Fronts." *Plays and Players* Apr. 1978: 12–16.

———. *Disrupting the Spectacle: Five Years of Experimental and Fringe Theatre in Britain*. London: Pitman, 1975.

Arden, John. *To Present the Pretense: Essays on the Theatre and its Public*. London: Methuen, 1977.

Barker, Clive. *British Alternative Theatre*. London: Macmillan, 1985.

Barker, Howard. *Arguments for a Theatre*. London: Calder, 1989.

Barnes, Philip. *A Companion to Post-war British Theatre*. Totowa: Barnes, 1986.

Bigsby, C.W.E. "The Language of Crisis in British Theatre: The Drama of Cultural Pathology." *Contemporary English Drama*. Ed. C.W.E. Bigsby. Stratford-upon-Avon Studies 19. London: Arnold, 1981. 11–51.

———. "The Politics of Anxiety: Contemporary Socialist Theatre in England." *Modern Drama* 24 (1981): 393–403. Rpt. in Brown, *Modern British Dramatists* 161–76 and in Zeifman and Zimmerman 282–94.

Boon, Richard. *Brenton The Playwright*. London: Methuen, 1991.

Brenton, Howard. "Writing for Democratic Laughter." *Drama* 157 (1985): 9–11. [On writing *Pravda*.]

Brown, John Russell, ed. *Modern British Dramatists (New Perspectives)*. Englewood Cliffs: Prentice, 1984.

———. *A Short Guide to Modern British Drama*. London: Heinemann, 1982.

Browne, Terry W. *Playwrights' Theatre: The English Stage Company at the Royal Court Theatre*. London: Pitman, 1975.

Buckley, Michael. "Rapping About *Rapture*." Interview with Blair Brown, Frances Conroy and Mary Beth Hurt. *TheaterWeek* 30 Oct. 1989: 22–25.

Bull, John. *New British Political Dramatists: Howard Brenton, David Hare, Trevor Griffiths and David Edgar*. Rev. ed. London: Macmillan, 1991.

Calder, Angus. *The People's War: Britain 1939–1945*. London: Cape, 1969.

Callow, Simon. *Being an Actor*. London: Methuen, 1984.

Cardullo, Bert. "Brecht and *Fanshen*." *Studia Neophilologica* 58 (1986): 225–30.

———. "*Fanshen*, Western Drama, and David Hare's *Oeuvre*." *San José Studies* 10.1 (1984): 33–41.

———. "Hare's *Plenty*." *Explicator* 43 (1985): 62–63.

———. "Playing on Words: Four Notes on the Drama of David Hare." *USF Language Quarterly* 24 (1986): 44–46.

Carpenter, Charles, comp. *Modern Drama Scholarship and Criticism 1966–1980: An International Bibliography*. Toronto: University of Toronto Press, 1986.

Cave, Richard Allen. *New British Drama in Performance on the London Stage 1970–1985*. Gerrards Cross: Smythe, 1987.

Chambers, Colin and Mike Prior. *Playwrights' Progress: Patterns of Postwar British Drama*. Oxford: Amber Lane, 1987.

Cohn, Ruby. "Modest Proposals of Modern Socialists." *Modern Drama* 25 (1982): 457–68. Rpt. in Zeifman and Zimmerman 267–81.

———. *Retreats from Realism in Recent English Drama*. Cambridge: Cambridge University Press, 1991.

———. "Shakespeare Left." *Theatre Journal* 40 (1988): 48–60. [Partly on *Slag*.]

Cook, Judith, ed. *Directors' Theatre: Sixteen Leading Directors on the State of Theatre in Britain Today*. London: Hodder, 1989.

Cornish, Roger N. "David Hare." *British Dramatists Since World War II*. Ed. Stanley Weintraub. Vol. 1. Detroit: Gale, 1982. 2 vols. 234–42.

Courtney, Richard. *Outline History of British Drama*. Totowa: Littlefield, 1982.

Coveney, Michael. "Turning Over: The Background to *Fanshen*." *Plays and Players* June 1975: 10–13.

Craig, Sandy, ed. *Dreams and Deconstructions: Alternative Theatre in Britain*. Ambergate: Amber Lane, 1980.

Davies, Andrew. *Other Theatres: The Development of Alternative and Experimental Theatre in Britain*. London: Macmillan, 1987.

Davison, Peter. *Contemporary Drama and the Popular Dramatic Tradition in England*. London: Macmillan, 1982.

Dean, Joan FitzPatrick. *David Hare*. Boston: Twayne, 1990.

Delmer, Sefton. *Black Boomerang*. London: Secker, 1962.

Doty, Gresdna A. and Billy J. Harbin, eds. *Inside the Royal Court Theatre, 1956–1981: Artists Talk*. Baton Rouge: Louisiana State University Press, 1990.

Dunn, Tony. "Joint Stock—The First Ten Years." *Plays and Players* Jan. 1985: 15–18.

———. "The Play of Politics." *Drama* 156 (1985): 13–15.

———. "Writers of the Seventies." *Plays and Players* May 1984: 12–13; June 1984: 35–36.

Edgar, David. *The Second Time as Farce: Reflections on the Drama of Mean Times*. London: Lawrence, 1988.

———. "Ten Years of Political Theatre, 1968–78." *Theatre Quarterly* 8.32 (1979): 25–33.

Elsom, John. *Post-war British Theatre*. Rev. ed. London: Routledge, 1979.

Findlater, Richard, ed. *At the Royal Court: 25 Years of the English Stage Company*. Ambergate: Amber Lane, 1981.

Free, William J. "Mischief and Frustration in David Hare's *Knuckle*." *The Legacy of Thespis*. Ed. Karelisa V. Hartigan. Lanham: University Press of America, 1984. 23–30.

Gale, Steven H. "Sex and Politics: David Hare's *Plenty*." *Drama, Sex, and Politics*. Ed. James Redmond. Themes in Drama 7. Cambridge: Cambridge University Press, 1985. 213–20.

Gaskill, William. *A Sense of Direction: Life at the Royal Court*. London: Faber, 1988.

Golomb, Liorah A. "Saint Isobel: David Hare's *The Secret Rapture* as Christian Allegory." *Modern Drama* 33 (1990): 563–74.

Gooch, Steve. *All Together Now: An Alternative View of Theatre and the Community*. London: Methuen, 1984.

Goodwin, Tim. *Britain's Royal National Theatre: The First 25 Years*. London: Hern, 1988.

Grant, Steve. "David Hare." *Contemporary Dramatists*. Ed. D.L. Kirkpatrick and James Vinson. 4th ed. London: St. James Press, 1988. 236–39.

———. "Voicing the Protest: The New Writers." In Craig 116–44.

Grindin, James. "Freedom and Form in David Hare's Drama." *British and Irish Drama since 1960*. Ed. James Acheson. London: Macmillan; New York: St. Martin's, 1993.

Gussow, Mel. "Profiles: Play Agent." *New Yorker* 23 May 1988: 35–60. [A profile of Hare's agent, Peggy Ramsay.]

Hall, Peter. *Peter Hall's Diaries: The Story of a Dramatic Battle*. Ed. John Goodwin. London: Hamilton, 1983.

Hammond, Jonathan. "David Hare." *Contemporary Dramatists*. Ed. James Vinson. 2nd ed. London: St. James, 1977. 361–64.

Hayman, Ronald. *British Theatre since 1955: A Reassessment*. Oxford: Oxford University Press, 1979.

———. *The Set-up: An Anatomy of the English Theatre Today*. London: Methuen, 1974.

Hobson, Harold. *Theatre in Britain: A Personal View*. Oxford: Phaidon, 1984.

Homden, Carol. "A Dramatist of Surprise." *Plays and Players* Sept. 1988: 5–7.

Innes, Christopher. *Modern British Drama 1890–1990*. Cambridge: Cambridge University Press, 1992.

Itzin, Catherine. *Stages in the Revolution: Political Theatre in Britain since 1968*. London: Methuen, 1980.

Itzin, Catherine and Simon Trussler. "Petrol Bombs Through the Proscenium Arch." Interview with Howard Brenton. *Theatre Quarterly* 5.17 (1975): 4–20. Excerpted in Trussler 85–97.

Johnstone, Richard. "Television Drama and the People's War: David Hare's *Licking Hitler*, Ian McEwan's *The Imitation Game*, and Trevor Griffiths's *Country*." *Modern Drama* 28 (1985): 189–97. Rpt. in Zeifman and Zimmerman 295–306.

Kareda, Urjo. "Nelligan's Leaps." Interview with Kate Nelligan. *Saturday Night* Aug. 1985: 22–29.

Kauffmann, Stanley. *Theater Criticisms*. New York: PAJ, 1983.

Kerensky, Oleg. *The New British Drama: Fourteen Playwrights since Osborne and Pinter*. London: Hamilton, 1977.

Klotz, Günther. *Britische Dramatiker der Gegenwart*. Berlin: Henschel, 1982.

Lambert, J.W. *Drama in Britain 1964–1973*. London: Longmans, 1974.

Lloyd Evans, Gareth and Barbara. *Plays in Review 1956–1980: British Drama and the Critics*. London: Methuen, 1985.

Ludlow, Colin. "Hare and Others." *London Magazine* July 1978: 76–81. Excerpted in Brown, *Modern British Dramatists* 149–52.

McDonald, David. "Unspeakable Justice: David Hare's *Fanshen*." *Critical Theory and Performance*. Ed. Janelle G. Reinelt and Joseph R. Roach. Ann Arbor: University of Michigan Press, 1992. 129–45.

McGrath, John. *The Bone Won't Break: On Theatre and Hope in Hard Times*. London: Methuen, 1990.

———. *A Good Night Out: Popular Theatre. Audience, Class and Form*. London: Methuen, 1981.

Mitchell, Tony, comp. *File on Brenton*. London: Methuen, 1987.

Morley, Sheridan. *Shooting Stars: Plays and Players 1975–1983*. London: Quartet, 1983.

Myerson, Jonathan. "David Hare: Fringe Graduate." *Drama* 149 (1983): 26–28.

Oberholzner, Werner. "'This is a woman's world': David Hare, *Slag* (1970)." *Strukturen des Vorurteils im modernen britischen Drama*. Ed. Werner Oberholzner. Trier: WVT, 1989. 63–77.

Oliva, Judy Lee. *David Hare: Theatricalizing Politics*. Ann Arbor: UMI, 1990.

―――. "From Brass to Crass: Brenton and Hare's Collaborative Plays *Brassneck* and *Pravda*." *Howard Brenton: A Casebook*. Ed. Ann Wilson. New York: Garland, 1992. 29–38.

Page, Malcolm, comp. *File on Hare*. London: Methuen, 1990.

Page, Malcolm and Ria Julian, comps. "David Hare Checklist." *Theatrefacts* 2.4 (1975): 2+.

Patraka, Vivian M. "Contemporary Drama, Fascism, and the Holocaust." *Theatre Journal* 39 (1987): 65–77.

Peacock, D. Keith. "Chronicles of Wasted Time." *Historical Drama*. Ed. James Redmond. Themes in Drama 8. Cambridge: Cambridge University Press, 1986. 195–212. [Partly on *Plenty* and *Licking Hitler*.]

―――. "Fact versus History: Two Attempts to Change the Audience's Political Perspective." *Theatre Studies* 31–32 (1984–86): 15–31. [Partly on *Plenty*.]

―――. *Radical Stages: Alternative History in Modern British Drama*. Westport: Greenwood, 1991.

Peter, John. "Meet the Wild Bunch." *Sunday Times* 11 July 1976: 31.

Rabey, David Ian. *British and Irish Political Drama in the Twentieth Century: Implicating the Audience*. London: Macmillan, 1986.

Raymond, Gerard. "The Truth About *Pravda*." *TheaterWeek* 6 Feb. 1989: 24–31.

Ridgman, Jeremy. "'A Shameful Conquest of Itself': Images from the Empire in Post-War British Drama." *Australasian Drama Studies* 1.1 (1982): 89–108.

Ritchie, Rob, ed. *The Joint Stock Book: The Making of a Theatre Collective*. London: Methuen, 1987.

Roberts, Philip. *The Royal Court Theatre, 1965–1972*. London: Routledge, 1987.

―――. *Theatre in Britain*. London: Pitman, 1974.

Rusinko, Susan. *British Drama 1950 to the Present: A Critical History*. Boston: Twayne, 1989.

Stokes, Geoffrey. "The Secret Rupture." *Village Voice* 28 Nov. 1989: 37–39. [An account of the Jack Kroll/Frank Rich/*Secret Rapture* controversy in New York.]

Taking the Stage: Twenty-one Years of the London Theatre. Photographs John Haynes. Intro. Lindsay Anderson. London: Thames, 1986.

Taylor, John Russell. *The Second Wave: British Drama of the Sixties.* Rev. ed. London: Methuen, 1978.

Trussler, Simon, ed. *New Theatre Voices of the Seventies: Sixteen Interviews from Theatre Quarterly 1970–1980.* London: Methuen, 1981.

Wandor, Michelene. *Carry on, Understudies: Theatre and Sexual Politics.* Rev. ed. London: Routledge, 1986.

––––––. *Look Back in Gender: Sexuality and the Family in Post-war British Drama.* London: Methuen, 1987.

Wardle, Irving. *The Theatres of George Devine.* London: Cape, 1978.

Wilcher, Robert. "*Pravda*: A Morality Play for the 1980s." *Modern Drama* 33 (1990): 42–56.

Williams, Christopher and Gaetano D'Elia. *La scrittura multimediale di David Hare.* Fasano: Schena, 1989.

Winkler, Elizabeth Hale. *The Function of Song in Contemporary British Drama.* Newark: University of Delaware Press, 1990.

Young, B.A. *The Mirror up to Nature: A Review of the Theatre 1964–1982.* London: Kimber, 1982.

Zeifman, Hersh and Cynthia Zimmerman, eds. *Contemporary British Drama 1970–90.* London: Macmillan; Toronto: University of Toronto Press, 1993.

Index